THE C WORKBOOK

THE C WORKBOOK

Sathis Menon
College of Computing
Georgia Institute of Technology

McGraw-Hill, Inc.
New York . St. Louis . San Francisco . Auckland . Bogotá . Caracas . Lisbon
London . Madrid . Mexico . Milan . Montreal . New Delhi . Paris . San Juan
Singapore . Sydney . Tokyo . Toronto

THE C WORKBOOK

Copyright © 1993 by McGraw-Hill, Inc. All rights reserved. Printed in the United States of America. Except as permitted under the United States Copyright Act of 1976, no part of this publication may be reproduced or distributed in any form or by any means, or stored in a data base or retrieval system, without the prior written permission of the publisher.

1234567890 DOC DOC 909876543

ISBN 0-07-041576-5

The editor was Eric M. Munson;
the production supervisor was Denise L. Puryear;
the cover was designed by Caliber/Phoenix Color Corp;
the book was typeset by the author.
R. R. Donnelley & Sons Company was printer and binder.

UNIX is a trademark of UNIX System Laboratories.

Library of Congress Catalog Card Number: 92-63301

Table of Contents

	Preface	xi
1	**Introduction**	**1**
	About the Workbook	1
	From K&R C to ANSI C	1
	Programming Style	2
2	**I/O, I/O, so off to Work I Go**	**5**
	Our First Program	5
	How Deep is Mariana Trench?	8
	Detailed explanation of the depth conversion program	9
	Program design: Sequential computation	13
	Simple Input and Output	15
	Output using the `printf` library function	15
	Control codes in printing using `printf`	20
	Input using the `scanf` library function	21
	All about Program Variables	25
	Rules for naming variables	25
	Declaring the type of the variable	27
	Common problems	28
3	**Dealing with Data**	**31**
	Math Tutor Program	31
	All about Data Types	35
	Attributes of variables	37
	Size of the basic data types	38
	Changing the Size of a Data Type	41
	Specifying the sign of a variable	43
	Qualifiers for variables that do not change values	44
	Displaying data using `printf`	46
	Data Type `char`	48
	Constants	51
	Integer constants	52
	Floating point constants	53
	Character constants	54
	Character conversion: An example	55
	Character conversion functions	58

	String constants	60
	Automatic type conversions	61
	Common Problems	65

4 Decision Time — 67

Arithmetic Operators	67
Precedence of arithmetic operators	68
Relational Operators and Decision Making	72
True and false, as seen by C	73
`if` statements: The rest of the story	75
Nested `if` statements	78
Multiway decision making using the `else if` clause	80
Exiting from the program	82
Logical Operators	84
Short-circuiting of logical operators	89
Precedence of relational and logical operators	91
Iterative Execution Using `while` Loop	93
Common Problems	100

5 File I/O — 103

All about Stream I/O	104
Opening a file	105
Read and write operations on files	108
Text Files and Data Conversion	111
Testing for end-of-file and error	115
Working with Binary Files	117
File application: Simple report generator	121
Keyboard and Terminal as Files	127
The Cast Operator	129
Common Problems	133

6 Preprocessor: Language within a Language — 137

The C Preprocessor	137
File Inclusion	139
Macro Substitution	141
Macros with arguments	145
Converting tokens to strings using the `#` operator	149
Debugging Aid: The `assert` Macro	151
Conditional expressions: A digression	155
Common Problems	159

7 Case for do Loops — 161

Multiway Branching Using the `switch` Statement	161
`switch` statement and "falling through effect"	163

	`case` values	165
	Data type `enum`	165
	Integer-valued branch and control expressions	167
	Increment and Decrement Operators	173
	Prefix and postfix application of ++ and --	173
	Looping Using the `for` Statement	175
	Nested loops	178
	Combining expressions using the comma operator	179
	Iteration Using the `do` Statement	181
	Understanding Input Operations	185
	Skipping the Execution in a Loop: `continue` Statement	189
	`for` loops: A complete example	190
	The `goto` Statement	195
	Updated precedence table	197
	Common Problems	198
8	**Grouping Data, Using Arrays**	**201**
	Arrays	201
	Declaring arrays and accessing elements	202
	Accessing elements of an array	203
	Sorting the elements of an array	210
	Array initialization	214
	Problem with arrays: Lack of bounds checking	216
	Compile-time memory allocation	217
	Sorting an array without shuffling the elements	217
	Binary search: Program development	222
	Multidimensional Arrays	224
	Common Problems	232
9	**Accessing Memory Directly: Pointers**	**233**
	Pointers	234
	Variables and address locations	235
	Finding the address of variables	238
	What is an address?	239
	Declaring pointer variables	240
	Initializing pointer variables	242
	Invalid addresses	245
	The null pointer	246
	Pointers and Arrays	248
	Pointer arithmetic is different from integer arithmetic	250
	Strings	255
	String-handling functions	259
	Pointer Arrays	261
	Sample program: Pointer arrays	263

		Defining data types using `typedef`	265
		`typedef` vs. `#define`	266
		Arrays and `typedef`	268
	Common Problems		274

10 Reusing Code by Using Functions — 277

- Functions — 279
  - Function declaration: Function prototypes — 281
  - Function call — 284
  - Function definition — 284
  - Argument names vs. parameter names — 286
  - Returning from a function: `return` statement — 287
  - Function prototyping and non-ANSI C — 290
  - Functions: A complete example — 291
- Function Arguments: Call by Value — 295
  - Implementing call by reference by using pointers — 297
  - Functions vs. macros — 301
  - Returning more than one value from a function — 302
  - Arrays as function arguments — 304
  - Functions: A complete example — 306
  - Functions with variable number of arguments — 309
- Functions: Separate Compilation — 310
- Function Prototypes: ANSI C vs. Old C — 313
  - Conditional compilation to manage code — 313
- Common Problems — 317

11 User-Defined Data Types: Structures — 319

- Structure — 320
  - Accessing structure members — 322
  - Problem with mixing formatted and unformatted I/O — 325
  - Structures and files — 329
  - Structures and binary files — 332
  - Structures and pointers — 334
  - Structures as function arguments — 341
  - Searching through the records — 343
  - Structure containing structures — 345
- Unions — 350
- Common Problems — 355

12 Types of Memory — 357

- Automatic Variables — 357
- External Variables — 360
  - Functions and external variables — 361
- Storage Class `register` — 365

Storage Class `static`	366
Scope Rules	372
Global visibility	372
Block visibility	372
File visibility	375
Storage classes: A complete example	375
Quick sort: A complete example	383
Common Problems	387
Near, but not complete, equivalence of arrays and pointers	387
13 Best of the Rest	**393**
Dynamic Memory Allocation	393
Dynamic memory allocation and linked lists	396
Command Line Arguments	402
Recursive Functions	408
Binary search: A complete example	413
Random Access	417
Random access: A complete example	418
Bitwise Operators	425
Octal and hexadecimal representation of data	425
Bitwise AND, OR and exclusive-OR	427
Shift operators	430
Assignment operators	432
Common Problems	435
Appendix A	**437**
Appendix B	**439**
Appendix C	**442**
Appendix D	**443**
Index	**447**

Preface

The popularity of the C language requires no elaboration. Ever since its introduction in the late 70s, C has been slowly and steadily climbing into the upperechelons of mainstream computing.

Why yet another book on C? My experience has shown that trying to teach programming in C from books written in "textbook style" is a difficult task. On the one hand, a voluminous amount of detail had to be covered to reach interesting and challenging topics. On the other hand, classic books such as *The C Programming Language* by Kernighan and Ritchie proved too difficult to be used as an introductory textbook. Thus I undertook the task of writing a "workbook style" book for self-guided study:

- Using the workbook, the student is introduced to topics on a "need to know" basis.
- Emphasis is placed on becoming proficient at writing correct and efficient programs with whatever language constructs have been presented at any point.
- Obvious and subtle problems with the language are presented.
- Students are also encouraged to use the style of programming preferred by proficient C programmers.

When given a programming problem to solve, the novice programmer is faced with two different hurdles: coming up with a plan to solve the problem (the algorithmic development) and translating the plan into C (syntactic and semantic translation). Studies show that expert programmers often solve a problem by reducing it to a sequence of techniques that they have mastered over the years. Thus the algorithmic development process is a very important part of programming. Once the outline of the algorithm has been developed, breaking down the steps of the algorithm into a set of manageable units (or modules) follows naturally. The actual translation process involves the selection of the appropriate language constructs that will actually implement the steps of the algorithm. It is the intent of this book to illuminate both of these aspects of program development.

Finally, the best way to master a concept is by making mistakes and trying to figure out what went wrong. A program that compiles and runs the very first time is not an interesting program at all! Unsuccessful programs are more challenging: Fixing them helps reinforce the basic concepts, allows the student to experience the nuances and pitfalls of the language, etc. So don't fear making mistakes, but learn by fixing them.

Acknowledgments

First and foremost, I wish to thank Arnold Robbins who read the manuscript thoroughly, pointed out numerous problems, suggested solutions and made me rewrite entire sections and add new ones. I also acknowledge the contribution from the reviewers whose suggestions helped fine-tune the book: Gary Newell, Carl McConnell, Ranjit John, Jay Lofstead, Adarsh Sethi, Douglas Hung, Gautam Shah, Paul Amer and Henry Etlinger and many others. Special thanks to Richard Fujimoto who suggested that I turn my class notes into a workbook for self-guided study and Jim Greenlee for adopting the book for CS 4801. Thanks to all those CS 4801 students who sent me comments and reported problems with the earlier versions of the notes. Thanks to my editor Eric Munson for seeing the book through from inception to production.

This book is dedicated to my wife Padma for her patience and support.

Sathis Menon

1
Introduction

1.1 About the Workbook

This workbook contains material suitable for a beginning level, self-study course in learning to program in the C language. No prior programming language experience is necessary to use this book. However, if you are familiar with at least one other high-level programming language (such as Pascal, FORTRAN, BASIC or COBOL), you will find the transition to C relatively painless. Assembly language programmers need not feel left out — C can chew bits and bytes as well as any low-level mnemonic language.

1.1a From K&R C to ANSI C

The C programming language was designed and implemented around 1972 by Dennis Ritchie, at AT&T Bell Labs. Why the name C? C was influenced by a language called B, designed by Ken Thompson, also at Bell Labs. Thompson and Ritchie were the principal designers of the UNIX® operating system. Why B? B was influenced by a language called BCPL, which was designed in the late 60's by Martin Richards. BCPL was a high-level language, yet was very machine-oriented.

The original version of C was popularized by the now classic book called The C Programming Language by Brian Kernighan and Dennis Ritchie. The language description contained in the book was the "official word", and compilers followed this description in what came to be known as "K&R C" (for Kernighan and Ritchie). Most of the older C compilers that exist today follow this standard.

K&R C had some flaws, due to the imprecise nature of the language grammar. Some of the language constructs were ambiguous. The language did not lend itself suitably for *type checking* (a technique that compilers perform to see if in fact you are using the language safely). Also, due to the lack of an official standard, compiler writers were free to interpret the language specification, leading to a plethora of C compilers that were not compatible with each other.

In spite of its deficiencies, the language was becoming tremendously popular among programmers. The time was ripe to officially standardize the language. In 1983, the American National Standards Institute convened a committee to draft an official standard. This standard came to be known as ANSI C, or Standard C.

Why do you need to know all this trivia? If you did not, you might get confused trying to compile your ANSI C compliant program on a K&R compiler or vice versa. Programs in this workbook are written in ANSI C. However, there are still many K&R compilers out there, and chances are that your system may still be using a K&R compiler. Luckily, the major differences between K&R C and ANSI C will not show up until we talk about *functions*, later in the workbook. All the programs in the workbook before we get to the chapter on functions will safely compile on any C compiler. Further, when a new feature introduced by the ANSI standard is discussed in the workbook, techniques to transform and to compile it under a K&R compiler will also be shown.

1.1b Programming Style

While writing programs, it is very important that you follow some stylistic conventions. Notice the use of indentations, placement of the curly braces, etc., in the sample programs shown in this text, and try to follow the style in the programs that you write, however trivial the programs may be. It is no fun to try and follow unreadable code. For example, shown below is a valid C program (albeit non-ANSI C), presented at an Obfuscated C Programming Contest, which generates a maze when it is compiled and run.

```
char*M,A,Z,E=40,J[40],T[40];main(C){for(*J=A=scanf(M="%d",&C;
--                E;              J[              E]             =T
[E   ]=   E)    printf("._");   for(;(A-=Z=!Z)   ||(printf("\n|"
)    ,   A    =                 39              ,C             --
```

```
)       ;     Z     ||      printf     (M    ))M[Z]=Z[A-(E =A[J-Z])&&!C
&       A     ==                T[                                   A]|
6<<11<rand()||!C&!Z?J[T[E]=T[A]]=E,J[T[A]=A-Z]=A,"_.":"|"];}
```

Needless to say, it is impossible to read the above program. For your own sanity, as well as the sanity of others who may read your code, use tabs, spaces, etc., to beautify your code.

2
I/O, I/O, so off to Work I Go

Input/output is an integral part of program development. Programs that run silently without producing any output are not very interesting. In this chapter, you will learn to compose, compile and run simple programs that are able to display the results of their computation. You will also learn the structural composition of C programs.

2.1 Our First Program

Using your favorite editor/word processor, type in the following vintage program and save it into a file called **hello.c**. All C program files have names that end with a **.c** (read as *dot-c*) extension.

Do not omit any text shown below, when you type it in, as it will lead to *syntax errors* when compiling the program.

Definition *Syntax Errors*

Errors due to grammatically incorrect programs. The C compiler expects the program to be compliant with its grammar rules. Typographical errors, imperfect understanding of the grammar rules, etc., will cause errors which will be flagged by the compiler. These errors only cause minor annoyance and can be corrected easily.

```
#include <stdio.h>

main()
{
```

```
        printf ("Hello world\n");
}
```

After you have typed in the program and saved it in the file called **hello.c**, compile the program using the C compiler on your computer.

The name of the C compiler varies from system to system. On most UNIX systems, the C compiler is named as **cc**. The Borland C compiler is named **tcc**. In this text, we will assume that your compiler is named **cc**. Find the name of the C compiler on your system, and substitute that name in place of **cc** in the examples shown here. In the commands shown below, the system prompt is shown as a dollar sign ($) and is not a part of the command.

```
$ cc hello.c
```

If no error messages were reported by the compiler and your system prompt is reissued, then your program has been successfully compiled. The compiler has created an output file, which contains the machine executable binary code corresponding to your program. On UNIX systems, the executable file is named **a.out**, by default. Most compilers running on DOS give the executable file the same name as the program file, without the **.c** suffix.

Verify that the compiler has created the executable file, by listing the contents of your directory.

If you have made any typographical mistakes in your program file, the compiler will flag these errors as syntax errors. For example, if you omit the semicolon at the end of the word that begins with the line `printf` and type it in as

```
printf ("Hello world\n")
```

when you compile the program, you will get an error message that looks similar to:

```
"hello.c", line 5: syntax error at or near symbol }
```

Note *The error is really on line 4. The compiler does not discover it until line 5 and flags the error on or near line 5.*

The program must be recompiled after you fix the syntax problem. If you get any other syntax errors and cannot figure out the problem, refer to the section on common problems (Section 2.5) at the end of this chapter.

After a successful compilation, execute (or *run*) the program by typing the name of the file containing the machine executable code.

```
$ a.out
```

or,

```
$ hello
```

You will see the following result:

```
Hello world
```

If you are working on a UNIX system and you compile another program file using the compilation command shown above, the C compiler will again create the executable program, store it in the file **a.out** and overwrite its previous contents. To avoid this problem, you can use the **-o** option flag to the C compiler, along with a file name. The **-o** flag indicates to the compiler that the executable program is to be named as you have specified.

On a UNIX system, recompile the previous program and create a new executable file:

```
$ cc -o hello hello.c
```

A new file called **hello**, which contains the executable program, will be created in your directory. Execute the new file

```
$ hello
```

and you get the same result as before:

```
Hello world
```

2.1a   Exercise

Write a program that prints the words, "My first C program." Save the program in a file called **first.c**. Compile and run the program.

2.2   How Deep is Mariana Trench?

Composing and running a bit more meaningful program reveals the structuring of C programs in more detail. We will write a program to convert the depth of Mariana Trench (the deepest explored depth of the oceans) from feet to miles.

Type in the following program into a file **mariana.c** (remember that C program file names end with a **.c** extension). Do not forget to include the semicolons at the end of the *statements* as shown and the curly braces.

Definition   **Statement**

A statement is a construct that expresses the flow of control through a program.

```
/* Program to compute the depth of Mariana
 * Trench (the deepest known point in the oceans)
 * in miles
 */

#include <stdio.h>

main()
{
   int depth_in_feet;
   float depth_in_miles;

   depth_in_feet = 35800;
   depth_in_miles = depth_in_feet / 5280.0;
   printf("Mariana Trench is %f miles deep\n",
             depth_in_miles);
}
```

Compile the program by issuing the appropriate command (command on UNIX systems shown):

```
$ cc -o mariana mariana.c
```

If the compilation produces no errors, run the program as shown below. Otherwise, fix the syntax errors in the program, recompile it until you get no more errors, and run the program.

```
$ mariana

Mariana Trench is 6.780303 miles deep
```

2.2a Detailed explanation of the depth conversion program

To explain the various C program lines that make up the depth conversion program, the program listing is shown again with line numbers.

```
1)     /* Program to compute the depth of Mariana
2)        Trench (the deepest known point in the oceans)
3)        in miles
4)     */
5)
6)     #include <stdio.h>
7)
8)     main()
9)     {
10)        int depth_in_feet;
11)        float depth_in_miles;
12)
13)        depth_in_feet = 35800;
14)        depth_in_miles = depth_in_feet / 5280.0;
15)        printf("Mariana Trench is %f miles deep\n",
16)                    depth_in_miles);
17)    }
```

Explanation follows:

```
1)      /* Program to compute the depth of Mariana
2)         Trench (the deepest known point in the oceans)
3)         in miles
4)      */
```

The above four lines are comments. You can insert any text (hopefully useful comments) in a C program between the sequence beginning with a /* and ending with a */. Text within the /*   */ is ignored by the C compiler. Comments should be used as a documentation tool to describe what the program does.

The C compiler also ignores blank lines (line numbers 5, 7, etc.) in program text. Blank lines are used for clarity in reading the programs.

```
6)      #include <stdio.h>
```

The above line instructs the C compiler to include along with your program a file called **stdio.h** (read as *standard-i-o-dot-h*), which is necessary for performing input/output operations from your program. Always remember to include this line at the top of your C programs that perform input/output.

```
8)      main()
```

All C programs must have a statement called **main**, which is also called the *main function*. This is the entry point where your program starts executing when it is run.

```
9)      {
```

Start of the main block, i.e., the *statements* that belong to the **main** function. Statements are higher-level program instructions (usually program lines terminated by a *semicolon*). C is a *block structured* language. The significance of block structuring will be explained in a later chapter.

```
10)         int depth_in_feet;
11)         float depth_in_miles;
```

Statements declaring the memory locations that will be used to hold data. The above statements have two components. The first word in both statements indicates the type of data, and such words are known as *data types*. The rest of the words are names of memory locations and are called *variable identifiers* or, simply, *variables*. Thus `int` and `float` are the data types, and the words `depth_in_feet` and `depth_in_miles` are the variables. The memory locations named by the variables may contain values that change during program execution. The nature of the values stored at these locations is specified by using the data type.

The data type `int` signifies that the values will be interpreted as integers (whole numbers). The data type `float` signifies that the values will be floating point (decimal numbers).

C requires that the type of all variables be declared before they are used.

13)   `depth_in_feet = 35800;`

The depth of the Mariana Trench is approximately 35800 feet. Since the conversion requires the use of this number in the formula (discussed below), the variable `depth_in_feet` is assigned this value. Once the variables have been declared as shown in lines 10 and 11 above, you can assign values to them and perform other operations on them. Note that the assignment of the integer value 35800 to the variable `depth_in_feet` is consistent with the declaration of the variable as type `int`.

14)   `depth_in_miles = depth_in_feet / 5280.0;`

Next, the conversion is performed (on the right-hand side of the *assignment operator* "="), and the computed value is assigned to the variable on the left-hand side. The conversion formula is derived from the following unit conversions:

       `1 mile = 5280 feet`

The value contained in the variable `depth_in_feet` is converted into its equivalent value in miles, by dividing it by `5280.0`. The division is performed by using the division operator (`/`). Other arithmetic operators are multiplication (`*`), subtraction (`-`), addition (`+`), and modulus or the remainder of division (`%`.).

Notice that we use a floating point value (`5280.0`) as the divisor, instead of an integer value (`5280`). The reason is that in C's rule for division, if an integer value is divided by another integer value, we get an integer value as the result (truncation of any fractional part occurs). We can avoid this problem by using a floating point value as the dividend or divisor (or both). You will learn more about this rule in Chapter 4.

The converted value on the right-hand side of the assignment operator is assigned to (stored into) the variable **depth_in_miles** on the left-hand side. Notice that the type of the converted value (floating point) is consistent with the type of the variable **depth_in_miles** (`float`).

```
15)     printf("Mariana Trench is %f miles deep\n",
16)                     depth_in_miles);
```

These two lines (which are really one statement, split into two lines to fit the page) display the results of the conversion. Using a *function* called `printf` (read as *print-f*), the value stored in the variable **depth_in_miles**, which holds the result of the conversion, is displayed on the terminal. The function `printf` is a utility program used for output purposes, available from the *standard library* associated with the C compiler. A collection of commonly used functions supplied by the system, which can be included with your programs, is known as a *library*.

Note that the above two lines are really one statement, split into two to fit the page. C allows you to split most statements across lines, subject to a set of rules described later.

Notice the funny looking sequence \n at the end of the *string* inside the `printf` statement.

Definition **String**

A string is a sequence of characters enclosed in a pair of quotes.

The \n sequence is called a *new line* and is used to introduce a carriage return and line feed at the end of the string being printed. This causes the cursor on your screen to move to the beginning of the next line. Remove the \n from the string, recompile the program, run it and see what happens.

```
17)     }
```

End of the `main` block.

2.2b Program design: sequential computation

Think about the program that you just examined. Try to correlate it with your understanding of how the computer operates. At the heart of the machine, the central processing unit (CPU) performs operations on data stored somewhere in memory. Memory is *addressable*; i.e., each memory location has a number assigned to it, and given the number, it is possible to get the data stored at the number. Since it is a bit inconvenient to deal with these numbers in our programs, the compiler hides these tedious details from us by allowing us to name the locations where data is stored. These are the variables in the program.

The depth conversion program is a *sequentially*[*] executed program. There is no branching or decision making involved anywhere in the program. Abstractly, the steps involved in computing the mile equivalent of the depth of the Mariana Trench are:

- Declare the name of the memory locations and the type of the data stored at the locations

    ```
    int depth_in_feet;
    float depth_in_miles;
    ```

- Store values into the variables

    ```
    depth_in_feet  = 35800;
    ```

- Compute the result using the conversion formula

    ```
    depth_in_feet / 5280.0
    ```

- Store the results into a memory location set aside for holding the result (assignment into variable **depth_in_miles**).
- Print the result (**printf** statement).

The above program design is typical of programs that perform unit conversions. Now it is your turn to write a few similar programs.

---

[*] The usage of the term is not in the same vein as the more traditional usage of sequential programming.

2.2c **Exercises**

1 Write a program to compute the number of centimeters in a foot (1 inch equals 2.54 centimeters).

The program design is similar to the depth conversion program: Assign memory to hold the number of inches in a foot and memory to hold the resulting centimeter value. Initialize the variable holding the inch value to the number of inches in a foot. Convert the number of inches in a foot to the equivalent centimeter value by applying the formula, and assign the result to the variable declared to hold the result. Finally, print the result.

The program should have the following features:

- The names selected for variables should reflect their usage.
- The output should be appropriately worded.
- The program should look similar to the depth conversion program in its appearance, use of tabs, parentheses, etc.
- The printed output should be meaningful.

2 Write a program to print the kilometer equivalent of a marathon race. The marathon distance is 29 miles and 385 yards. The unit conversions are as follows:

```
1 mile = 1760 yards.
1 mile = 1.609 kilometers.
```

Thus, you will have to use the following formula:

```
kilometers = 1.609 * (miles + (yards/1760.0))
```

The parentheses are necessary, in the above formula, to order the operations correctly (i.e., the division before the addition, and the multiplication following the addition). C has a set of built-in rules for ordering operations. We will discuss these orderings in detail in Chapter 4.

As you may have observed, all that complicated circuitry on your computer is redundant if all you are going to do is straight formula conversions that a simple calculator can perform with greater ease. In the remaining chapters you will learn to program the computer to make decisions, interact with the user from within the program, repeatedly compute results, and more.

2.3 Simple Input and Output

The conversion program would be a lot more useful if you could write a general-purpose program that converts from any number of inches to its equivalent centimeter value. This requires the program to take input from the user at execution time. In this section you will learn the essential techniques to perform input/output (I/O) operations from C programs.

A surprising fact is that C does not provide any features for performing I/O. I/O is accomplished by using a set of library programs, which calls on the computer's operating system to perform the task. Since the peripheral hardware differs from system to system, C chose to leave out the implementation of I/O from the base language.

The library that provides programs for input/output is known as the *standard I/O library* or, simply, the *standard library*. By default, the **cc** command includes the standard library with your program. There are many other libraries available on your system (such as the *math* library, which provides a variety of functions implementing mathematical operations), and in the next chapter you will learn how to include these libraries with your programs.

Functions in the standard library are *declared* in the header file **stdio.h** (remember the `#include <stdio.h>` line in your program?).

2.3a Output using the `printf` library function

You have seen the use of the `printf` function already:

```
printf("Mariana Trench is %f miles deep\n", depth_in_miles);
```

When this line was executed in your program, the displayed result was something similar to:

```
Mariana Trench is 6.780303 miles deep
```

Notice that the `%f` sequence within the string

```
"Mariana Trench is %f miles deep\n"
```

is replaced by the numeric value of the variable `depth_in_miles`. The replacement is done using the floating point format (which is what the *f* in the `%f` stands for). Character sequences that begin with a `%` are special to the `printf` function and are known as *format specifiers*.

A format specifier instructs the `printf` function how to interpret its corresponding *data-item*, which is the value to be printed. In our example, the data-item is the value of the variable `depth_in_miles`, and the `%f` format specifier instructs the `printf` function to interpret the data-item as a floating point value.

The `\n` (read as *backslash-n*) character sequence is a control code that inserts a new line at the end of the string being printed. Other control codes used in printing will be discussed later.

Syntax **`printf` statement for output**

```
printf ("output-string with formats", data-items);
```

Data-items can be variables (such as `depth_in_miles`), constant values (such as the numbers 100, 3.24), or even *expressions*.

Definition *Expression*

An expression is a combination of numerals, variables and operators (such as + and =) that produces a value. For example 6, 7 * (8 + 2), i + 1, etc., are all expressions. C permits the use of expressions in most places where variables are used.

Example **Print the value of PI**

```
printf("The value of PI is %f\n", 3.14);
```

will be printed as:

```
The value of PI is 3.140000
```

More than one data-item can be printed using the **printf** function. Each item must have its own format specifier, placed in the order in which the data-items are placed. The next example shows the printing of two data-items using a **printf** statement.

Example Printing two data-items using one **printf** statement

```
/* The following program fragment computes area and
 * circumference of a circle. Note that this is only a
 * fragment: To run this program, you must enclose this
 * in a main block
 */

int radius;
float area, circumference, pi;

pi = 3.14;
radius = 2;
area = pi * (radius * radius);
circumference = 2 * pi * radius;
printf("Area = %f, Circumference = %f\n", area,
        circumference);
```

When the program is run, the results will be printed as:

```
Area = 12.560000, Circumference = 12.560000
```

Some often used format specifiers are given below:

Format sequence	Use
%d	Normal integer format (decimal system)
%c	Character format
%f	Floating point format
%s	String format

In addition, you can specify an optional *field width*, which is the minimum width of the datum to be printed, and an optional *precision*, which is the number of significant digits after the period (in the case of floating point values), as shown below: format specification;field width

    %field-width.precision

The field width specifies the *minimum* number of digits to be printed. An optional minus (–) placed before the field width left-justifies the item printed.

For floating points the precision specifies the number of digits to be printed to the right of the decimal point. The following examples illustrate these formatting options:

Note   *If no precision is specified, a precision of 6 is assumed. This is the reason why numbers such as* 6.780303 *were being generated without specifying the precision.*

The next example describes the specification of width and precision, and its effect when printed.

Example   **Specifying the width and precision in printing**

Format sequence	Effect when printed
%5d	Print an integer using at least 5 spaces for width.
%.2f	Print a **float** value with 2 places after the decimal.
%5.2f	Print a **float** value with total width 5 and precision 2.

Note   *If the number of digits after the decimal point is larger than the specified precision, rounding of the digits to the specified precision takes place.*

The next example shows the computation and printing of the value of PI using the approximation of PI = 22/7.

```
printf("%.2f\n", 22.0/7.0);    /* Print with precision 2 */
3.14
```

Simple Input and Output

```
printf("%.5f\n", 22.0/7.0);    /* Print with precision 5 */
3.14285

printf("%3.2f\n", 22.0/7.0);   /* Minimum width is 3 */
3.14

printf("%5.2f\n", 22.0/7.0);   /* Minimum width 5,
                                  including period. Notice
                                  the blank before 3 */
 3.14

printf("%7.4f\n", 22.0/7.0);   /* Width = 7,
                                  precision = 4 */
 3.1429

printf("%11.9f\n", 22.0/7.0);  /* Precision = 9,
                                  width = 11 */
3.142857143
```

Note *The requested width is only a minimum; actual width may be greater, but will not be less than requested.*

```
printf("%10d\n", 22);          /* Width of integer = 10
                                  Notice the blanks */
        22
```

Note that attempting to print the value of PI, as shown below, will not work:

```
printf("%.2f\n", 22/7); /* Print with precision 2 */
```

The above line will not work due to two reasons:
- According to C's rules for integer division, dividing **22** by **7** yields the integer value **3**, truncating any fractional part.
- Printing the integer value **3**, using floating point format **%f** is not correct, as the representation of integers and floating point numbers are not the same.

If any of the operands is a floating point number (or a floating point variable), C will perform floating point division and produce floating point values as the result. This is the reason why we used the floating point number `5280.0` in the depth conversion program:

```
depth_in_miles = depth_in_feet / 5280.0;
```

These rules are discussed in detail in a subsequent section. Meanwhile, to avoid these problems, write floating point constants with explicit decimal points even when the constants have integral values.

The next example shows how we can use the `printf` function to print values of different type by using the format specifiers.

Example **Using two different format specifiers**

```
int radius;
float area;

radius = 2;
area   = 3.14 * radius * radius;
printf ("Area of a circle of radius %d is %5.2f\n",
         radius, area);
```

Notice that the radius of the circle is printed in decimal integer format, while the area is printed in floating point format.

2.3b **Control codes in printing using `printf`**

You may have observed that the character sequence `\n`, when printed, forces a new line at the end of the line being output. Many other special character sequences are available. Some most often used sequences and the effect they produce when used in a print string are given below.

Character sequence	Result when used in an output string
\n	Skips to the beginning of the next line.
\t	Skips one tab stop.
\b	Backspaces by one.
\a	Beeps at the terminal.

2.3c Exercise

1. Modify the depth conversion program to print the result of the computation with a precision of 2 digits. Similarly, modify the centimeter conversion and the marathon conversion program to use a precision of 1 decimal digit.

2.3d Input using the `scanf` library function

The depth conversion program, as it is written, is not very general. It is used to convert 35,800 feet to its equivalent value in miles, something that an ordinary (nonprogrammable) calculator can compute with much less hassle. A general program should be able to take the value to be converted as input from your keyboard and perform the conversion. To read input from the keyboard, the `scanf` function available in the standard library can be used.

To illustrate the use of `scanf`, the program that computes the area and the circumference of a circle of given radius is modified to take the radius as a user input. Instead of using any preset value for the variable `radius`, we will use the number input by the user. Type in the following program and run it, after successfully compiling.

```
#include <stdio.h>

main()
{
   int radius;
   float area, circumference, pi;

   pi = 3.14;
   printf("Enter the radius of the circle --> ");
   scanf("%d", &radius);/* Read input value into radius */
   area = pi * radius * radius;
   circumference = 2 * pi * radius;
   printf("Area of a circle of radius %d is %5.2f\n",
           radius, area);
   printf("Circumference of a circle of radius %d is \
%5.2f\n", radius, circumference);
}
```

Observe that the program is expecting the user to input an integer value as the radius of the circle. If you type in a floating point number at the prompt, the program will simply read the integer part of the floating point number and thus will produce incorrect results.

The informal syntax of `scanf` is shown below.

Syntax **`scanf` statement for input**

```
scanf ("format-control-string", &variable-to-hold-value);
```

The *format-control-string* instructs `scanf` to interpret the input value according to the format specified by the format character. The format codes are the same as those used by `printf`.

The format control string may also contain *white space* (blanks, tabs (horizontal and vertical), new lines and form feed), which are ignored.

Note the strange `&` (ampersand), before the variable name, which is to receive the value input by the user. When using `scanf`, due to reasons too complicated to explain here, it is necessary to place an `&` before every variable.[*]

The `scanf` function can be used to input more than one value at a time: provide a format specifier for each value to be read in, and list the variables that will hold the values, in the corresponding order. The next example illustrates this:

Example **Using `scanf` to input two values**

```
/* Read two values input by the user
 * into the variables age and salary
 */
scanf ("%d %f", &age, &salary);
```

The `scanf` function shown above reads the first input value in integer format into the variable `age` and the second input value in floating point format into the variable `salary`. Input values can be entered, separated by white space.

---

[*] There are some exceptions to this rule. You will realize why this is necessary after you learn about C's *call by value* semantic in function calls.

Thus the following input is valid to the above `scanf` call:

```
30      30000
30 30000
```

Whereas, the following input is not valid:

```
30, 30000
```

The reason is that the comma (,) is not considered a white space character.

If any other character besides white space appears in the control string, the input to `scanf` must match the character in the control string. For example, if we were to modify the previous `scanf` function call as shown

```
scanf("%d, %f", &age, &salary);
```

then the valid input to the `scanf` statement will be

```
30, 30000
```

For the input shown above, the comma matches the comma in the format control string, and thus the input is valid. However, the following input is invalid:

```
30      30000
```

In this case, the input does not contain the comma specified in the format control string. Hence, the input is invalid.

As noted above, the format code instructs the `scanf` function to interpret the input value according to the format character. But bear in mind that it is the user's responsibility to ensure that the input value entered is in the form expected by `scanf`.

2.3e Exercises

1. Compile and run the following program, and verify its behavior by giving it sample inputs:

```
#include <stdio.h>

main()
{
   int age, salary;
   printf("enter age and salary\n");
   scanf("%d, %d", &age, &salary);
   printf("age = %d, salary = %d\n", age, salary);
}
```

When the program runs, type some sample input and validate the behavior of the program. Next, modify the `scanf` statement as shown below, recompile and run the program, and verify its behavior by entering some sample data.

```
scanf("%d %d", &age, &salary);
```

2 The variable name(s) used for storing input values using the `scanf` function is always preceded by an `&`. If you omit the `&` by mistake and run your program, your program may "crash" (terminate prematurely) with warning messages such as "segmentation violation" or "memory fault — core dumped." In the centimeter conversion program, delete the `&` preceding the variable `inches`, recompile and run the program, and see what happens.

3 Write a program to convert from Fahrenheit to Celsius values. The program should prompt the user for Fahrenheit value and then accept the user input (a floating point value). After the input is read into a variable (called `fahr`), convert the Fahrenheit value according to

```
celsius = (5.0 / 9.0) * (fahr - 32.0)
```

In the above program, change the *expression* `(5.0 / 9.0)` to `(5 / 9)`, recompile and run the program, and study the output. Why is the answer wrong?

2.4 All about Program Variables

You have used variables such as `inches`, `fahr`, etc., in the programs seen so far. In this section you will learn the complete rules for declaring variables. Variables are also known as *identifiers*.

Variables must be declared before they are used in programs. Variable declaration has two components: naming the variable and specifying its type.

Think about the role variables have in programs: *variables hold (possibly) changing data values of appropriate type.*

Tip *Choose meaningful variable names: A variable called* `value` *(as in* `float value`*) which is used for storing values representing miles is better declared as* `float miles`*. Some programmers are notorious for choosing inappropriate variable names — if you are studying or modifying someone else's program, check to see if the variable names really reflect program usage. More often than not you will be surprised!*

Tip *Use the underscore (_) character to compose more readable, more meaningful variable names, such as* `num_of_miles`, `std_deviation`, *etc.*

Referring to the earlier example, `inches` is a variable that can hold floating point values that represent inches in a program. The variable `radius` represents integer-valued radius measurements of a circle.

2.4a Rules for naming variables

- Variable names are made up of letters, digits and underscores (_). However, the first character must be a letter or underscore.
- In ANSI C, a variable name may contain up to 31 characters. Note that 31 significant characters are the required minimum; some compilers exceed this requirement. Beware that some older, non-ANSI C compilers limit variable names to 7 or 8 characters.
- Uppercases and lowercases are distinct. Thus the variable names `inches` and `Inches` are two distinct variables (which could cause much confusion when used in a program and should be avoided!).

Example Valid and invalid variable names

Variable name	Validity	Explanation
`circumference`	Valid	Up to 31 characters OK
`Radius`	Valid	Capital letters OK
`1flag`	Invalid	Cannot begin with a digit
`num_of_miles`	Valid	Underscore allowed in names
`num-of-miles`	Invalid	Hyphen is not allowed
`$amount`	Invalid	Special symbols such as $ are not allowed
`amount1`	Valid	Digits allowed in name
`default`	Invalid	C reserved word (see below)

The following is a list of reserved words, which have special meaning for C programs. They cannot be used as program variables:

```
auto       break      case       char       const
continue   default    do         double     else
enum       extern     float      for        goto
if         int        long       register   return
short      signed     sizeof     static     struct
switch     typedef    union      unsigned   void
volatile   while
```

Use of the above keywords as variables in a program will lead to syntax errors, some of which are hard to trace. If you are composing a program and see strange errors, check to see if you are using a reserved name as a program variable. If you are, change the name of your variable.

Note *In addition to the list of ANSI reserved words, most C compilers also reserve the usage of the word* `asm`, *which is used for embedding assembly language instructions in C code.*

2.4b Declaring the type of the variable

As mentioned before, every program variable that you use (such as **depth_in_feet, depth_in_miles**) must be declared before they are used in any other statement. The declaration of a variable specifies its data type (such as **int** or **float**) and a list of one or more names.

Syntax **Declaring variables**

data-type variable-name;

or

data-type variable-names-separated-by-commas;

Example **Valid and invalid declarations**

Declaration	Correctness	Remarks
`int radius;`	Valid	
`float area`	Invalid	Missing semicolon (;).
`int val1,val2;`	Valid	Can declare more than one variable.
`int v1,int v2;`	Invalid	Syntactically incorrect. Correct as `int v1,v2;` or `int v1; int v2;`
`char flag;`	Valid	**char** is a valid data type.

Each declaration must be *unique*. That is, you cannot have the same variable name declared twice in the *same block* (such as the **main** block).

2.4c Exercise

Write a program that accepts two integer-valued numbers and then prints their sum (in integer format) and average (in floating point format, with a precision of 2).

2.5 Common Problems

Some mistakes, common at this stage of program development are listed below:

1. Program file name does not end with a **.c** extension. Rename the file to end with a **.c** extension.

2. Missing "( )" after the `main`. Insert the "( )".

3. Missing beginning curly brace "{" or missing the matching closing brace "}". Insert them at the appropriate place, as shown in the original text.

4. Omission of the semicolon at the end of statements such as `printf(...)`. Fix it by inserting a semicolon as: `printf(...);`

5. Missing quotes inside the `printf` statement:

   ```
   printf("Hello world\n);
              or
   printf(Hello world\n");
   ```

   Correct as shown in the original program text.

6. String split across two lines without the use of escape character:

   ```
   printf("This is a very long string, which has
           been split improperly\n");
   ```

   Though C allows the splitting of a single statement across several lines, a string should be *escaped* before splitting, using a "\" (backslash) as shown below:

   ```
   printf("This is a very long string, which has \
   been split properly\n");
   ```

7. Hidden characters introduced by your word processor. If you are using a word processor/editor that introduces special symbols such as end-of-line

marker, end-of-paragraph marker, etc., into your program text file, the C compiler will flag these as errors. Unfortunately, you may not be able to see the offending characters until you turn on the viewing of hidden symbols or look at it using another full-feature ASCII editor. Find the extraneous characters and remove them.

8. Program terminates when a value is entered in response to an input statement in the program. If you see a system message such as "memory fault" or "segmentation violation" or "bus error," this could be due to the omission of the "&" before the name of the variable in the `scanf` statement.

9. Program behaves incorrectly for certain inputs: Make sure that the format for input variables in the `scanf` statements matches the type of the data input at the keyboard.

3
Dealing with Data

Programming is mainly about manipulating data. Thus it is necessary to master the topic of data representation in order to write correct, efficient and *portable* programs.

Definition *Portable program*

A program is portable if it compiles and runs with little or no modification on a computer system different from the original system on which the program was compiled and tested.

In this chapter, you will learn in detail about data representation in C. The basic data types are discussed, followed by the nature of *constant* data (i.e., data values that cannot change).

3.1 Math Tutor Program

In this section you will start developing a simple arithmetic tutor program that tests the user's skills in addition. The bare bones of the program will be developed here. Through the remaining chapters, the program will be enhanced by the addition of functionality as well as techniques to make the program more solid.

The program development is simple. First you need two numbers generated at random. After the numbers have been generated, the user should be prompted for the result of addition of the numbers. The user's input should be read in and compared with the actual result of the addition, and an output message indicating success or failure should be printed. If the user's input was incorrect, the correct result should also be displayed. Each of the above steps is discussed in more detail below:

The first step is the generation of a pair of random numbers. For this you can use the **rand** function from the C standard library. The function **rand** returns a new pseudo-random number each time it is called. The random number will be in the range from zero to at least 32,767 (actual upper bound is a value defined by the *macro* **RAND_MAX** — you will learn what a macro is, shortly). Before **rand** is called, the generator needs to be initialized by supplying a *seed* value to it. This is accomplished by calling a function called **srand**, which takes a *seed* value: a number necessary to –jump-start— the engine of the random number generator. We will use an arbitrary number as the seed value.

Code for seeding the generator and obtaining a random number is shown below:

```
/* Program to generate a random number */
#include <stdlib.h>   /* ANSI C file. If not present,
                         use math.h */

main()
{
    int number;         /* To hold the random number */

    srand(17);    /* Initialize the generator,
                    * using a seed value 17 */
    number = rand();
    /* For testing, print the number generated */
    printf("number generated was %d\n", number);
}
```

Before the random number can be used in the tutor program, the number needs to be sized down. The random number generated by **rand** is in the range from 0 to a very large value. How many people can multiply the numbers 31,784 and 22,375? The common technique used to scale a number to a desired upper bound is by dividing the number by the upper bound value and then taking the remainder of the division (which will never be larger than the divisor). This can be accomplished by using the *modulus operator* (**%**) provided by C. Choosing an upper bound of 20 and using the modulus operator, the random number can be scaled down, as shown below:

```
number = rand() % 20;
```

The resulting number will be in the range from 0 to 19.

After two random numbers are generated, a prompt string should be printed, instructing the user to total the two numbers. Next, the user's input should be stored in a suitable variable. Assuming that the first random number is stored in the variable **number1** and the second number is stored in the variable **number2**, the code for prompting the user and then storing the user's response into an integer variable called **response** is shown below:

```
printf("%d + %d ? ", number1, number2);
scanf("%d", &response);
```

The user's input is to be compared against the actual sum of the two numbers. The two numbers need to be summed and stored in an integer variable called **sum**.

```
sum = number1 + number2;
```

The next step is the checking of the user's input against the actual sum of the values in the variables **number1** and **number2**. This involves a decision-making process: Is the value entered by the user equal to the value stored in **sum**? For decision making, C provides the **if** statement. The nature of the **if** statement is as shown below and top of the next page:

```
if (the comparison performed here yields success)
{
   /* Execute these statements enclosed
      in the curly braces */
   statements
}
else /* The comparison failed */
{
   /* Execute these statements enclosed
      in the curly braces */
   statements
}
```

Note The **else** part of the statement is not necessary (syntactically) and may be omitted.

What constitutes success or failure? Success and failure are determined by the result of the comparison operation performed within the parentheses. C provides many comparison operators. For the purpose of testing whether the values in two variables are equal, the equality operator == can be used. Do not confuse the equality operator == (two equals signs) with the assignment operator = (one equals sign). If the comparison succeeded, an output message needs to be printed. If the comparison failed, then the output message should indicate failure and display the correct result. The code for this is shown below:

```c
if (response == sum) /* Comparison using equality
                                operator */
{
    printf("Correct\n");
}
else
{
    printf("Wrong. The correct answer is %d\n", sum);
}
```

The complete program is given below:

```c
/* Simple math tutor program. Tests addition skills */
#include <stdlib.h>     /* ANSI C file. If not present,
                         * use math.h */
main()
{
    int number1, number2; /* Hold 2 random numbers */
    int sum, response;    /* Hold actual sum and user's
                             response */
    srand(17);            /* Initialize the generator,
                           * using a seed value (17) */
    number1 = rand() % 20;/* First random number */
    number2 = rand() % 20;/* Second random number */

    sum = number1 + number2;
    printf("%d + %d ? ", number1, number2);
    scanf("%d", &response);
    if (response == sum)
    {
```

All about Data Types

```
        printf("Correct\n");
    }
    else
    {
        printf("Wrong. The correct answer is %d\n", sum);
    }
}
```

Now it's your turn to enhance the tutor program.

3.1a   Exercises

1 Modify the math tutor program to test the user's skills in multiplication, as well as addition. Generate a different pair of random numbers for each test.

2 Write a program that prompts the user for an integer. When the user inputs the value, print the number, the square and the cube of the number. (Sample output shown for an input value of 5.)

```
----------------------------------
|   5   |    25    |    125    |
----------------------------------
```

3.2   All about Data Types

Understanding the nature of data representation is essential to writing efficient, correct and portable programs. To illustrate why, consider the writing of a very simple conversion program that computes the energy equivalent of mass using Einstein's famous equation $e = mc^2$. In the equation, e is the energy value in joules, m is the mass in kilograms and c is the velocity of light in meters/second. Given the velocity of light (3×10^8 meters/second), you probably would be tempted to write the following program:

```
/* Program to compute the energy equivalent of given mass */
main()
{
    int velocity_of_light;
```

```
    float mass, energy;

    velocity_of_light = 300000000;
    printf("Enter the mass (in kilograms) \
to be converted: ");
    scanf("%f", &mass);
    energy = mass *
            (velocity_of_light * velocity_of_light);
    printf("Energy equivalent of %f kilograms of \
mass = %f\n", mass, energy);
}
```

The program appears to be quite simple and straightforward. Unfortunately, the program cannot be relied upon, until we verify that the number 300000000 will fit into a memory location of type `int` without overflowing. It is the programmer's responsibility to ensure that values used in programs will fit into memory locations designated to hold them.

Even if we find that the number 300000000 can fit into an `int` variable, we need to verify that the square of the number times the mass in the statement

```
    mass * (velocity_of_light * velocity_of_light);
```

will fit into the variable `energy`, which is of type `float`.

Definition *Bits, bytes and Size*

A byte is the smallest unit of addressable memory. When a C program is run, each of the variables in the program occupies a number of memory locations, which is an integral number of bytes.
Each byte is made up of a fixed number of bits (usually 8). Each bit can assume a value of 0 or 1. The size of a data type is the number of bytes occupied by a variable of the type.

The above example illustrates the need to know more about these data types before variables of these types can be used correctly. But before we get into these details, let us discuss data types, in general.

3.2a Attributes of variables

In general, a variable declared as a certain data type (e.g., `int miles`) has two attributes:
- The name assigned to the variable by you, the programmer.
- The size of storage allocated to it by the particular C compiler you are using. The storage size determines how large a value can be assigned to it.

Declaring a variable to be of a certain type provides information to the C compiler on how much storage to allocate for that variable and also on how that variable is to be interpreted when used in computations.

The most basic data types in C are:
- `char` — Data type to hold integral values corresponding to the representation of characters in the ASCII character set *
- `int` — Data type to hold integral values (natural numbers)
- `float` — Data type to hold single-precision floating point values (real numbers)
- `double` — Data type to hold double-precision floating point values (real numbers)

In addition to the basic types shown above, C provides the following types.
- `void` — Data type with no storage associated with it (hence no value can be stored in it). The use for `void` will become apparent when you learn about *pointers*, in Chapter 9 and functions, in Chapter 10.
- `enum` — Data type to represent a list of values

C also provides the facilities to build user-defined data types from the basic data types. You will learn how to build and use these *aggregate data types* in later chapters that discuss *arrays* and *structures*.

---

* We assume that the encoding used by the machine is ASCII.

3.2b Size of the basic data types

Hopefully, you are convinced that it is important to know the sizes of various data types in order to use them correctly. In this section you will learn how to compute the size of the basic data types.

When a variable (of any type) is declared, storage is allocated to hold the variable in memory. The amount of storage required depends on the type of variable and your computer's architecture.

The following program can be used to compute the size in bytes of the various data types on your computer. Type in the program, compile and run it, and write its output in the space below. Edit the first **printf** statement, and replace the underscores with the name of the computer that you are working on (such as Sun SPARCstation, IBM AT, VAX 11/750, etc.).

Example Compute sizes of fundamental types on your computer

```
#include <stdio.h>
main()
{
    printf("Size of various data types on the _____\n");
    printf("Size of a char is %d byte\n", sizeof(char));
    printf("Size of an int is %d bytes\n", sizeof(int));
    printf("Size of a float is %d bytes\n", sizeof(float));
    printf("Size of a double is %d bytes\n", sizeof(double));
}
```

Note that **sizeof** is an *operator*, which when applied to a data type (or a variable of a particular data type) gives the size in bytes of that data type.

Write down the output, in the space provided. You will have use for this information later.

```
Size of various data types on the

    Size of a char is                    byte
    Size of an int is                    bytes
    Size of a float is                   bytes
    Size of a double is                  bytes
```

Note that these sizes are not absolute. C does not guarantee that these sizes will remain the same on all machine architectures. The only guarantee that C makes is that the size of a character will be 1 byte.

Given the sizes of the various data types of the computer that you are using, you can calculate the range of the values that can be placed into a variable of that type. For example, a character (data type `char`) has a size of 1 byte, or 8 bits. Thus, a variable declared as a `char` should be able to hold a positive value from 0 (all bits 0) to 255 (all bits 1).

It is appropriate at this point to ask the question, "Why should a variable declared as a character hold integer values?" One would assume that the data type `char` is meant to hold characters such as `'a'`, `'b'`, `'c'`. The answer to this question is revealed in the next section, in which the data type `char` is discussed in more detail. For now, just think of the character type as an integer type which is smaller in size.

A negative value is represented by the most significant bit (which is the leftmost bit on most computers' architectures) being a 1. Thus if a negative value is stored in a character variable, the most significant bit will be set to 1 to indicate that the value is negative. Only the remaining 7 bits will be available for holding the value, which can be from −128 to 127.

If it is 2 bytes (16 bits) wide, an integer variable can hold a value from −32,768 (-2^{15}, since the leftmost bit is used as the sign bit) to 32,767 ($2^{15} - 1$). If integers are 4 bytes wide, the range of values will be from −2,147,483,648 (-2^{31}) to 2,147,483,647 ($2^{31} - 1$).*

Fortunately, you don't have to remember all these crazy numbers. The system header file **limits.h** has all the information you need. On UNIX systems, the header file can be found in the directory **/usr/include**. On DOS systems, the header file will usually be in a subdirectory under the directory in which the compiler is installed. Shown below are some of the definitions from **limits.h**. You should examine the header file **limits.h** on your system. The lines in the file are of the form:

---

* All values shown, assuming 2's complement encoding.

```
#define    data_type_MIN      -number
                   or
#define    data_type_MAX      number
```

In the above construct, *data_type* stands for the name of the data type in uppercase (such as CHAR, INT), and the suffixes MIN and MAX stand for the smallest and the largest values assignable to a variable of the type. The construct **#define** is a *macro* definition facility provided by the *C preprocessor*.

Definition Macro

A macro is a symbolic name that gets translated into a program construct. A macro is composed of a name followed by a construct. The C preprocessor replaces the name, wherever it appears in a program, with the construct that follows the name. You will learn more about the C preprocessor in Chapter 6.

An excerpt from the file **limits.h** is shown below:

```
#define CHAR_BIT     8     /* Width of character in bits */
#define SCHAR_MIN    -127  /* Minimum value of signed char */
#define SCHAR_MAX    127   /* Maximum value of signed char */
#define UCHAR_MAX    255   /* Maximum value of unsigned
                              char */
#define SHRT_MIN    -32767 /* Minimum value of short int */
#define SHRT_MAX     32767 /* Maximum value of short int */
```

It is a very good idea to look up **limits.h** before you write programs that require the use of large values. Thus, according to the **limits.h** header file, the energy conversion program may be unsafe the way it is presented here. Can this problem be fixed by using **double** in place of **ints** and **floats**? This in turn depends on the size of **double** and the maximum value that may be placed in a variable of size **double**.

Values pertinent to the floating point data types (**float** and **double**) are given in the header file **float.h**. Given below is a section from **float.h**.

```
#define FLT_DIG    6  /* Number of decimal digits of
                         precision */
#define DBL_DIG    10
#define FLT_MIN    1.17549435e-38
```

```
#define FLT_MAX    3.40282347e+38
#define DBL_MIN    2.2250738585072014e-308
#define DBL_MAX    1.7976931348623157e+308
```

Notice the line

```
#define FLT_MAX    3.40282347e+38
```

The macro **FLT_MAX** represents the maximum representable finite number, which fortunately is large enough to hold the results from our conversion program. Thus, the choice of the data types is safe for the energy conversion program.

So, what's the moral of the story? Pay attention to the choice of data types in your program.

3.2c **Exercise**

Write a program that computes and displays the volume and weight of liquids held in a tank of dimensions specified by the user. The program should prompt for the length, the width and the height of the tank and the density of the liquid.

3.3 Changing the Size of a Data Type

As noted previously, the basic data types **char** and **int** can hold positive or negative values. But how do you notify the compiler that you intend to use only positive or positive/negative values in a program? This can be achieved by using a *modifier* or a *qualifier* for the data type.

Definition *Qualifier*

Qualifiers are additional attributes that you specify to a data type to (possibly) change the size and/or the interpretation of the sign bit of a data type.

The syntax for declaring a variable using a qualifier for the basic data type is as shown below:

Syntax **Declaring qualifiers for a data type**

```
qualifiers data type variable-name;
```

The qualifiers for changing the size are:

Qualifier	Use
short	Changes the size of **ints**
long	Changes the size of **ints** and **doubles**

Examples   **Using qualifiers**

```
short int miles;
long int sound_velocity;
short loop_index;   /* Same as short int loop_index */
long ss_no;         /* Same as long int ss_no */
long double e;
```

Now, the inevitable question: Why is it necessary to change the size of a data type?

The size of the data type **int** is the same as the size of a memory *word* on most computers. Consider a computer with a word size and integer size of 4 bytes. You have already learned that by using all 32 bits, one can store a large value in a variable of type **int**. However, empirical studies have revealed that most integer data values used in a program will fit within 8 to 12 bits.

So for variables that may contain small values, why waste 2 or more bytes? This conservation of memory is especially important for programs that have to fit into smaller memories (such as programs that run under DOS without any extended or expanded memory support).

An integer that occupies 2 (instead of 4) bytes may be large enough to hold most data values in your programs. By declaring a variable to be of type **short int** (or **short**), you are notifying the compiler that the variable will only contain relatively small values and thus to allocate less memory for the integer variable *if possible*.

In order to justify why the qualifier **long** is necessary, we will use the same line of reasoning as above. Computers with a word size of 2 bytes will have data type **int** allocated in 2 bytes. The range of values that can be placed in variables of type **int** is relatively small. If you need to use values larger than

Changing the Size of a Data Type 43

what will fit into a normal `int`, you may *try* to achieve this by declaring the variable to be `long int` (or `long`).

Unfortunately, there is no guarantee that a `short int` will be smaller than an `int` or that a `long int` will be larger than an `int`. The only guarantee provided by C is that an `int` may not be smaller than a `short` and a `long` may not be smaller than an `int`. Once again, you need to refer to the files **limits.h** and **float.h** to verify the actual range of values.

3.3a Specifying the sign of a variable

The second use of qualifiers is in specifying the —signedness— of a variable. The qualifiers for specifying the nature of the variable (positive or positive/negative) are:

Qualifier	Use
`signed`	Positive or negative values may be assigned to a variable of this type (default).
`unsigned`	Only positive values may be assigned to a variable of this type.

The qualifier `signed` is the default and may be omitted from declarations. Using the qualifier `unsigned` instructs the compiler to use all the bits in the storage to represent the value stored in a variable.

Example **Using qualifiers to specify sign**

```
unsigned char flag;    /* Always treat flag as positive */
unsigned int loop_index;
signed int kelvin;     /* Same as int kelvin */
```

In the example above, all 8 bits of the variable `flag` will be available to store values. Thus the range of values can be from 0 to 255. Similarly, for integers of width n bits, the range of values can be from 0 to $2^n - 1$. The range of values is given in the header file **limits.h**, with the letter U prefixing the data type name. For example, the following may be defined for a certain computer architecture.

```
#define UCHAR_MAX      255      /* Maximum value of
                                 * unsigned char */
#define UINT_MAX       65535    /* Maximum value of
                                 * unsigned int  */
```

Note *The qualifier* `signed` *was introduced in ANSI C and may not be available in older C compilers.*

Note *Using a qualifier does not change the nature of the data type. For example, an* `int` *will always hold integral values (whole numbers) regardless of whether it is a* `short int` *or a* `long int`.

3.3b Qualifiers for variables that do not change values

Another qualifier of interest is `const`. Qualifying a data type as `const` notifies the compiler that the variable of the type should not change its value after an initial value has been assigned to it. The initial value for the variable is assigned at the point of declaration. Any subsequent assignment to the variable will be flagged as an error by the compiler.

Example Declaring constant values

```
const float pi = 3.14; /* Variable pi should not change */
const int miles = 26;
```

To summarize, here's the list of all qualifiers:

Qualifier	Use	Example
short	To store small integers	`short int small_val;`
long	To store large integers	`long int large_val;`
long	To store large floating point values	`long double very_large_val;`
unsigned	To store positive values only	`unsigned int pos_val;`
signed	To store positive as well as negative values	`signed int fahrenheit;`

Changing the Size of a Data Type

Qualifier	Use	Example
const	To store values that do not change after initialization	const int my_age = 26;

The depth conversion program, modified to take advantage of the topics discussed above, is shown below:

```
/* Modified program to compute the depth of Mariana
 * Trench (the deepest known point in the oceans)
 * in miles
 */

#include <stdio.h>

main()
{
    const unsigned int depth_in_feet = 35800;
    float depth_in_miles;

    depth_in_miles = depth_in_feet / 5280.0;
    printf("Mariana Trench is %f miles deep\n",
            depth_in_miles);
}
```

In reality, programmers do not write such stringent code. So do not be surprised if you do not see all possible qualifiers used in declarations where they may be really appropriate. For example, most programmers would write:

```
const int depth_in_feet = 35800;
```

As mentioned before, there is no guarantee that a **short** will be smaller than an **int** or that a **long** will be longer. If you are using an older, non-ANSI compliant compiler, you may not have the file **limits.h** on your system. In any case, you should verify the facts mentioned above by completing the exercise at the end of this section.

3.3c Displaying data using `printf`

So far we only learned to display integers, floating points, characters and strings, using the format specifiers d, f, c and s, placed after the % (%d, %f, %c and %s). How do we instruct `printf` to display the value in a variable that is declared **unsigned**? If we don't notify `printf` that a variable has been declared as **unsigned**, `printf` will treat the value in the variable as normal (signed). If the variable contains a value large enough to turn the most-significant bit on, `printf` will display the value as negative.

To display the value in a variable that has been declared **unsigned**, the format specifier u can be used.

Example Display value in an **unsigned** variable

```
unsigned int value;
/* Input a number into value */
printf("Variable value contains %u\n", value)
```

In addition to format conversion letters, it is possible to specify a *size modifier* letter in the format specification. The size modifier is to indicate the *width* of the datum — **int**, **short** or **long** for integer data and **double** or **long double** for floating point data. The size modifier is placed before the conversion letter. The following table contains the commonly used size modifiers.

Data Type	Conversion Letter	Size modifier
int	d	*none*
short	d	h
long	d	l
double	f	*none*
long double	f	L

Note that **floats** are treated as **double**, for printing. The following example shows how the size modifier is used in a `printf` statement.

Changing the Size of a Data Type

Example **Using a size modifier in `printf`**

```
long large_val;
unsigned long even_large_val;
long double large_float;
/* Input values into the variables declared above */
printf("Large value is %ld\n", large_val);
printf("Even large value is %lu\n", even_large_val);
printf("large float value is %Lf\n", large_float);
```

Note *The size modifier `L` may not be available on some older compilers.*

The size modifiers are applicable to `scanf` statement also. The next example shows how to to read a value into a variable declared as `short`.

Example **Using a size modifier in `scanf`**

```
short small_value;    /* short int small value */
scanf("%hd", &small_value);
```

3.3d Exercise

Write a program to compute the size of the fundamental types along with the qualifiers. Your output should like:

```
Size of a char               __ byte
Size of an unsigned char     __ bytes
Size of an int               __ bytes
Size of a short              __ bytes
Size of a long               __ bytes
Size of a float              __ bytes
Size of a double             __ bytes
Size of a long double        __ bytes
```

3.4 Data Type `char`

By now, the data types `int` and `float` should be obvious to you. Variables of type `int` hold integral values and type `float` hold floating point values. However, the data type `char` requires some discussion. The author is willing to bet a small amount (even though gambling is illegal here in Georgia, as of this writing) that you are a little confused about what characters (data type `char`) really are. Any takers?

Characters are nothing but very small integers. Since characters are always 8 bits in size, we can fit a value from 0 through 255 (unsigned, all 8 bits) or −128 to 127 (signed) into a `char`. Thus character variables are sufficiently large to hold all possible ASCII values.

What is all this about? What is ASCII and why should you care about it?

Well, you know that computers can only deal with numbers (in the form of binary digits or bits). This implies that all our printable characters — such as alphabetics (a to z, A to Z), digits (0 to 9), special characters (!@#$%^&*()-_+":';?/.,~') and even nonprintable characters (beep) need to be converted to numeric values before they can be stored in the computer.

ASCII (American Standard Code for Information Interchange) is a code devised to represent these characters inside your computer.

Here's a sample for the ASCII code set. The table shows a character and its numeric ASCII equivalent. The complete table is given in Appendix A.

Note *ANSI uses the ISO 646 codeset to specify characters. However, since ISO 646 is an invariant subset of ASCII, we use the ASCII codeset here.*

Character	ASCII code	Character	ASCII code
A	65	a	97
B	66	b	98
Z	90	z	122
0	48	9	57

As you can see from Appendix A, the maximum value is 127, which will fit nicely into 7 bits of a signed or unsigned character.

Now, if you want to print the character **A** from your program, how do you do it?

From a somewhat limited knowledge of `printf` (do not despair! this is only the third chapter!), you can easily do this:

```
printf("A");
```

You may be tempted to just print the ASCII code for **A**, which is an integer:

```
printf("%d\n", 65);
```

Unfortunately, that does not work, as 65, an integer printed in decimal format will just display that — *an integer*. What you need to do is to print the ASCII code for **A** (which is 65) and instruct the print routine to treat 65 as a character value. How do you tell `printf` that? Just use the character format specifier.

```
printf("%c\n", 65);  /* Print 65, in character format */
```

The following will be printed:

A

You could also have performed:

```
char alpha;
alpha = 65;
printf("%c\n", alpha);
```

However, it is inconvenient to remember these meaningless numbers (that's what computers were invented for, right?). A better way is needed to initialize the variable **alpha**. You can perform the initialization as

```
char alpha;
alpha = 'A';
printf("%c\n", alpha);
```

or

```
const char alpha = 'A';
printf("%c\n", alpha);
```

Note that when you perform the assignment

```
alpha = 'A';
```

the C compiler is really performing the assignment

```
alpha = 65;
```

You could also have declared **alpha** as **int** and written the program as:

```
int alpha;            /* Or even, short alpha */
alpha = 'A';
printf("%c\n", alpha);
```

The %c format specifier takes the integer value contained in the variable **alpha** and prints a character according to the conversion in the ASCII table.

So what does that tell you? Just that *characters and integers are essentially the same data type.* The only distinction is that characters will usually be smaller than integers and that characters will always be 1 byte.

Okay, enough said about the data types and their sizes. It's time to move on. But, just in case you haven't noticed, here's the scoop about sizes, as C guarantees it:

```
sizeof (char)      =  1
sizeof (short)     <= sizeof (int) <= sizeof (long)
sizeof (unsigned)  =  sizeof (int)
sizeof (float)     <= sizeof (double) <= sizeof (long double)
```

3.5 Constants

So far, you have been dealing with two kinds of data values:
- Data values stored in variables that may change during program execution. For example, the variable **miles** may be assigned an initial value and can be subsequently reassigned.
- Constant data values. For example, the number 35,800 in the declaration **int depth_in_feet = 35800;** is a constant integer value. Obviously, the constants cannot be reassigned — it does not make any sense to perform **35800 = 36800**.

Using constant values in a program is not just limited to integers. You may specify floating point constants as well as character and string constants in your program. Recall that a string is a sequence of characters enclosed within a pair of double quotes ("). Examples of using constant values are shown next.

```
int age;
char alpha;
float pi;
age = 26;                    /* 26 is an integer constant */
alpha = 'A';                 /* 'A' is a character constant */
pi = 3.14;                   /* 3.14 is a floating point
                              * constant */
printf("Hello world\n");     /* "Hello world\n" is a string
                              * constant */
```

Note the difference between character and string constants. A character constant is surrounded by single quotes, whereas a string is enclosed by double quotes. Regardless of the type of the constant, these constant values cannot appear on the left-hand side of an assignment and cannot be reassigned. Thus, the following assignments are all invalid:

```
'A' = 62; /* Invalid: character constant on LHS */
"hello" = "world"; /* Invalid: string constant on LHS */
```

Even assignments that may seem to be valid may not be so. For example, the following assignments are not valid in C.

```
char alpha;
alpha = "Hello world\n";/* Invalid: alpha can only
                            hold one char and not a
                            string */
```

The next few sections examine C's rules concerning the use of the above constant types.

3.5a Integer constants

Integer constants consist of an optional sign, a sequence of digits and an optional suffix, as shown below:

Syntax **Specifying an integer constant**

optional-prefix integer-value optional-suffix.

The following table shows the valid prefixes and examples of usage.

Prefix	Meaning	Example
+	Positive value	`int miles = +26;`
-	Negative value	`int penalty = -10;`
0x, 0X	Hexadecimal (base 16)	`int full = 0xff;`
0	Octal (base 8)	`int full = 077;`

In the list of valid prefixes shown above, the suffix "+" is not of much interest, since a constant integer value is positive by default. Often, integer constants are expressed in a base other than the decimal system (base 10). C allows octal (base 8) and hexadecimal (base 16) representations. Representing in bases which are powers of 2 allows us to view *bit patterns* with natural ease. This is often useful in systems programming. Octal and hexadecimal representation of integer constants is outlined in Chapter 13. For now, we will only deal with the decimal system.

Constants

3.5b Floating point constants

Floating point constants may also have the optional prefixes and suffixes. The syntax for specifying a floating point constant is:

Syntax **Specifying floating point constants**

```
optional-prefix real-value optional-suffix
```

Valid prefixes are:

Prefix	Meaning	Example
+	Positive value	`float pi = 3.14;`
-	Negative value	`float neg_pi = -3.14;`

Valid suffixes are:

Suffix	Meaning	Example
e, E	Exponent	`314e-2`
f, F	`float` (ANSI C)	`1.0f`
l, L	`long double` (ANSI C)	`3.8e12L`

The suffix **e** or **E** is used to represent floating point numbers in the scientific notation. Thus, the constant **314e-2** is interpreted as:

$$314 * 10^{-2}, \text{ or } 3.14$$

Dealing with Data

3.5c Character constants

Character constants, which are enclosed within a pair of single quotes (,), are characters from your machine's character set.*

Usually, only one character is allowed within the quotes. However, certain character constants, called *escape sequences*, can be used in programs to control printing, produce audible beeps, backspace and so on.

An escape sequence is a character from the ASCII character set that is preceded by a backslash (\). Putting a backslash in front of a character is called –escaping— the character and thus the term *escape sequence*. Note that the escape sequences are single characters, even though they appear to have more than one character inside the quotes (such as ' \n'). They have a numeric value in the ASCII character set. For example, ' \n' or new line has value 10 (refer to Appendix A).

You have used some of these escape sequences under the pretext of print codes in an earlier section. For example, the sequence ' \n' is an escape sequence, which when sent to the output puts a new line (carriage return and line feed) at the point where the sequence is encountered. The commonly used escape sequences and their effect when used in output are given in the following table:

Escape sequence	Effect on output
\n	New line
\t	Horizontal tab
\a	Audible alert (bell) (ANSI)
\f	Form feed
\r	Carriage return

---

* We assume that character set is represented by ASCII character set.

Constants

Example **Using character constants**

```
char BELL = '\a'; /* ASCII bell character */
printf("%cError: Please try again\n", BELL);
```

From the ASCII tables in Appendix A, you may observe that a lowercase character and an uppercase character always differ by a constant numeric value. For example, `'a'` has the value 97, `'A'` has the value 65, and the difference is 32. Similarly, `'t'` has the value 116, `'T'` has the value 84, and the difference is again 32. Thus, given an uppercase character, you can very easily convert it to lowercase and vice versa. Similarly, given ASCII values for the characters `'0'` through `'9'`, one can easily convert it to its numeric equivalents (and vice versa). If the user inputs a digit x in character format, you can convert it to its numeric value as

```
'x' - '0'
```

Let us see how this works: If the character `'8'` is to be converted, `'8' - '0'` evaluates to 56 − 48 (ASCII value of character 8 minus ASCII value of character 0), yielding the numeric value 8.

3.5d Character conversion: An example

To illustrate character conversions, the following program takes input in the form of a mix of lowercase and uppercase letters and characters and prints them out as uppercase only.

The program design is as follows:

Step ❶ – Read a character from the keyboard.

Step ❷ – Check if the character read is a lowercase letter. If it is a lowercase letter, convert it to its uppercase equivalent and print it. Otherwise, just print it.

Step ❸ – Go to step 1 and repeat until there are no more characters.

To read characters from the keyboard, the function `getchar` from the standard library can be used. The function `getchar` is used to read one character at a time. Note that the function **scanf** can also be used to read one character, as shown below:

```
char ch;
scanf("%c", &ch);
```

However, it is simpler to use **getchar** for reading one character at a time, as shown:

```
char ch;
ch = getchar(); /* Read a character from input
                   and place in ch */
```

Moreover, when there is no more input, the function **getchar** will return a special value called EOF (End Of File), which is defined as an integer value in the header file **stdio.h**. Characters input by using **getchar** can be tested against **EOF** to determine whether the user has finished input. How does the user signal the end of input? By typing the appropriate end-of-input character, which on most systems will be a *<control>d* (the keyboard representation for typing —d— while holding down the *control* key). Since **EOF** is defined as an integer value, a slight modification needs to be made to the above program stub:

```
int ch;
ch = getchar();   /* ch can be tested against EOF */
```

For writing one character to the output, the function **putchar** can be used as

```
putchar(ch);        /* Write the character contained in
                       ch to output */
```

The program also uses the **if** construct to test whether character input is an uppercase letter or not. To read all the characters in a line input by the user, a loop construct is required, and for this, we will employ the **while** construct. To terminate the loop, the character input can be tested against **EOF**. The usage of the **while** construct is as shown:

```
while(the loop test here remains true)
{
   /* Loop body: execute the statements
    * within the braces */
```

```
        statement1;
        statement2;
        ...
} /* Go back to the while and check if the
      condition still remains true */
```

The statements within the braces following the **while** will be repeatedly executed as long as the **while** condition remains true. To terminate the execution in the loop, the condition should become false at some point. In our program, we will terminate the loop when the user signals end of input (by typing a <*control*>*d*). Thus our loop condition will be

```
while ((ch = getchar()) != EOF)
{
   /* Loop body */
   statements;
}
```

The value returned by **getchar** is assigned to the variable **ch**, and that is the result of the expression inside the parentheses **(ch = getchar())**. This value is then compared for inequality against **EOF**. The comparison is performed by using the *not-equals* operator **!=**. If the comparison succeeds, the end of input has not been seen yet and the loop body is entered. If the loop body is entered, the statements within the braces are executed. When the the closing brace (**}**) is encountered, control is transferred back to the top of the loop for the loop test to be executed again.

If the comparison fails (i.e., user has indicated end of input), the loop is exited (execution resumes after the loop body).

To test whether the input is a character in the range *a* through *z*, we will use two comparison operators **>=** (greater than or equal to) and **<=** (less than or equal to). If the comparison succeeds, the body of the **if** statement will be entered and the statements within the curly braces will be executed.

The complete program is given below:

```
#include <stdio.h>
main()
{
   int ch;
```

```
        while( (ch = getchar()) != EOF)
        {
           /* Test to see if character input is a lowercase
            * letter, i.e., if it is in between 'a' and a 'z'
            */
           if (ch >= 'a')
           {
              if (ch <= 'z')
              {
                 ch = ch + 'A' - 'a'; /* Transform to upper
                                                case */
                 putchar(ch); /* Send to output */
              } /* Close of inner if */
           } /* Close of outer if */
        } /* Close of the while loop */
} /* End of main */
```

Examine the following statement closely:

```
        ch = ch + 'A' - 'a';
```

In ASCII representation, 'a' has the value 97 and 'A' has the value 65. Suppose the user entered the character 'g', which has the ASCII value 103. The arithmetic yields

```
        103 + 65 - 97 = 71
```

which is the code for 'G'. Thus the lowercase character is converted to uppercase. Since the sequence of values for lowercase alphabets is contiguous, the conversion works in all cases for the ASCII character set.

Compile and run the above program and test it for a few inputs. In the input list, include nonletters, such as $, %, &, etc. What happens in these cases?

3.5e Character conversion functions

If conversions such as the ones shown above are too cumbersome for you (justifiably), the standard library provides a variety of functions that perform the character conversions and character testing. The system header file **ctype.h** contains declarations for functions that aid in character conversion and character testing. The conversion functions have names that are prefixed with *to*, followed by the type of conversion. For example, the function `toupper(c)` returns the uppercase equivalent of its argument (shown here as an integer variable `c`). The testing functions have names that are prefixed with *is*. For example, the function `isupper(c)` returns true if its argument `c` is 1 of the 26 uppercase letters. All the testing functions return false if the intended test fails.

The commonly used conversion functions are given below:

Function	Use
`tolower(c)`	Returns the lowercase letter corresponding to uppercase letter c.
`toupper(c)`	Returns the uppercase letter corresponding to lowercase letter c.

The commonly used testing functions are given below:

Function	Use
`isalnum(c)`	Test if c is an alphanumeric character (a–z,A–Z,0–9).
`isalpha(c)`	Test if c is an alphabetic character (a–z,A–Z).
`iscntrl(c)`	Test if c is a control character.
`isdigit(c)`	Test if c is a decimal digit (0–9).
`islower(c)`	Test if c is a lowercase letter (a–z).
`isprint(c)`	Test if c is a printable character.
`isspace(c)`	Test if c is a white space character (tab, newline, space, carriage return).
`isupper(c)`	Test if c is an uppercase letter (A–Z).

3.5f <u>Exercises</u>

1. Modify the lowercase to uppercase conversion program to use the standard library routines. Use `islower` and `toupper` functions.

2. Write a program that takes an input line typed by the user (terminated by a new line) and counts the number of white space characters in the input. Recall that white space characters are new lines, tabs (horizontal and vertical), form feed and blanks. You only need to count the number of horizontal tabs and spaces. Print the count at the end of the program.

   To read an input line, read one character at a time (using `getchar`), till you read a new line (`'\n'`). Check each character to see if it is a blank or a tab, and increment a counter variable if a match is found.

3.5g <u>String constants</u>

A sequence of 0 or more characters surrounded by double quotes is called a *string constant*. You have already used string constants in program lines such as

```
printf("Hello world\n");
```

Examples **String constants**
```
"This is a string"
""      /* The null (empty) string */
"Sunday"
"Monday"
```

Strings are zero (`'\0'`) terminated by the compiler. This means that the compiler always adds the ASCII NUL character (which has the decimal value 0) to the end of your string when you declare a string. The strings in the above example will be transformed as shown:

Examples **Strings padded with null character**
```
"This is a string\0"
"\0"
```

Constants

```
"Sunday\0"
"Monday\0"
```

Thus the size (length) of a string is one more than the number of characters between the quotes. Thus the character `'x'` is not the same as the string `"x"`, since the string `"x"` is really the characters `'x'` appended by the character `'\0'`. Thus the following are not valid statements:

```
char   ch = "x"; /* ch is a char whereas
                  * "x" is a string */
printf("%s\n", 'x');
```

In the first statement, `ch` can only hold one character. Hence the correct version is

```
char   ch = 'x';
```

In the second statement, the `%s` format specifier is applicable for strings only. The correct version is

```
printf("%s\n", "x");
```

3.5h   Automatic type conversions

In expressions involving the operation on two values of different types, C converts the values to a common type by using a set of built-in rules. These rules are shown in the following table.

Type of one operand	Type of other operand	Converted type
`long double`	*any*	`long double`
`double`	*any*	`double`
`float`	*any*	`float`
`unsigned long`	*any*	`unsigned long`
`long`	`unsigned`	`long` *or* `unsigned long`
`long`	`int`	`long`

Type of one operand	Type of other operand	Converted type
unsigned	int *or* unsigned	unsigned
int	int	int

3.5i **Exercises:**

1. Write a program that prompts the user for a month code (a value between 1 and 12), a date code (a value between 1 and 31) and a year. After the values are input, print the day, date and month in verbose form. Program output should be similar to the following:

    ```
    Enter the month (1-12): 3
    Enter the date (1-31): 30
    Enter the year (1-1999): 1958

    March 30, 1958.
    ```

    The program would be more appealing if we could enter the input as: *mm/dd/yyyy* where *mm* is the month, *dd* is the date and *yyyy* is the year. This requires the knowledge of character arrays and string processing, which are beyond the scope of this chapter and will be presented later.

2. Write a program that plays a number-guessing game. To play the game, generate a random number between 0 and 100 and ask the player to guess the number. If the player guesses incorrectly, hint whether he/she needs to guess a higher or lower value, depending on whether the input was smaller than or larger than the random number generated. If the player guesses the correct value, print a string congratulating him/her and print the number of steps it took to guess the value.

    A sample run of the program is shown below:

    ```
    Guess a number between 0 and 100: 50
    Incorrect: guess higher: 75
    ```

```
Incorrect: guess lower: 60
Incorrect: guess higher: 65
Incorrect: guess higher: 68
Correct: You took 5 guesses.
```

Hint: to generate a random number from 0 to 100, review the math tutor program. To repeatedly prompt for the correct value, use a `while` loop, the basic structure of which is shown below:

```
#define INCORRECT   0
#define CORRECT     1
int answer;
int count;

answer = INCORRECT;
generate a random number and store in a variable
while (answer == INCORRECT)
{
  read user's input to variable
  if (input is equal to the generated value)
  {
     answer = CORRECT;
     print correct and number of guesses
  }
  else
  {
     print incorrect.
     increment count.
     if (input is lower than the generated value)
     {
         print higher
     }
     else
     {
         print lower.
     }
  } /* End of outer else */
} /* End of while */
```

3 It can be shown analytically that in the worst case, the correct value can be guessed in *ceiling* of $\log_2$ value steps, where value is the upper bound of the number generated (100, in our sample case). Ceiling of a number x is the smallest whole number not less than x. For example, the ceiling of 3.2 is 4.0 and the ceiling of 4.56 is 5.0.

To illustrate the above claim, assume that the computer has generated the number 33. The $\log_2$ of 100 is 6.643 and its ceiling is 7. Let us see how we can guess the number in at most 7 steps:

```
Enter the guess: 50          (half of the maximum number 100)
Incorrect: guess lower: 25   (half of 50)
Incorrect: guess higher: 38  (ceiling of 25 + (50 - 25)/2)
Incorrect: guess lower: 32   (ceiling of 25 + (38 - 25)/2)
Incorrect: guess higher: 35  (ceiling of 32 + (38 - 32)/2)
Incorrect: guess lower: 34   (ceiling of 32 + (35 - 32)/2)
Incorrect: guess lower: 33   (step 7)
Correct: It took you  7 guesses
```

As shown above, at most 7 steps were made to arrive at the correct guess.

Using the `ceil` (ceiling) and the `log2` functions available in the math library, compute the worst-case number of guesses. When the player finally guesses the correct value, print the number of guesses it took and the number of steps over or under the worst-case number of guesses.

The `log2` and the `ceil` functions both take an argument which is a `double` and return a `double` value. Use the following declarations and statements to operate the `log2` and the `ceil` functions.

```
#include <math.h>
int random_no, worstcase_guess;
worstcase_guess = ceil(log2( (double) random_no));
```

In the inner loop of the above statement, the integer variable **random_no** is converted to a `double`, as required by the `log` function. The `log` function returns a **double**, which is the argument to the **ceil** function. The **ceil** function returns a **double**, which is stored in the integer variable **worstcase_guess**.

3.6 Common Problems

Problems common at this stage of program development are:

1. Compilation problems due to nonmatching of the parentheses ({ ... }). Every opening brace "{" should have a matching closing brace, such as:

   ```
   main()
   {   /* Start of main */
       if ( ... )
       { /* Start of if */
           ...
       } /* End of if */
       else
       { /* Start of else */
           ...
       } /* End of else */
   }   /* End of main */
   ```

2. Compilation problems due to "dangling else statements." Every **else** construct should be a part of an **if** statement. Also, there should not be any statements between an **if** statement and its corresponding **else** construct. For example, the following set of statements would yield compile time errors:

   ```
   if (response == sum)
   {
      printf("Correct\n");
   }
   printf("Good guess\n");
   else    /* Error: Dangling else */
   {
      printf("Wrong. The correct answer is %d\n", sum);
   }
   ```

Remove the `printf` statement before the `else` construct.

3. Program behaves incorrectly. For reasons that are explained later, it is *not* syntactically incorrect to perform the comparisons as:

```
if (response = sum)
{
    ....
}
```

If you haven't spotted it yet, the comparison is attempted using the assignment operator = rather than the equality operator == . If the variable `sum` has a value greater than zero, the set of statements corresponding to the success part of the `if` construct will always be executed, producing incorrect results.

4. Compilation problems may due to missing parentheses around the comparison expression in the `if` construct.

4
Decision Time

C provides operators for performing arithmetic computations, relational operators for comparisons and many other operators. Expressions containing the relational operators can be combined using logical operators to form more complex relationships. These relational expressions are often used along with decision-making constructs such as the `if` statement and iterative constructs such as the `while` statement. In this chapter you will learn about arithmetic, relational and logical operators and more about the `if-else` and the `while` statements.

An operator may be a *binary operator* or a *unary* operator. A Binary operator performs operations on two operands: A left operand and a right operand. A unary operator applies the operation to only one (left or right) operand.

4.1 Arithmetic Operators

The arithmetic binary operators defined for integer and real operands are:

Operator	Purpose
+	Addition
−	Subtraction
*	Multiplication
/	Division

Operator	Purpose
%	Modulus (valid for integers only)

Example   **Using arithmetic operators**

```
val = x % y;
x = (x + 1) / (x - 1);
```

In addition, the following unary operators are used to change the sign of a data item.

Operator	Purpose
-	Negate the operand.
+	Make the operand positive (default).

4.1a Precedence of arithmetic operators

Arithmetic expressions raise the interesting question about the order of evaluation of the operators.

The term precedence (as applied to operators) defines the order in which operators will be applied in an expression if it contains more than one operator.

For example, given the following arithmetic expression

```
5 + 3 * 2
```

there are two possibilities for evaluation. If the + operator is applied before the *, the result will be 16. If the * operator is applied before the +, the result will be 11. It is clear from this example that the order of evaluation must be known to write these expressions correctly.

There are two factors that control the order of evaluation in an expression: The *precedence* of the operators in the expression and the *associativity* rule for the operator.

Arithmetic Operators

Definition *Precedence and associativity*

Precedence defines the priority with which each operator in an expression will be applied.

Associativity defines the order of evaluation of operators in an expression containing operators of the same precedence. If the evaluation is from left to right, the operator is termed left-to-right associative. Otherwise, the operator is right-to-left associative.

Example **Evaluation of the expression 5 + 3 * 2**

From the table on page 91 we see that the * operator has a higher precedence than the + operator. Thus the * operator will be applied before the + operator, and the expression will be evaluated as `5 + (3 * 2)`.

All arithmetic operators are left-to-right associative. Thus the expression

```
5 + 4 - 2
```

is evaluated from left to right as

```
(5 + 4) - 2
```

The expression

```
a * b * c
```

is evaluated as

```
(a * b) * c
```

The assignment operator = is evaluated right to left. In the expression **a = b = c**, the value contained in variable **c** is assigned to the variable **b**, which is then copied to the variable **c**.

The precedence and associativity of all the arithmetic operators are given below. Operators in the same row have the same precedence. We will assign each row a number indicative of its precedence, larger numbers signifying higher precedence.

Operator	Meaning	Precedence	Associativity
-, +	Sign change (unary)	3 (high)	Right to left
*, /, %	Multiplicative	2	Left to right
-, +	Additive	1 (low)	Left to right

Now, let us examine how **5 + 3 * 2** will really be evaluated. Since ***** has a higher precedence than **+**, **3 * 2** will be evaluated first yielding the value 6, and then the addition of the value 5 will be performed, yielding the value 11.

Let's try another example that illustrates precedence as well as associativity: We will trace the evaluation of the arithmetic expression **4+4+3*2+5+6.**

Expression	Comment on evaluation
4 + 4 + 3 * 2 + 5 + 6	Original expression
4 + 4 + 6 + 5 + 6	"*" has higher precedence
8 + 6 + 5 + 6	Within the group left-to-right associative
14 + 5 + 6	Due to left-to-right associativity
19 + 6	Due to left-to-right associativity
25	Result of evaluation

You can force your own order of evaluation by using parentheses to supersede the default. In an expression, evaluation starts with the innermost pair of parentheses.

For example, consider the evaluation of the following expressions. In the first

```
x + y * 2
```

is evaluated as:

```
x + (y * 2)
```

Arithmetic Operators

In the expression

```
(x + y) * 2
```

(x + y) is evaluated first; then multiplied by **2**.

The expression

```
(((4 + 2) / 3) + 2)
```

is evaluated as shown in the following steps:

```
(((4 + 2) / 3) + 2)    /* Original expression */

((6 / 3) + 2)          /* Innermost () is evaluated */

(2 + 2)

4
```

Tip *It is a good idea to use parentheses to make sure that the order of expression evaluation is what you expect it to be, rather than relying on the default. This also makes the expression more readable.*

Example **Using parentheses in expressions**

```
/* Compute the average of two values */
int value1, value2;
float average;

average = value1 + value2 / 2.0;   /* Incorrect */
average = (value1 + value2) / 2.0; /* Correct */
```

Notice the use of the floating point constant **2.0** in the above statements. When expressions combine different data types, the result of the evaluation depends on the data types used. The following list shows the type of result when real (**float**) and integer (**int** or **char**) data types are used as the two operands for arithmetic operations:

Operand types	Result	Example
`int, int`	`int`	4 * 2 yields 8; 5 / 2 yields 2
`float, int`	`float`	4 + 12.0 yields 16.0; 5 / 2.0 yields 2.5
`float, float`	`float`	3.2 / 1.6 yields 2.0

4.1b Exercise

Modify the math tutor program to implement subtraction and division. For division, drop the fractional part while testing against the users' input. This can be achieved by assigning the floating point result of the division to an integer variable and then testing the result.

4.2 Relational Operators and Decision Making

Relational operators are used for comparing values. These operators are binary. The operator compares the value of its two operands and produces a value, which can then be used in decision-making constructs (such as the `if` statement).

The list of all relational operators is given below:

Operator	Meaning
`<`	Less than
`<=`	Less than or equal
`>`	Greater than
`>=`	Greater than or equal
`==`	Equal
`!=`	Not equal

Relational Operators and Decision Making

Example **Using != relational operator**

```
/* If the input value is not a predefined signal
 * (-1, in this case), compute the sum
 */
if (input_value != -1)
   sum = sum + input_value;
```

Example **Using >= relational operator**

```
/* If your bank account earned more than $400 in
 * interest, use schedule B to report interest */
if (interest >= 400)
   printf("Use Schedule B to report interest\n");
```

The next example computes the accumulated principal on a deposit (contained in a **float** variable named **principal**), over a number of years (**int** variable **no_of_years**), at a given interest rate (**float** variable **rate**):

Example **Compute accumulated principal**

```
/* Rate is given as percentage points */
while(no_of_years > 0)
{
   interest = (principal * rate) / 100.0;
   /* New principal */
   principal = principal + interest;
   no_of_years = no_of_years - 1;
}
```

4.2a True and false, as seen by C

As you have seen earlier, the decision-making and iterative constructs of C have the following form:

```
if (expression evaluates to true)
{
   /* Execute these statements */
   statement-list
}
else /* If the evaluation yielded false */
```

```
{
    statement-list
    /* Execute these statements */
}
```

or

```
while(expression remains true)
{
    statement-list
    /* Execute these statements */
} /* Go back and retest the while condition */
```

The **if** and the **while** statements expect the expression inside the parentheses to evaluate to true or false. But what constitutes truth or falsity (no, this is not a philosophical question)? In C, the answer is very simple.

> 0 is false.
> Everything else is true.

Don't you wish the answer to the philosophical question concerning truth and falsity were that simple? Wishful thinking aside, in C, any expression that yields a value other than 0 can be used in an **if** or a **while** statement to satisfy the true condition. If the expression yields 0 as the value, the statements corresponding to the **else** part of the **if** statement (if any) will be executed and the **while** loop will be terminated.

How does all this tie in with relational operators? Relational operators, upon evaluation, returns the value 1 if the comparison operation succeeds and the value 0 if the comparison fails.

Run the following program and verify the results.

```
#include <stdio.h>
main()
{
    int result;

    result = 35 < 23; /* The relation 35 less than 23 should
                         produce a false or a zero result */
    printf("Result of 35 < 23 is %d\n", result);
```

Relational Operators and Decision Making

```
    result = 0 > -1;  /* Should be true */
    printf("Result of 0 > -1 is %d\n", result);
}
```

Running the above program should reveal that the value 0 is produced when a relational operator fails in its comparison and the value 1 is produced when the comparison succeeds. The result of the evaluation can be used in the **if** or **while** constructs, or it can be assigned to a variable. For example, in the program fragment above, the relational expression `35 < 23` produces the value 0, which is then assigned to the variable **result**.

Now type in and run the following program, and explain its outcome.

```
main()
{
    int result;
    if ( result = (1 < 2) )
        printf ("Result of 1 < 2 is %d\n", result);

    if ( result = (1 > 2) )
        printf ("Result of 1 > 2 is %d\n", result);
}
```

4.2b if statements: The rest of the story

The time has come to talk about the **if** statement in detail. The syntax of the **if** statement is once again shown below:

Syntax **if statement**

```
if (expression)
{
    statements
}
else
{
    statements
}
```

If only one statement follows the **if** or the **else** clause, the use of curly braces around the statement is optional. The **else** part is not necessary (syntactically) and may be omitted. It is a good idea to indent the code inside the `if` and `else` blocks as shown in this book.

The evaluation of the `if` statement proceeds as follows. First, the expression inside the parentheses following the word `if` is evaluated. If the expression evaluation yields a *nonzero* value, the statements following the `if` clause are executed. If the expression yields the value *zero* and the `else` clause is present, then the statements following the `else` clause are executed.

Example **Compute the minimum of 2 values**

```
if (a < b)
   minimum = a;
else /* b is less than or equal to a */
   minimum = b;
```

The next example shows how you can swap the values stored in two variables `high` and `low`. Our program checks if the value stored in `high` is less than the value stored in `low`, and if it is, the values are swapped.

Example **Swapping the values in 2 variables**

```
/* Swap values if value in high is
 * less than the value in low */
int high, low;
int temp; /* To swap two values, we need a third
           * variable for temporary storage */

assign values to high and low
if (high < low)
{
   temp = high; /* Save high to temp */
   high = low;  /* Store low to high */
   low = temp;  /* Store old high to low */
}
```

If curly braces are not used to enclose statements that logically belong to the `if` clause, you may get compile time errors. The following example shows an invalid `if` statement.

Example Invalid if construction

```c
if (age < 25)
   printf("Major Credit Card required\n");
   /* Need {} for multiple statements */
   denied = 1;
else
   printf("OK to rent\n");
   denied = 0;
```

The above example may appear as a valid **if** statement. However, note that indenting code within the **if** statement is done for improving readability of the code only. Indenting several statements together by using white space does not imply that they will be grouped together logically by the C compiler. The C compiler will simply ignore all the white space and the comments. Thus the C compiler will see the above code as shown below. Comments have been added to explain what is really going on.

```c
if (age < 25)
printf("Major Credit Card required\n"); /* If ends here */
denied = 1;               /* Stand alone statement. OK */
else                      /* Dangling else: Syntax Error */
printf("OK to rent\n"); /* Everything from here on
                           is error */
denied = 0;
```

Here's the correct version:

```c
if (age < 25)
{
   printf("Major Credit Card required\n");
   denied = 1;
}
else
{
   printf("OK to rent\n");
   denied = 0;
}
```

The next example is an **if** statement that is syntactically correct but semantically wrong:

Example **Incorrect if statement**

```
if (age < 25);
{
   printf("Major Credit Card required\n");
   denied = 1;
}
```

In the above example, which will compile correctly, the only statement applicable to the **if** clause is the null statement at the end of the line (recall that without curly braces, the **if** statement is applicable to the following *one* statement. Semicolon (;) is a valid null statement. Hence the compiler does not flag this as an error.

Most systems have a program called **lint** that is useful for finding apparent faults with your program that the C compiler may not catch. Running **lint** on a C program file may reveal many surprising facts about a seemingly trivial program.

4.2c Nested if statements

if statements may be nested within **if** statements, as shown:

```
if (expression)
   if (expression)
      statement
   else
      statement
else
   statement
```

Care should be taken to ensure that a particular **else** statement belongs to the appropriate **if** statement. Curly braces can be used to ensure that the grouping is as you desire. For example, if the inner **else** statement is not necessary in your program, the above **if** statement will appear as:

```
if (expression)
   if (expression)
      statement
```

```
else /* Which if does this belong to? */
   statement
```

Even though the intent may have been to lump the **else** statement with the outer **if** loop, that will not happen in this program. The above statements can be made more readable by using curly braces:

```
if (expression)
{ /* Outer if */
   if (expression)
   { /* Inner if */
      statements
   } /* End inner if */
} /* End outer if */
else
{ /* Else belongs to the outer if */
   statements
}
```

Example   **Compute the minimum of 3 values**

```
if (a < b)
{
   /* a is smaller than b */
   if (a < c)
   {
      /* a is smaller than c also */
      min = a;
   }
   else
   {
      /* c is less than or equal to a */
      min = c;
   }
}
else
{
   /* b is less than or equal to a */
   if (b < c)
   {
      /* b is also less than c */
```

```
        min = b;
    }
    else
    {
        /* c is less than or equal to b */
        min = c;
    }
}
```

4.2d Multiway decision making using the `else if` clause

The `if` statement is useful for two-way decisions. If you need to decide among multiple choices, the `else` clause of an `if` statement can be combined with another `if` clause, as shown below:

```
if (expression₁)
{
    statement
}
else if (expression₂)
{
    statement
}
else if (expression₃)
{
    statement
}
else
{
    statement
}
```

Notice that the last `if` statement does not contain the `else if` clause

Example Multiway decision using `else if` clause

```
/* From the guessing game */
if (answer == number)
{
    printf("You guessed correctly\n");
}
```

```
            else if (answer > number)
            {
               printf("Guess lower\n");
            }
            else
            {
               printf("Guess higher\n");
            }
```

Here's another example of multiway decision making. This one is from a simple tax program (you know: the one that has only two steps: 1. How much money did you make last year? 2. Send it in).

Example **Multiway decision using `else if` clause.**

```
/* From the dreaded 1040 */
if (line_22 == line_24)
{
   printf ("You somehow managed to break even\n");
}
else if (line_22 > line_24)
{
   printf ("I owe, I owe, so, off to work I go\n");
}
else
{ /* Getting some money back!!! */
   printf ("***IRS Audit Warning***\n");
}
```

For multiway decision making, C provides a somewhat more readable and elegant construct called the `switch` statement. You will learn about the `switch` statement in Chapter 6.

One final note has to be made on true and false evaluations. Since 0 is equivalent to false and anything else is true in C's lingo, the following statements are all valid and the statement list associated with the `if` clause will always be executed.

```
      if (1)
      { /* Always true */
         statement-list
```

```
}
if (-44)
{ /* Always true */
    statement-list
}
```

We could even run into problems due to this. For instance, the next **if** statement is valid C code. Whether or not it is a valid program is up to you to decide:

```
if (a = 10)   /* Same as if (10) */
{ /* These statements will always be executed */
    statement-list
}
else
{ /* These statements will never be executed */
    statement-list
}
```

In the above **if** statement, the programmer's intent may have been to test the value of the variable **a** (using ==), rather than assign a value to it. C is less forgiving though. To C, evaluation of the expression **a = 10** yields the value 10, which satisfies the criterion for a true value, and the statement list following the **if** clause will always be executed. This is a potential problem and is caused by the fact that C does not have any true boolean data type. You can catch problems like this by running **lint** on all your programs.

❑ **Exiting from the program**

Program execution terminates when the outermost enclosing curly brace in the **main** function is encountered. Termination can also be achieved by using the **return** statement (from the **main** function) or, by using the **exit** function. We will use the **exit** function to terminate the program and return back to the command prompt.

By using the **exit** function, it is possible to return a value to the environment indicating whether the program succeeded or failed. ANSI has defined 2 predefined macros for this purpose. The macros, defined in the header file **stdlib.h**, are:

Relational Operators and Decision Making 83

```
                EXIT_SUCCESS    /* Indicate successful termination */
                EXIT_FAILURE    /* Indicate unsuccessful termination */
```

Example **Using `exit` to terminate a program**

```
if (something bad happened)
{
   print something bad happened
   exit(EXIT_FAILURE);
}
/* Otherwise, indicate successful termination */
exit(EXIT_SUCCESS);
```

Note *If your older C compiler does not define the* **EXIT_SUCCESS** *and* **EXIT_FAILURE** *macros, you will get an error message from the compiler indicating that the variables* **EXIT_SUCCESS** *and* **EXIT_FAILURE** *are undefined. In this case, including the following two lines at the top of your program:*

```
                #define    EXIT_SUCCESS      0
                #define    EXIT_FAILURE      1
```

4.2e Exercises

Turn the last example into a complete program, and compile it. Does it report any errors or warnings? Next run **lint** on your program, and check if **lint** catches problems with the code.

1. Modify the guessing game to use the `else if` construct.

2. Write a program that computes the interest earned at the end of the year on a starting principal and an interest rate. The program should contain the following steps:

   Prompt the user for a starting principal in the range 1 to 10,000. If the user enters any other value, quit the program. To quit the program, use the `exit` function.

Prompt the user for the interest rate in percentage points (1.0 to 20.0). If the user enters any other value, quit the program.

Compute the interest at the end of the year (principal X rate/100.0). Print the interest earned.

If interest earned was more than $100, print a message indicating that the interest will be reported as earned income.

4.3 Logical Operators

Logical operators || (OR) and && (AND) allow us to combine relational expressions to form more complex relations. Also, the logical operator ! (negation, or NOT) computes the logical negation of its operand.

The list of logical operators available in C are:

Operator	Purpose
!	Logical negation (unary)
&&	Logical AND
||	Logical OR

Evaluation of a logical operation always yields 0 for false and 1 for true conditions.

Example Using the logical && operator

```
/* Decide where to enter the interest income */
if ( (interest > 0) && (interest <= 400) )
{
   /* Will enter here if interest earned was greater than
    * 0 AND less than or equal to 400
    */
   printf("Enter interest earned on line 8a\n");
}
```

Logical Operators 85

```
        else if (interest > 400)
        {
           printf("Report interest earned on Schedule B\n");
        }
```

Example   **Using the logical || operator**

```
/* Check to see if form 1040EZ can be used */
#define SINGLE   1
#define MARRIED  2

if ( (filing_status != SINGLE) || (income > 50000) )
{ /* Will enter here if filing status is not
   * single OR income is greater than 50000 */
   printf("Cannot use the easy form\n");
}
```

The following rules apply when combining relational expressions using logical operators of the following form:

expression1 && expression2

expression2 || expression2

- The logical AND expression will yield a true value (value 1) only if *both* the relational expressions yield true values. Thus

   (*expression1* **&&** *expression2*)

   will yield a true value only if *expression1* **and** *expression2* yield true values. The result of evaluation of the logical expression will be false if either of the relational expressions yields a false value.

- The logical OR expression will yield a true value if *either* or both of the relational operations yield true values. Thus

   (*expression1* || *expression2*)

   will yield a true value if either *expression1* **or** *expression2* yields a true value. The logical OR expression will yield a false value if both of the relations yield false values.

The evaluation of the AND and the OR operators are summarized in the following *truth tables*.

Definition **Truth table**
A truth table is a systematic tabulation of possible input/output combinations produced by a binary circuit (in our case, a binary operator).

Truth Table for AND

Expression1	Expression2	Result
True	True	True
True	False	False
False	False or true	False

Truth Table for OR

Expression1	Expression2	Result
True	False or true	True
False	True	True
False	False	False

The following examples illustrate the evaluation of the logical && and || operators.

Expression1	Operator	Expression2	Result
(1 < 0)	&&	(anything)	False
(24 < 35)	&&	(0 > -1)	True
(1 == 1)	&&	(1)	True

Expression1	Operator	Expression2	Result
(1 < 0)	||	(0 > -1)	True
(anything)	||	(24 < 35)	True
(0)	||	(1 == 0)	False

Let us examine how the second line in the table evaluates:

```
(24 < 35)   && (0 > -1) /* Will evaluate to: */
(1) && (0 > -1)  /* First operand evaluates to 1 */
(1) && (1)       /* Relation1 and relation2 are TRUE */
(1)              /* Expression is TRUE */
```

Since the logical operator is only interested in whether value of its left and right operands are 0 or not, we can concoct relations similar to the third table item:

```
(1 == 1) && (1)    /* Is a valid expression (though
                    * it does not make much sense) */
```

The unary logical NOT operator ! allows us to reverse the truth value of its operand. The operand could be a relational expression or simply a variable. If the operand has a false value (the value 0), the ! operator changes it to a 1. If the operand has a true value (anything but 0), the ! operator changes it to a 0.

The next example illustrates the use of the ! operator. In our earlier math tutor program, the division test requires that the denominator must have a nonzero value. This can be implemented as

```
random1 = rand() % 20; /* Numerator */
random2 = rand() % 20; /* Denominator */
if (!random2)
{   /* random2 is zero: Generate a new one */
    random2 = rand() % 20;
}
```

In the above example, if the variable `random2` gets assigned a 0 by the random number generator, the ! operator changes it to a 1 and the `if` clause succeeds. Inside the body of the `if` statement, another random number is generated and assigned to the variable `random2` But there is a problem: What if the new number generated is also a zero? That's another problem to take care of — we will fix it in the next section.

Note *This use of the* ! *operator to test for numerical equivalence to 0 is considered bad style. We use it here as an example but do not recommend tests for 0 this way in programs. The recommended usage is:*

```
if (random2 == 0)
{
    random2 = rand() % 20;
}
```

Now an exercise using logical operators follows.

4.3a   Exercise

Write a program to compute whether a given year is a leap year or not. A year is a leap year if it is divisible by 4 and not divisible by 100. A year is also a leap year if it is divisible by 400. Your program must prompt the user to input the year and should output whether the user input was a leap year or not. Use the logical AND and logical OR operators.

4.3b Short-circuiting of logical operators

Notice the following lines in our table on page 86:

```
(1 < 0) && (anything) yields False

(anything) || (24 < 35) yields True
```

Since the success of the logical AND operation implies that both the operands must yield true values, evaluation stops when the first operand expression yields a false value. Similarly, since the success of the logical OR operation depends on only any one of its operand expressions yielding a true value, evaluation stops if the first operand expression yields a true value.

The partial evaluation of the operands of the && and || operators due to the conditions described above is called *short-circuiting* of expression evaluation.

Since C allows arbitrarily complex expressions in loops and decision constructs, you can inadvertently write faulty programs by using assignment operations inside the right operand of the && and || operators. For example, the following program is faulty:

```
if ((principal > 0) &&
((interest = (principal * rate)) >= 400) )
{
   /* Use Schedule B */
   statements
}
printf("Interest = %f\n", interest);
```

In the above example, we cannot rely on the value of the variable **interest** to be "correct." If the first relation happens to be false, the second expression

```
((interest = (principal * rate)) >= 400)
```

will never be evaluated (as the result is going to be false anyway), and **interest** may contain an invalid value. The program could be rewritten as

```
/* Initialize interest */
interest = 0;
```

```
if (principal > 0)
    interest = principal * rate;

if (interest >= 400)
    printf ("Interest will be reported to IRS\n");
```

The next program segment is equally dangerous:

```
if ((maximum > 50) ||
     ((difference = (maximum - minimum)) > 10))
{
    printf("Difference = %d\n", difference);
}
```

If the variable **maximum** has a value greater than 50, the second part of the OR expression will never be evaluated. Subsequently, the variable **difference** may have an undefined value inside the **if** body.

The program could be rewritten as

```
difference = maximum - minimum;
if (maximum > 50 || difference > 10)
{
    printf("Difference = %d\n", difference);
}
```

The program is much more readable this way too!

Tip *Never include an assignment expression as the second operand of a logical operator (&& or ||) in an **if** clause. The assignment may never take place, and you can never depend on the variable that was to receive the value to hold anything useful. Perform the assignment outside the **if** statement or as the first operand of the logical operator.*

4.3c Precedence of relational and logical operators

Relational and logical operators are subject to precedence rules similar to arithmetic operators. The relative precedence of relational and logical operators, along with the arithmetic operators and the assignment operator, is shown in the following table. As before, each operator has been assigned a number indicative of its precedence. The larger the number, the higher the precedence. Operators of the same precedence have been assigned the same number.

Operator	Meaning	Precedence	Associativity
!	Logical NOT	9 (high)	Right to left
-, +	Sign change	8	Left to right
*, /, %	Multiplicative	7	Left to right
-, +	Additive	6	Left to right
<, >, <=, >=	Relational	5	Left to right
==, !=	Equality	4	Left to right
&&	Logical AND	3	Left to right
||	Logical OR	2	Left to right
=	Assignment	1 (low)	Right to left

Now let us see how an expression such as **x = y == 2** will be evaluated. From the precedence table, observe that the equality operator == has a higher precedence than the assignment operator =. Hence the relation **y == 2** will be tested first. If the variable **y** has a value 2, the comparison will yield the value 1, which will be assigned to the variable **x** by the assignment operator. If the variable **y** contains any value other than 2, the comparison will produce the value 0, which will be assigned to **x**.

Here's another example of operator precedence in evaluations. In the example, the variable **x** contains the value 2 and variable **y** contains 3.

```
x = x && y != !x;          /* Weird looking expression */
```

Parenthesizing the expression obeying the precedence rules produces the following expression:

```
x = (x && (y != (!x)))
```

The operator ! has the highest precedence among the various operators in the expression and is enclosed in the innermost parentheses. Next, the operator != has a higher precedence than the operator && and is enclosed in the outer set of parentheses.

The evaluation is shown below:

```
x = (2 && (3 != (!2)))   /* Parenthesized weird expression */
x = (2 && (3 != 0))      /* !2 evaluates to 0 */
x = (2 && 1)             /* 3 != 0 is true; evaluates to 1 */
x = 1                    /* 2 is true and 1 is true; result is true */
```

Tip *In reality, no one should be writing expressions as strange as the ones shown above. But if you come across situations where you have to write arbitrarily complex expressions, do use parentheses to make sure that you are getting exactly what you think you are getting. Redundant use of parentheses will not hurt anything.*

4.3d Exercises

1. Modify the above expression to force the evaluation of the && operator before the other operators (using parentheses to force the order of evaluation). What result does the evaluation of the expression produce?

2. Evaluate the following expressions:

```
4.0 + 9 / 4

x = 1; y = 2; /* Assume these initial values */
(!x + y) || (x + !y)
```

3. Modify the earlier exercise (compound interest program) to use a variable interest rate. If the deposit is in its last year (**no_of_years** is equal to 1)

and the current principal has doubled from its original value, then increase the rate to the old rate times 1.5. Otherwise, use the old rate.

4.4 Iterative Execution Using `while` Loop

To iterate means to perform an action repeatedly — an activity that the computer performs without boredom. The `while` construct in C is a simple and intuitive iterative construct. In this section we will discuss the nuances of the `while` loop.

Syntax   `while` **statement**

```
while (expression)
{
    statements-list
}
```

or

```
while (expression)
    statement;
```

The evaluation of the `while` statement proceeds as follows: The expression enclosed in parentheses next to the keyword `while` (called the *loop-control expression*) is evaluated. If it yields a true value (value other than 0), the body of the `while` statement is entered. After the *statement-list* is executed, control passes back to the top of the `while` statement, and the loop-control expression is evaluated again. The iteration continues until the loop-control expression evaluates to false (returns a 0). This implies that the variables in the loop-control expression should be modified inside the `while` loop's body or else the `while` loop will never be exited.

As in the case of the `if` statement, the curly braces can be omitted if there is only one statement to be executed inside the `while` loop.

Example   `while` **loop for finding the sum of numbers from 1 to 25**

```
int count, sum;
count = 25;
sum = 0;
```

```
while (count > 0)
{
   sum = sum + count;
   count = count - 1;
}
```

In the above example, the loop will not exit until the value in `count` becomes zero. This is achieved by decrementing the value in `count` inside the `while` body. Notice that outside the loop, we initialized the variable `sum` to zero. Why is this necessary?

Consider the statement

```
sum = sum + count;
```

The current value contained in variable `sum` is added to the value in `count`, and then it is assigned to `sum` again. If `sum` were not initialized, what would its value be when the loop was first entered? *Garbage!* We need to explicitly give it a good value.

Tip *Make sure that all the variables used in your program contain valid values before the values are used. The program* **lint** *may be used to check if you are using any variable without initializing it first.*

Since false and true evaluation depends on a value being zero or not, we might as well have written the above loop as

```
while (count)
{
   sum = sum + count;
   count = count - 1;
}
```

In the example above, the expression being tested is just the value in the variable `count`. As long as the variable `count` has a value that is not zero, the loop body will be entered. When `count` finally becomes equal to zero, the loop will be exited.

Iterative Execution Using `while` *Loop*

Example Count down using `while` loop

```
int i = 365;
while (i)
{
   printf ("%d days left till XMAS\n", i);
   i = i - 1;
   /* Sleep for a day ...*/
}
```

In the above example, the expression that controls the `while` loop is `i`. When `i` becomes zero, the loop is terminated.

The next example will illustrate how the factorial of a number (an integer) can be computed using the `while` loop. The factorial of *n* (represented as *n!*) is *n*(n-1)*(n-2)*...2*1*. For example, 5! is 5*4*3*2*1, or 120. By definition, 0! is 1.

Factorial values can get very large, even for seemingly small numbers. For example, 8! is 40,320 and 16! is 2,004,189,184. We will use an `unsigned long` variable to hold the computed factorial, and to display the value, we will use the `%lu` format specifier, as discussed in page 46.

Example Compute the factorial using `while` loop

```
#include <stdio.h>

main()
{
   unsigned int number, saved_number;
   unsigned long fact;

   /* Input a value into number */
   number = 7; /* For testing */
   saved_number = number; /* For display */
   fact = 1; /* Initialize */
   while (number > 0)
   {
      fact = fact * number;
      number = number - 1;
   }
```

Decision Time   *Chapter 4*

```
        printf("The factorial of %d is %lu\n",
               saved_number, fact);
}
```

Compile and run the above program. Modify the program to use keyboard input for the initial value. At what point do you sense an arithmetic overflow?

The next example shows an infinite **while** loop — one that never quits!

Example   **An infinite loop**

```
while (1)  /* There is no escaping this one */
    ;      /* The null statement. nothing to do */
```

How do we break out of an infinite loop? C provides the **break** statement that allows control to transfer out of the innermost enclosing loop. The following program reads in as many values as the user wants to enter inside an infinite **while** loop. When a value less than zero is entered, the loop is terminated.

Example   **Breaking out of a loop**

```
/* Read the user's input and exit on bad value */
short input;
while (1) /* Forever */
{
   printf("Enter a positive value ");
   scanf("%hd", &input);
   if (input < 0) /* Bad value */
   {
      /* Terminate input */
      break; /* Out of the while loop */
   }
   statements
} /* End while loop */
statements after the while loop
```

In the above example, when the **break** statement is executed, control transfers to the statements after the **while** loop.

The next program shows how to keep a running count of items satisfying specific criteria and how to break out of a loop when there is no need to continue the iteration. The program reads in student GPAs and counts the number of students with a GPA greater than or equal to 3.5.

```
/* File count.c: Count the number of students with
 * grade point average (GPA) greater than 3.5
 */

#include <stdio.h>

main()
{
   float gpa;
   short count = 0; /* Initialize count */

   while (1)
   {
      printf("Enter the GPA: ");
      scanf("%f", &gpa);
      if (gpa == 0.0)
      {
          /* Sentinel value */
          break; /* Break out of the loop */
      }
      count = count + (gpa >= 3.5);
   }
   printf("%hd Students have GPA 3.5 or higher\n", count);
}
```

Inside the body of the while loop, if the **break** statement is encountered, iteration terminates and control is passed to the statement after the **while** body (in our case, the **printf** statement).

Notice the use of the expression **count + (gpa >= 3.5)**. If **gpa** is greater than or equal to 3.5, the relation returns a value 1, which is then added to count. Otherwise, the relation returns 0, which is added to count. Cute, eh? Also, observe the comparison **gpa == 0.0**. Since **gpa** is a **float** variable, we should check it against a floating point constant.

Now, let us modify the math tutor program to make sure that the denominator of the division test will always be greater than zero. The program design is quite simple:

- Generate a random number for the denominator.
- If the generated random number is zero, generate a new number. Repeat this step until the random number generated is not zero.

```
/* Test the user's skill in division */
random1 = rand() % 20;   /* Numerator */
random2 = rand() % 20;   /* Denominator */

while (random2 == 0)
{
    random2 = rand() % 20;
}
/* Will get here only when random2 is nonzero */
```

C programmers tend to write cryptic code, which sometimes makes the program somewhat unreadable. If writing cryptic code is of interest to you, you may even modify the above program as shown below:

```
/* Test the user's skill in division */
random1 = rand() % 20;   /* Numerator */
while ( !(random2 = (rand() % 20) ) )
    ;  /* Null statement */ }
/* Will get here only when random2 is non zero */
```

In the example shown above, all the work is done in the loop control expression itself. Here is how the loop-control expression works:

The random number generated inside the inner parentheses is assigned to the variable **random2**. Next, the value is logically negated using the logical NOT operator **!**. Thus if **random2** was assigned a value zero, the logical negation would turn it into 1, which is a true value, and the loop body will be entered. Since the generation and assignment of the random number is done as part of the loop-control expression, there is nothing to initialize. Control goes back to the evaluation of the loop-control expression. If a nonzero random number is generated, the logical NOT of the value assigned to **random2** turns it into a zero, and the iteration will be terminated. Upon exiting the loop, we will always have a nonzero value in **random2**.

Which version of the program is preferred? The first version is more readable and is recommended. However, beware that C programmers tend to write cryptic code. If you have to read and understand programs written by other people, you need to know these language quirks.

4.4a   Exercises

1 Write a program that prompts the user to enter two values. When the user enters the values, compute the minimum of the values, the maximum, the sum and the average. Perform this in a loop, and terminate the program when the user enters a negative value.

2 Modify the math tutor as follows:

Implement division and multiplication testing fully.

For the division test, increase the upper bound of the random number to 100. Ensure that the numerator will always be larger than the denominator. To ensure that the numerator will always be larger than the denominator, check the values against one another and swap them if necessary (as shown in an earlier example).

Dealing with fractions when performing the division test is messy. We want to make sure that the division yields integral results. For this, generate two random numbers, and use the product of the two numbers as the numerator and one of the two numbers as the denominator. This will ensure that the result will be integral.

Enclose the whole series of tests in a `while` loop, and administer all the tests for a total of 10 times. Keep a count of the number of correct answers, and at the end of the test print out the percentage of correct answers.

3 Write a program that computes the accumulated principal amount in a bank account. The user should be prompted for the starting principal, the interest rate, and the number of years the deposit remains in the bank. The interest is to be computed annually and added to the principal (compounded annually). At the end, print out the value of the principal amount.

Shown below is a sample session. Make sure that the values are printed with the precision shown.

```
******* Welcome to Decadent Federal Savings & Loan ********

Enter the starting principal: 3000.00
Enter the interest rate: 5.5
Enter the number of years of deposit: 2

Principal at the end of year 1 of deposit = $3165.00
Principal at the end of year 2 of deposit = $3339.07
```

4.5 Common Problems

1. Incorrect understanding of the precedence of operators can lead to incorrect execution of programs. When writing complex expressions, use parentheses to order the operators the way you intended them to be evaluated.

2. Incorrectly placing semicolons at the end of statements such as the **while** will lead to unexpected behavior. The following statement is syntactically valid:

    ```
    while (i < 10);
    {
        printf("%d, %d\n", i, i * i);
    }
    ```

    Semantically, the program may be incorrect and the semicolon at the end of the **while** statement needs to be removed.

3. When using the **if** statements, programmers often omit the pair of curly braces following the conditional expression if only one statement needs to be associated with the **if** condition. This may lead to problems if you use statements such as the following:

```
if (debug) /* If debugging is turned on */
    printf("Value of i = % d\n", i);
/* Normal program statement */
statement
```

In order to turn debugging off, programmers sometimes comment out the line that prints the debugging statement, as shown:

```
if (debug) /* If debugging is turned on */
    /* printf("Value of i = % d\n", i); */
/* Normal program statement */
statement
```

Unfortunately, this causes a serious programming bug, as the statement following the commented-out **printf** statement now gets controlled by the evaluation of the **if** conditional.

The right solution is to turn debugging off by setting the value of the variable **debug** to 0.

5
File I/O

It is not very convenient to deal with just keyboards and screens when dealing with input/output. Terminal screens have no *permanence*: Data written to the screen is lost. Data input from keyboard is slow, and keyboard data entry will have to be repeated each time the program is run. Consider writing a program that keeps track of the test scores for students in a programming class. It would be very convenient to store all the test scores on a permanent storage medium, such as a hard disk. If the program can be made to take input from the hard disk, cumbersome keyboard entry can be avoided. Also generated reports can be saved on the hard disk and displayed, without having to rerun the program that produces the reports.

C programs can access hard disks as well as terminals through an abstraction known as *streams*.

Definition Stream

A stream is a source or sink for data. Streams provide a uniform representation for different physical devices such as hard disks (files), terminals, etc.

A file is a container for data: whatever the user wants to store in it. Once stored in a file, data can be retrieved later, either sequentially (i.e., starting at the top of the file, byte by byte) or randomly by moving to any arbitrary location in the file and reading or writing at that location. The former is called *sequential access*, the latter *random access*. We will limit our discussion to sequential access in this chapter and discuss random access in Chapter 13.

If we store the test scores in a file called **SCORES.TXT**, the file can be visualized as shown in Figure 5.1.

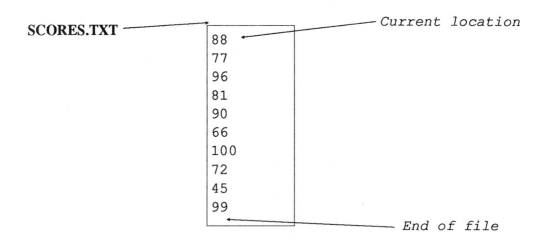

Figure 5.1 Conceptual view of a file

5.1 All about Stream I/O

Recall that C does not provide any facilities for I/O. Stream I/O is implemented by a set of functions available in the standard library. These stream I/O functions allow us to access hard disks and terminals as files. In the remainder of this workbook we will refer to streams, simply, as files. Please bear in mind that a file can be a hard disk, a terminal, a tape device, or some other physical device connected to the computer.

The following operations can be performed on files:
- *Open* the file — prepare the file for access from the C program.
- *Read* the file — copy the data from the file, to a location in the program.
- *Write* the file — copy data from a location in the program, to the file.
- *Close* the file — detach the file from the program.

A file has two components that facilitate access:
- The *name* of the file. The file name is specified as a string, in the program. For example, the file **SCORES.TXT** will be represented as `"SCORES.TXT"`.
- The *handle* to the file. When a file is opened from the program, the function call that performs the open returns an internal identifier for the file. After the file has been opened, only the internal identifier is used for further operations on the file (reading, writing, closing). The name of the file is only used for opening the file.

The internal identifier for the file contains information about the number of bytes contained in the file, the *current location* in the file and so on. Every time you read or write the file, the current location is advanced past the data item that you read or wrote. The internal identifier is a variable of type **FILE** `*`. It would be too complicated to explain here what **FILE** `*` (pronounced *file star* or *file pointer*) really means. This will become clear when you learn about *structures* and the derived data type *pointers*. In this chapter we hope to show you the mechanisms to access files. To learn how it all really works requires the knowledge of some of the advanced topics mentioned above.

5.1a   Opening a file

The function call to open a file is **fopen** (pronounced *f-open*). Most file operation calls begin with the letter "f." The syntax for opening a file is as shown:

Syntax   **Opening a file**

```
/* Declare a handle for the file */
FILE *fhandle;   /* File handle */
fhandle = fopen(name, modes);
```

The name of the file is a string (enclosed in double quotes). The mode is also a string that dictates how the file should be opened. The valid modes for opening a file are given below:

Mode	Purpose
`"r"`	Open an existing file, for reading.
`"w"`	Create a new file (or *truncate* an existing file), for writing.
`"a"`	Create a new file (or *append* at the end of an existing file), for writing.
`"r+"`	Open an existing file for updating (reading/writing), starting at the beginning of the file.
`"w+"`	Create a new file (or truncate an existing file), for updating.
`"a+"`	Create a new file (or append at the end of an existing file), for updating.

If the file resides in the same directory from which you run the program, then the name string contains just the name of the file. If the file is not in the same directory, then the string must include the path name to the file.

Example **Opening an existing file for reading**

```
/* Assuming that a file called "SCORES.TXT"
 * exists in the current directory */
FILE *fhandle;
fhandle = fopen("SCORES.TXT", "r");
```

What happens if the file that you tried to open did not exist? The **fopen** function call will return the value defined by the macro **NULL**. The macro **NULL** is defined in **stddef.h** (ANSI) and may also be defined in other header files, such as, **stdio.h**. You should always check the value returned by **fopen**.

Example **Opening a file and testing for success and failure**

```
FILE *fhandle;
fhandle = fopen("SCORES.TXT", "r");
if (fhandle == NULL)
{
    printf("Could not open file called SCORES.TXT\n");
    exit(EXIT_FAILURE);
}
```

Note *If the macro* `EXIT_FAILURE` *is not defined by your system, please include the following two lines at the top of your program:*

```
#define EXIT_SUCCESS 0
#define EXIT_FAILURE 1
```

A function called `perror` (pronounced *p-error*) available in the standard library is useful in determining the exact cause of the failure of a prior call to the library. We can use `perror` to find why an `fopen` function call failed.

Example Using `perror` to find why an `fopen` call failed

```
FILE *fhandle;
if ((fhandle = fopen("SCORES.TXT", "r")) == NULL)
{
   perror("SCORES.TXT (fopen)");
   exit(EXIT_FAILURE);
}
```

In the above example, if the file **SCORES.TXT** does not exist in the current directory, `perror` will display a message similar to

```
SCORES.TXT (fopen): No such file or directory
```

Closing the file using the `fclose` function detaches the file from the program. The function `fclose` returns `EOF` if an error is detected; otherwise, it returns zero. The syntax for using `fclose` is shown below:

Syntax Closing a previously opened file

```
/* Assuming that fhandle contains a
 * valid file handle from opening SCORES.TXT
 */
if (fclose(fhandle) == EOF)
{
   perror("SCORES.TXT (fclose)");
   exit(EXIT_FAILURE);
}
```

Tip *Always check the return value from library calls for any possible errors. Incorrectly assuming that a library function call returned successfully will*

lead to breakage of the program in seemingly unrelated places. For example, if a **fopen** *call failed and you did not check the return value, your program will crash when you try to read or write the file later in the program.*

Note *We don't always follow what we just preached! Some error checking has been left out to save space in the text. The comments in the code point out the omissions, and you should replace the comments with actual code to check the return values.*

5.1b Read and write operations on files

Before we start reading and writing files, let's discuss the nature of data contained in files. Files can be classified according to the type of the data stored in them: *text files* for character data and *binary files* for all other types of data. Text files contain lines of characters, each line terminated by the new line character '**\n**'. Binary files contain a sequence of bytes. Binary files are useful for storing data items such as integers, floating point numbers and database records.

To perform read and write operations on text files, the following functions can be used. For the functions listed below, **FILE *** indicates that the functions expect a valid file handle of type **FILE ***, obtained by opening the file using **fopen**, to be passed to it.

Function name	Purpose
fgetc(FILE *)	Read one character at a time from the file.
getc(FILE *)	Same as above.
fgets(*buffer*, *nbytes*, FILE *)	Read a line of input into buffer of size *nbytes*.
fputc(char, FILE *)	Write one character at a time to the file.
putc(char, FILE *)	Same as above.
fputs(*buffer*, FILE *)	Write a line of output from buffer.

We will explain the nuances of these functions as we use them. The functions `fgetc` and `getc` return the predefined value `EOF` upon reaching the end-of-file (no more characters to read).

Example **Reading from a file using `getc`**

```
int ch;
FILE *fhandle;
open file and assign file handle to fhandle.
ch = getc(fhandle);
```

In the example above, the function `getc` places in the variable `ch` the next character read from the file referred to by `fhandle`. The function `getc` returns `EOF` when there is nothing more to read.

Example **Checking for `EOF` when reading files**

```
/* Read one character at a time till
 * there are no more characters */
while( (ch = fgetc(fhandle)) != EOF )
{
    statements
} /* End while. No more data in the file */
```

Each time it passes through through the loop, the function `fgetc` gets the next character from the file represented by the file handle `fhandle`. The returned character is assigned to the variable `ch`. After the assignment, the value in `ch` is tested against the predefined value `EOF`. If the comparison fails, the end of input has not been seen and the loop body is entered. Otherwise, the loop is terminated.

When reading from a file or writing to a file, two error conditions

Example **Writing to a file using `putc`**

```
char ch;
FILE *fhandle;
open file and assign file handle to fhandle.
putc(ch, fhandle);
```

In the example shown above, `putc` writes the value in `ch` to the file indicated by `fhandle`.

To illustrate reading and writing text files, we will write a simple program that reads the character data contained in one text file, converts it to uppercase and writes it into another text file. First, let us create a file called **"INFILE.TXT"** that has the following data:

```
To err is human. To really screw things up takes a computer.
```

List the contents of the file, and check if the file has been created properly. The program is given next:

```
/* File convert.c: Reads from a file called "INFILE.TXT",
 * converts characters to uppercase and writes it into
 * another file called "OUTFILE.TXT"
 */
#include <stdio.h>
#include <ctype.h>

main()
{
   FILE *ifhandle, *ofhandle; /* Input & output
                               * file handles */
   int inchar; /* For input character */
   /* Open the file for the reading */
   ifhandle = fopen("INFILE.TXT", "r");
   if (ifhandle == NULL)
   {
      perror("INFILE.TXT (fopen)");
      exit(EXIT_FAILURE);
   }
   /* Create a file called OUTFILE.TXT for writing */
   ofhandle = fopen("OUTFILE.TXT", "w");
   if (ofhandle == NULL)
   {
      perror("OUTFILE.TXT (fopen)");
      exit(EXIT_FAILURE);
   }
   while ((inchar = fgetc(ifhandle)) != EOF)
   {
      fputc(toupper(inchar), ofhandle);
   }
```

```
        /* Close the input and output files and */
         * check return values (not shown)
        fclose(ifhandle);
        fclose(ofhandle);
}
```

After compiling and running the above program, you can examine the contents of the output file by listing it.

Inside the body of the `while` loop, the character contained in `inchar` is converted to its uppercase equivalent by calling the function `toupper` and then written to the output file represented by `ofhandle`. Notice the use of a function call within a function call (`toupper` called within `fputc`).

5.2 Text Files and Data Conversion

Text files contain a sequence of characters composed into *lines*. Each line consists of zero or more characters and is terminated by a new line character (except the last line, which may or may not contain a new line). For example, if a text file contains the data `1234`, the data will be in character form; i.e., the data really is character `'1'` followed by the character `'2'`, etc.

If the data contained in a file is to be read into an integer variable, first it needs to be *converted* to an integer. There is nothing unusual about it — the function `scanf` converts the character data that you type at the keyboard into a form suitable for storing into the variable that you specify (according to the format specifier). Similarly, to read from files, the function `fscanf` can be used. The function `fscanf` is similar to `scanf` except that `fscanf` reads the input from files, instead of from the standard input (keyboard). Similarly, the function `fprintf` writes the output values to a specified file. The syntax for these calls is shown below:

Syntax **`fscanf` and `fprintf` calls**

```
fscanf(file handle,"formats", arguments);
fprintf(file handle,"string with formats", arguments);
```

The function `fscanf` returns the value `EOF` upon reaching the end of input. The function `fprintf` returns `EOF`, upon encountering an error in writing to the file.

The following program illustrates the use of **fscanf**. The program reads a list of scores from a text file and computes the average, the number of A's (scores above 90), the number of B's (scores from 80 to 90), the number of C's (scores from 70 to 80) and the number of D's (scores below 70 — we will be kind and not flunk anyone!). But first, let's create a file and put some scores in it. Using your editor or word processor, create a file called **SCORES.TXT** and enter the following ten scores in it:

```
88
77
96
81
90
66
100
72
45
99
```

Notice that since the data in the file is in character form, you can list the file and read its contents. We will use the function **fscanf** and give it an appropriate format code specifier to read the character input and convert it to a numeric form. Here's the program:

```c
/* File grades.c - Reads a file called "SCORES.TXT" and
 * computes the average, number of A's, B's, C's and D's.
 */
#include <stdio.h>

main()
{
   FILE *fhandle; /* File handle */
   int score, sum;
   int no_a, no_b, no_c, no_d, no_grades;
   float average;

   fhandle = fopen("SCORES.TXT", "r");
   if (fhandle == NULL)
   {
      perror("SCORES.TXT (fopen)");
```

Text Files and Data Conversion

```
            exit(EXIT_FAILURE);
    }
    /* File has been opened and we will start
       reading at the top */
    sum = no_a = no_b = no_c = no_d = no_grades = 0;
    while (fscanf(fhandle, "%d", &score) != EOF)
    {
        /* Read an integer from file and store in score */
        sum = sum + score;
        no_a = no_a + (score >= 90);
        no_b = no_b + (score >= 80 && score < 90);
        no_c = no_b + (score >= 70 && score < 80);
        no_d = no_d + (score >= 0 && score < 70);
        no_grades = no_grades + 1;
    }
    /* Compute average. We will drop the fractional
     * part by using integer division (see Exercise 1
     * at the end of this chapter.
     */
    average = sum / no_grades;
    /* Print the sum, number of a's etc */
    printf("\nAverage score = %4.2f\n\n", average);
    printf("No. of A's = %d\n", no_a);
    printf("No. of B's = %d\n", no_b);
    printf("No. of C's = %d\n", no_c);
    printf("No. of D's = %d\n", no_d);
    fclose(fhandle);   /* Check return value */
}
```

By now, statements such as

```
no_b = no_b + (score >= 80 && score < 90);
```

must be familiar to you. If the comparison inside the parentheses is satisfied, the expression produces a 1, which is added to the variable **no_b**. Otherwise, 0 is added to **no_b**. Also, notice the loop-control expression in the **while** statement:

```
while (fscanf(fhandle, "%d", &score) != EOF)
```

`fscanf` will return the number of items input in the normal case. When there is no more data to input, `fscanf` returns the value `EOF` and the loop will be terminated.

Compile and run the above program. Your output should appear as follows:

```
Average score = 81.00
No of A's = 4
No of B's = 2
No of C's = 2
No of D's = 2
```

To trace the execution through the `while` loop, insert the following `printf` statement into the body of `while` loop

```
printf("Score read is %d\n", score);
```

Compile and run the program again. Your output should appear as

```
Score read is 88
Score read is 77
Score read is 96
Score read is 81
Score read is 90
Score read is 66
Score read is 100
Score read is 72
Score read is 45
Score read is 99

Average score = 81.00

No. of A's = 4
No. of B's = 2
No. of C's = 2
No. of D's = 2
```

5.2a Testing for end-of-file and error

So far we have been testing for the end-of-file by checking return values from functions dealing with stream I/O. It is also possible to test for end-of-file as well as error by using the `feof` and `ferror` functions available in the standard library.

Function name	Purpose
`feof(filehandle)`	Returns nonzero if the end-of-file has been reached for file indicated by *filehandle*.
`ferror(filehandle)`	Returns nonzero if an error indicator is set for file indicated by *filehandle*.

Using these functions, we can rewrite a segment of the previous program as shown:

```c
while(!feof(fhandle) && !ferror(fhandle))
{
   /* Read an integer from file and store in score */
   fscanf(fhandle, "%d", &score);
   sum = sum + score;
   no_a = no_a + (score >= 90);
   no_b = no_b + (score >= 80 && score < 90);
   no_c = no_b + (score >= 70 && score < 80);
   no_d = no_d + (score >= 0 && score < 70);
   no_grades = no_grades + 1;
}
```

Note *When designing nontrivial applications, you should always check for end-of-file conditions and error conditions. Such checking must be done even when performing I/O from terminals and keyboards. We omit most such checking in this text for the sake of brevity.*

5.2b Exercises

1 Test the program shown above by adding a few more test scores.

2. Rather than using an editor or word processor to create the text file containing the data, write a program to create the file, using the `fprintf` call. The program design is given below:

Open a file for output.

Prompt the user for the test score, inside an infinite `while` loop.

Read the user's input into a suitable variable.

If the user enters a score of less than 0, exit the `while` loop (using the `break` statement).

Inside the `while` loop, write the input into the file using `fprintf`. Don't forget to add a new line to terminate each line.

Outside the `while` loop (which is exited when the user has typed a test score of less than 0 to end input), close the file.

5.3 Working with Binary Files

In the above program, we used a text file that contained character data and used the function `fscanf` to perform the conversion for us. Binary files contain data that is not in character form. Rather, the data is written as is. For example, if the value contained in an integer variable is written to a file in binary form, the internal binary representation of the integer variable will be written to the file.

To illustrate the difference between text files and binary files, we will redo the above example with a few minor modifications. Since we cannot create binary files by editing them, we will create the file from our program. Thus we will prompt the user for the scores and write the scores in integer format into the file. Next, we will write another program to read the file and compute the average and the number of A's, B's, etc., as before.

To read and write binary data, we will use the functions `fread` and `fwrite`. These functions perform no conversions: `fread` reads the binary data in the file into a variable of appropriate type. `fwrite` writes the data contained in a variable to the file, as is. The syntax for `fread` and `fwrite` are shown below:

Syntax `fread` and `fwrite` for binary files

```
fread(buffer, size, count, file-handle);
fwrite(buffer, size, count, file-handle);
```

For `fread`, the first argument, *buffer*, is some space large enough to hold *count* (the third argument), number of items. The second argument, *size*, is the size of the data item that we are reading.

For the function `fwrite`, *buffer* is a memory location that holds the data to be written out. Both `fread` and `fwrite` are capable of reading and writing multiple units of the data item. However, dealing with multiple units requires the knowledge of *arrays*, a topic yet to come. Hence we will only deal with units of one data-item at a time (count of 1).

The function `fread` returns the number of items read, which will be equal to `count` (unless end-of-file is detected, in which case it will return 0). The function `fwrite` returns the number of items written to the file, which should be the same as `count`, unless an error occurs.

As mentioned before, the first argument, *buffer*, is a memory location — not just a variable name. The memory location of a variable is given by the *address-of* operator (`&`), which we have used for `scanf`. The location is then converted to a type `void *` (`char *`, in non-ANSI compilers), by using the *cast* operator discussed later in this chapter. If all this sounds too sketchy, don't worry! The reason behind all these complications will become clear after you learn about *pointers* in Chapter 9.

The following example shows an integer variable called `score` being prepared for use as the first argument of `fread` or `fwrite`.

Example **Specifying a buffer for `fread` and `fwrite`**

```
/* To read 1 integer into variable score, from
 * file handle fhandle */
FILE *fhandle;
int score;     /* To read the data from the file */
int ret_value; /* To test the return value from fread */
open the file, etc.
ret_value = fread((void *)&score,sizeof(int), 1, fhandle);
if (ret_value != 1)
{
   perror("SCORES.DAT (fread)");
   exit(EXIT_FAILURE);
}
```

Off to our program now. The first part is the creation of the binary file. To distinguish between text files and binary files, we will name binary files with a ".DAT" suffix (we have been naming text files with a ".TXT" suffix).

```
/* File binfile.c: Creates a binary file called
 * SCORES.DAT containing test scores
 */
#include <stdio.h>

main()
{
   FILE *fhandle;
   int score, ret_value;
```

Working with Binary Files

```c
        /* Open the file for writing and check for error */
        fhandle = fopen("SCORES.DAT", "w");
        if (fhandle == NULL)
        {
           perror("SCORES.DAT (fopen)");
           exit(EXIT_FAILURE);
        }
        while(1) /* Forever */
        {
           printf("Enter the score (-1 to quit) => ");
           scanf("%d", &score); /* Read into variable score */
           if (score < 0)
           {
            /* Break out of the while loop */
              break;
           }
           /* Write to the output file and check for error*/
           ret_value = fwrite((void *)&score, sizeof (int),
                             1, fhandle);
           if (ret_value != 1)
           {
              perror("SCORES.DAT (fwrite)");
              exit(EXIT_FAILURE);
           }
        } /* End while loop */
        fclose(fhandle); /* check for return value */
}
```

Compile and run the program, and enter a few test scores into the file. To verify that the file created contains binary data, try listing the contents of the file. It will not be character data at all!

Notice the use of the four arguments to the **fwrite** call:

- **(void *)&score** — Buffer to hold one integer.
- **sizeof (int)** — Number of bytes in an integer.
- **1** — Number of items to read.
- **fhandle** — The file handle.

Next, let us rewrite the earlier program, which reads scores from a text file and computes the average, to work with a binary file.

```c
/* File binprint.c: Reads a file called "SCORES.DAT",
 * computes average and the number of each letter grades
 */
#include <stdio.h>

main()
{
   FILE *fhandle; /* File handle */
   int score, sum;
   int no_a, no_b, no_c, no_d, no_grades;
   float average;

   fhandle = fopen("SCORES.DAT", "r");
   if (fhandle == NULL)
   {
      perror("SCORES.DAT (fopen)");
      exit(EXIT_FAILURE);
   }
   /* File has been opened and we will start
    * reading at the top. But first, initialize
    * all the variables
    */
   sum = no_a = no_b = no_c = no_d = no_grades = 0;
   while (fread((void *)&score, sizeof (int), 1, fhandle)
          == 1)
   {
      /* Read an integer from file and store in score */
      sum = sum + score;
      no_a = no_a + (score >= 90);
      no_b = no_b + (score >= 80 && score < 90);
      no_c = no_b + (score >= 70 && score < 80);
      no_d = no_d + (score >= 0 && score < 70);
      no_grades = no_grades + 1;
   }
   average = sum / no_grades; /* Note: Truncation */
   /* Print the sum, number of a's etc */
   printf("Average score = %4.2f\n", average);
   printf("No. of A's = %d\n", no_a);
   printf("No. of B's = %d\n", no_b);
   printf("No. of C's = %d\n", no_c);
```

```
        printf("No. of D's = %d\n", no_d);
        fclose(fhandle);  /* check return value */
}
```

Compiling and running the above program should produce the same results as before. Examine the loop-control expression in the **while** loop:

```
while (fread((void *)&score, 1, sizeof (int), fhandle) == 1)
```

Upon reaching the end of the file, **fread** returns the count of items read as zero and we exit the **while** loop.

Building on the above topics, we will create an application that keeps track of student scores and produces a report. The application is composed of two parts: the file builder and the report generator. We will do the file builder part here and leave the report generator as an exercise to you.

5.3a File application: Simple report generator

Professor John Jollyfellow wants to create a file that not only contains the scores but also the average, number of A's, number of B's, etc. He can then write a program to produce a formatted report of test scores for all the students in the various classes he teaches.

If we were to write the average, number of A's, etc., into our binary file, the file will conceptually appear as shown in Figure 5.2.

```
┌─────────────┐
│ score1      │
│ score2      │
│ score3      │
│ ...         │
│ average     │
│ no. of A's  │
│ no. of B's  │
│ no. of C's  │
│ no. of D's  │
└─────────────┘
```

Figure 5.2 File format for report generator

Our report generator program should read all the scores and print them, followed by the average, number of A's, etc. But there is a problem. Prof. Jollyfellow teaches more than one class, and there are an unequal number of students in each class. If we were to write a general program, how do we know how many scores to read (or, in other words, where do the scores end and the rest of the information in the file begin?).

To circumvent this problem, we will make one modification to the file format. We will write the number of students in each class, as the first entry in the file. Thus the file format will appear as shown in Figure 5.3.

But there is yet another problem: The number of students will not be known until Prof. Jollyfellow enters all the scores. To take care of this, we will leave room for the number of students at the top of the file and come back and fill it in after all the scores have been written.

There are two ways to get to the beginning of the file. We can either close the file and open it again or use the `rewind` call. The function `rewind` resets the current location pointer in the file to the beginning. The syntax for `rewind` is as shown below:

The `rewind` function is discussed in detail in Chapter 13.

```
no. of students
score1
score2
score3
...
average
no. of A's
no. of B's
no. of C's
```

Figure 5.3 Modified file format

Syntax   **Rewinding to the beginning of the file**

```
rewind(file handle)
```

Here is the file builder part of the program:

```
/* File fbuild.c: builds a file called "SCORES.DAT"
 * containing student scores, averages, no. of A's, B's,
 * C's and D's. The file format is as follows:
 *   ---------------
 * |no. of students|
 * |student1 score |
 * |student2 score |
 * |student3 score |
 * |...            |
 * |average score  |
 * |number of A's  |
 * |number of B's  |
 * |number of C's  |
 * |number of D's  |
 *   ---------------
 */

#include <stdio.h>

main()
{
    FILE *fhandle;
    int score, sum;
    int no_of_students, ret_value;
    int no_a, no_b, no_c, no_d;
    float average;

    /* Open the file for writing, check for error */
    if ((fhandle = fopen("SCORES.DAT", "w")) == NULL)
    {
        perror("SCORES.DAT (fopen)");
        exit(EXIT_FAILURE);
    }
```

```c
/* Leave room for number of students at
 * the top of the file */
no_of_students = 0;
ret_value = fwrite((void *)&no_of_students, sizeof (int),
                  1, fhandle);
if (ret_value != 1)
{
   perror("SCORES.DAT (fwrite)");
   exit(EXIT_FAILURE);
}
/* Initialize all counts before starting */
sum = no_a = no_b = no_c = no_d = 0;
while(1)  /* Forever */
{
   printf("Enter the score (-1 to quit) => ");
   scanf("%d", &score);
   if (score < 0)
   {
      break;
   }
   /* Write score to the output file */
   ret_value = fwrite((void *)&score, sizeof (int),
                     1, fhandle);
   if (ret_value != 1)
   {
      perror("SCORES.DAT (fwrite)");
      exit(EXIT_FAILURE);
   }
   /* Increment number of students */
   no_of_students = no_of_students + 1;
   sum = sum + score;
   no_a = no_a + (score >= 90);
   no_b = no_b + (score >= 80 && score < 90);
   no_c = no_b + (score >= 70 && score < 80);
   no_d = no_d + (score >= 0 && score < 70);
} /* End while */

/* Compute the average */
average = sum / no_of_students; /* Note: Truncation */
```

Working with Binary Files

```c
            /* All the scores have been written. Now write average
             * and the count of number of A's, B's, etc
             */
            /* Write the average. Note: average is type float */
            if (fwrite((void *)&average, sizeof(float),
                        1, fhandle) != 1)
            {
               perror("SCORES.DAT (fwrite)");
               exit(EXIT_FAILURE);
            }
            /* Write the number of A's, B's, etc ..*/
            if (fwrite((void *)&no_a, sizeof(int), 1, fhandle) != 1)
            {
               perror("SCORES.DAT (fwrite)");
               exit(EXIT_FAILURE);
            }
            /* Checking for return value is omitted for the rest
             * of the fwrite calls, for the sake of space.
             * Please include error checking in your program.
             */
            fwrite((void *)&no_b, sizeof(int), 1, fhandle);
            fwrite((void *)&no_c, sizeof(int), 1, fhandle);
            fwrite((void *)&no_d, sizeof(int), 1, fhandle);
            /* Finally, at the top of the file, write the
             * number of students */
            rewind(fhandle); /* Rewind to the beginning of file */
            fwrite((void *)&no_of_students, sizeof(int), 1, fhandle);
            /* All done. Close the file */
            close(fhandle);
         }
```

Now, it's your turn to write the report generator. Since you know the layout of the file, this is a simple task. The details are given below:

5.3b Exercise

Write a program to read the score file created by the above program, and produce a report as shown below:

```
*************************************************************
* Midterm Grades for Intro to File Processing
* Instructor: John Jollyfellow:
* Number of students: 10
* Scores:
* Student 1:  88
* Student 2:  77
* Student 3:  96
* Student 4:  81
* Student 5:  90
* Student 6:  66
* Student 7:  100
* Student 8:  72
* Student 9:  45
* Student 10: 99
* Average Score = 81.00
* No. of A's = 4
* No. of B's = 2
* No. of C's = 2
* No. of D's = 2
*************************************************************
```

The program design is as follows:

Open the file for reading, check for error.

Read the number of students from the top of the file, check for error.

Print the report heading.

Build a **while** loop by using the number of students as the loop-control expression.

Inside the body of the **while** loop, read the score, check for error, compute the sum, the number of A's, B's, etc., as shown before. Don't forget to decrement the count of the students so as to exit the loop when all scores have been read. For debugging, print the scores as you read them.

At this point, all the scores would have been read. Next, outside the `while` loop, read the average (don't forget that it is in floating point format), the number of A's, B's, etc., checking for error in each case.

Print the average, number of A's, B's, etc. and close the file.

5.4 Keyboard and Terminal as Files

As mentioned before, a stream can be connected to any physical device: even keyboards and terminals. Thus even these devices can be accessed from a C program by using the stream interface.

When a C program is run, the system makes the keyboard and the terminal screen accessible to the program by providing three handles to these devices. The handles have predefined names and are called:

- `stdin` — The standard input file, connected to the keyboard.
- `stdout` — The standard output file, connected to the terminal.
- `stderr` — The standard error file, also connected to the terminal. This connection is normally used for writing error messages.

There is no need to open these files explicitly. When the program is run, the file handles named `stdin`, `stdout` and `stderr` are already initialized.

Example   Writing to `stdout`

```
fprintf(stdout, "Hello World\n');
```

Example   Writing an error message to `stderr`

```
fprintf(stderr, "Could not open file SCORES.TXT\n");
```

Tip   *It is a good idea to direct error messages, debugging output, etc., to `stderr`. If the user redirects the output of a program to a disk file (using command line redirection), anything written to `stdout` will be redirected to the file. However, any error or debugging output written to `stderr` will still be sent to the terminal screen, by default.*

For reading from the keyboard and writing to the screen, we have been using `scanf, printf, getchar`, etc. These functions are really shortcut versions of the following:

Function name	File equivalent
scanf(...)	fscanf(stdin, ...)
printf(...)	fprintf(stdout, ...)
getchar()	getc(stdin, ...)
putchar(...)	putc(stdout, ...)

When designing nontrivial applications, we can check for end-of-file and error conditions associated with keyboards and terminals by using the `feof` and `ferror` functions.

Example Read a list of numbers until end-of-file or error is detected

```
int number;
while(!feof(stdin) && !ferror(stdin))
{
    fscanf(stdin, "%d", &number);
    statements
}
```

Tip *Always check for end-of-file or error conditions. Murphy's Laws especially favors computer programs!*

Before we leave the topic of files, if you ever wondered about the advantages text files have over binary files and vice versa, here's the answer: Text files are portable across most machines. We store all data in character form in text files. Characters are standard across machines using the ASCII character set. Hence text files created on any machine using the ASCII character set may be read by the same program compiled on another machine with the same character set. We may not be that lucky if we deal with binary files across machines. As you all know, sizes of the data types vary across machines. Thus data created on one machine may not be correctly read by a program running on another machine which supports different sizes for data types. However, binary text files are more efficient for storing large and complex records.

Before we leave this chapter, let us discuss an operator that we have been using quite a lot without having talked about the need for using it. We mentioned in Chapter 3 that the *cast operator* is used to convert the type of one variable to another, as may be required in a situation.

In this chapter, we used the cast operator to convert the type of the buffer to read the data from one to another as shown below:

```
(void *)&score;    /* Cast operator (void *) */
```

The cast operator is discussed in detail next.

5.5 The Cast Operator

The cast operator is used to convert the type of a variable or constant from its original type to another type. The syntax of the cast operation is as shown:

Syntax **Cast operator**

```
(data type) expression
```

The *expression* can be a constant, a variable or a full-fledged expression. For example, the following are all valid uses of the cast operator:

Example **Applying the cast operator to a constant**

```
printf("%f", (float)5); /* Print integer constant 5 in
                         * floating point format */
```

Example **Applying the cast operator to a variable**

```
float i;
printf("%d", (int) i);  /* Convert type of i to int
                         * and print */
```

Example **Applying the cast operator to an expression**

```
float i;
int value1, value2;
i = (float) value1 / (float) value2;
```

To realize why the cast operator is really necessary, compile and run the following program:

```
#include <stdio.h>
main()
{
   printf("Printing 5 in floating point format \
gives: %f\n", 5);
}
```

On a Sun SPARCstation 1, the following result is produced:

```
Printing 5 in floating point format gives: 0.000000
```

Now fix the type of the integer constant 5 as shown below and recompile and run the program:

```
printf("Printing 5 in floating point format \
        gives: %f\n", (float) 5);
```

The following result is produced:

```
Printing 5 in floating point format gives: 5.000000
```

Here is another example of using the cast operator to convert a variable of one type to another type for printing purposes. When displayed as an integer, a floating point variable will not appear similar to the original value. Compile and run the following program! Seeing is believing:

```
main()
{
   float j = 10.0;
   printf("Value of j is %d\n", j);
}
```

Does the value look familiar at all? Probably not. On a Sun SPARCstation 1, the above program displays:

```
Value of j is 1076101120
```

Certainly, 10 ≠ 1076101120. We will modify the program as

```
main()
{
   float j = 10.0;
   printf("Value of j is %d\n", (int)j);
}
```

The following example illustrates the use of the cast operator in fielding problems with truncation of results in integer division. The example is about keeping tabs on a football running back's average yards per carry. Football statisticians keep all kinds of information about individual players, such as the total number of yards gained and the number of times the running back carried the ball, both of which are integral values. Thus, a declaration for these variables could be:

```
int total_yards, no_of_carries;
```

Players' average yards per carry are kept as real values: 4.3, etc. Thus we could compute the average yards per carry as

```
float average;
average = total_yards/no_of_carries;
```

Unfortunately, since both the operands for the division are integer values, C will perform integer division and truncate the fractional part. We can cast the integer values to be of type **float** and perform the division as

```
average = (float) total_yards/(float) no_of_carries;
```

In this case, the compiler will convert the type of the variable **total_yards** and **no_of_carries** to **float** when the expression is evaluated. Thus the result will be a **float** value.

Note *The type of the variables* `total_yards` *and* `no_of_carries` *is not permanently changed. It is temporarily converted in the expression in which the cast operators appear.*

5.5a Exercises

1. Modify the program **binprint.c** to compute the average score as a floating point value, avoiding truncation.

2. Suppose we wish to administer the math tutor test to a bunch of students. To ensure fairness in testing and evaluating the students, all the students should be given the same test; i.e., the numbers used for testing should be the same for all the students. We can do this by creating a file which contains all the numbers and using the numbers read from the file for testing. The file can be created either by editing it manually or by writing a program that generates a bunch of numbers and writes them to the file. The tutor program should then read a pair of numbers from the file and perform the testing.

   For part one of this program, create a text file by manually editing a file and putting these numbers into it:

   ```
   15   9
   16   4
   18   11
   21   7
   ```

   Modify the tutor program to read from the file and implement one round of testing. The order of testing should be addition, multiplication, subtraction and division. Use `fscanf` to read each pair of numbers.

   For part two of this program, create a binary file containing several numbers. Use the random number generator to create each pair of numbers (as we have done before). Before writing the numbers to the file, ensure that each pair of numbers is meaningful for the test performed: For subtraction, the first number should be larger than the second number and for division, the first number should be an integral multiple of the second number in the pair.

5.6 Common Problems

1 Opening a file using read mode ("r" as the second argument to **fopen**) fails. This may be because the file you are trying to read may be nonexistent. Either create the file or use mode "a".

2 Failure to test the return value from the **fopen** function can result in incorrect behavior when the file is being read or written to. Check the return value from all functions. Failure of the **fopen** function call may be due to several reasons such as:

    a No permission to create a file, in the current directory.

    b No permission to write the file (file has been created in read mode only).

3 Permission seems to be okay, but **fopen** still returns error. This may be due to incorrect specification of the open system call. For example, the following statement may appear to be correct

```
if ((fhandle == fopen("SCORES.DAT", "w")) == NULL)
{
   perror("SCORES.DAT (fopen)");
   exit(EXIT_FAILURE);
}
```

and does not produce compilation errors, but produces a run-time error. If the function **perror** does not show any valid error message and displays something similar to

```
    SCORES.DAT (fopen): Error 0
```

then there may be nothing wrong with the file **SCORES.DAT**: The problem may be an incorrect use of the equality operator ==. Correct as shown:

```
if ((fhandle = fopen("SCORES.DAT", "w")) == NULL)
{
   perror("SCORES.DAT (fopen)");
   exit(EXIT_FAILURE);
}
```

4   File gets opened properly, but the program dies when you attempt to read or write the file. This may be due to the incorrect usage of parentheses in the **fopen** statement. Consider the following statement:

```
if (ifhandle = fopen("SCORES.DAT", "r") == NULL)
{
   perror("SCORES.DAT (fopen)");
   exit(EXIT_FAILURE);
}
```

The above statement may compile on a C compiler (perhaps with warnings) . The problem here is that the operator == has a higher precedence than the operator =. Thus the evaluation will take place as:

```
ifhandle = (fopen("SCORES.DAT", "r") == NULL))
```

With the result that **ifhandle** will be assigned a 0 or a 1. Correct the program as shown:

```
if ((ifhandle = fopen("SCORES.DAT", "r")) == NULL)
{
   perror("SCORES.DAT (fopen)");
   exit(EXIT_FAILURE);
}
```

5   Incorrect use of the mode flag may in the **fopen** statement may cause subsequent problems while reading and writing the file. The following table outlines the capabilities and actions associated with the various mode flags.

Common Problems

	r	w	a	r+	w+	a+
File must exist before open	Y			Y		
Old file contents discarded on open		Y			Y	
File can be read	Y			Y	Y	Y
File can be written		Y	Y	Y	Y	Y
File can be written only at end			Y			Y

6
Preprocessor: Language within a Language

The C compiler includes a separate program called the *preprocessor* that extends the capabilities of the base language. Remember the lines in our program that begin with a "#"? We have been using it to include the **stdio.h** header file, which contains declarations for the I/O functions such as `scanf` and `printf`. Lines beginning with the # in a C program are processed by the *preprocessor*. The preprocessor is automatically invoked by the C compiler **cc** before the actual compilation.

The preprocessor provides three distinct services:
- File inclusion
- Macro substitution
- Conditional compilation

In this chapter, you will learn about the file inclusion and macro substitution services provided by the preprocessor. Conditional compilation is discussed in Chapter 10.

6.1 The C Preprocessor

Before we discuss the preprocessor in detail, let us digress a bit here and examine what really happens when you compile a C program. Figure 6.1 shows typical program compilation stages. The actual details of compilation may vary from system to system. We will describe the action taken by the C compiler on most UNIX systems.

The typical C compiler is a master program that does most of its work by calling other programs. The first program it calls is the *preprocessor*. Any line that begins with a # as the first character is a directive to the preprocessor. When the preprocessor runs, it scans the file for such lines and takes an action depending on the type of directive.

After the original source file is preprocessed, the output from the preprocessor is *compiled*. In this pass, the actual compilation takes a place. At the end of this stage, an intermediate file which contains the assembly language translation of the program will be generated. The intermediate file is then given as the input to the next program, the *assembler*. The assembler produces a binary

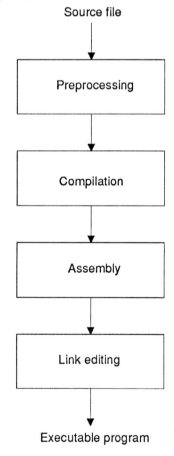

Figure 6.1 Typical compilation stages

file (called an *object file*) that contains actual machine instructions. The name of the object file is the same as the original program file name but with a **.o** suffix instead of the **.c** suffix (most compilers on DOS systems use **.OBJ** as the suffix).program;binary file

Next, the C compiler calls a program called the *link editor* . The link editor builds the actual executable program by linking the object file with the needed libraries.

Knowledge of the compilation process is required to build applications composed of multiple source files. You will learn how this is done in Chapter 10. Meanwhile, let's start at the top of the compiler food chain: the preprocessor.

6.2 File Inclusion

The preprocessor directive `#include` is used to read the named header file into your program. Usually, the header files contain useful declarations. As explained before, the compiler expects that all the variables used in a program will be declared before they are used. Similarly, all the functions that we use (such as `scanf` and `printf`) should be declared before they are used. Rather than remembering and typing in all the declarations ourselves, the compiler writers have created files (such as **stdio.h**), which we can include with our program. This file inclusion is done by the preprocessor before the actual compilation phase.

The syntax of the `#include` directive is shown below:

Syntax   **File inclusion directive**

```
#include    "user-file"
```

  or

```
#include    <system-file>
```

The need for user-defined header files will become apparent when we write applications that are composed from multiple source files. User-defined header files are searched for in the path name specified inside the double quotes. If no path name is specified, the file is searched for in the current directory. If the file is not found in the current directory, then the preprocessor searches the file in some well-known, implementation-dependent directories (where most of your system header files are kept). Refer to your compiler manuals for the location of these search directories.

Example **Include a user file from the current directory**

```
#include "my_file.h"
```

The directive shown above will search for the file **my_file.h** in the current directory. If the file is not present in the current directory, it is searched in compiler-specified directories (on most UNIX systems, the directory **/usr/include** is searched). If the search fails, a compiler error will be issued and the compilation will be terminated.

Example **Include a user file from the specified directory**

```
#include "/home/snm/my_file.h"
```

The directive shown above will search for the file **my_file.h** in the directory **/home/snm**. If the file is not present, a compiler error will be issued and the compilation will be terminated.

System files are searched for in well-known directories. On UNIX systems, the most common place where the system files are stored is the directory **/usr/include**. Thus for the directive below

```
#include <stdio.h>
```

on UNIX systems, the preprocessor will search the directory **/usr/include** for the file **stdio.h**. If the file is found, its contents will be read into the program.

6.3 Macro Substitution

Perhaps, a more immediate use of the preprocessor for us is its macro definition facility, implemented by using the `#define` directive. In its simplest form, the macro substitution performs straight *token replacement*. In simple token replacement, a token name is replaced by a string. The syntax for the `#define` directive is shown below.

Syntax Simple token replacement macro

```
#define     name     string
```

Once a name has been defined using the `#define` directive, any subsequent use of the token *name* in the source program will be replaced with the *string*. This is useful in specifying symbolic names for constants and providing a shorthand notation for a sequence of steps, among other things.

Here is an example of writing and using simple macros. In our math tutor program, we defined the upper bound of the random numbers to be the value **20**. What if we decided to lower the upper bound to **10** to make the test easier for lower-class students? This would require us to hunt down the statements in the program where the constant **20** is used and change it to a **10** everywhere. A better alternative is to use a simple token replacement macro as shown below:

```
#include <stdio.h>

#define LIMIT    20         /* Upper bound */

main()
{
   int random1, random2;

   /* Set the seed value, etc. */
   random1 = rand() % LIMIT;
   random2 = rand() % LIMIT;
   rest of the statements
}
```

After the preprocessor encounters the definition of the macro

```
#define LIMIT      20
```

every occurrence of the token `LIMIT` would be replaced by the string that follows it in the directive (here, the constant 20). Tokens inside quotes are not replaced.

To change the upper bound of the generated random numbers to 10, all we need to do is to modify the macro as

```
#define   LIMIT    10   /* New upper bound */
```

Upon recompiling the program, the preprocessor will replace `LIMIT` in the program with the constant 10.

Here are some more examples of macro definitions:

Example   **Macro definitions**

```
#define BAD_INPUT   -1

#define TRUE         1
#define FALSE        0

#define SUCCESS      1
#define FAILURE     -SUCCESS
```

Notice the last two macro definitions above. Token replacement works even in the `#define` construct. The only place in a program where the replacement is not done is inside a string. For example, if the program contained the statement

```
printf("The limit of the random number is LIMIT\n");
```

no replacement would take place inside the above string. If the program were compiled and run, you would see the following result:

```
The limit of the random number is LIMIT
```

Of course, you can modify the statement, as shown below, and things should work okay:

```
printf("The limit of the random number is %d\n", LIMIT);
```

Macro Substitution

Here is another example of the the macro definition facility. Fans of the programming language Pascal may wish to use the **begin** and **end** constructs to signify the start and end of a block in C. This can be easily accomplished:

```
#define begin   {
#define end     }
```

Now, programs such as the following can be written:

```
main()
begin
    statements
    while(1)
    begin
        statements
    end
end
```

The next example shows how we can use a token replacement macro for a filename.

Example **Using a macro for a filename**

```
#define INFILE   "SCORES.TXT"
FILE *fhandle;
fhandle = fopen(INFILE, "r");
if (fhandle == NULL)
{
    perror(INFILE);
    exit(EXIT_FAILURE);
}
```

If we changed the name of the file from **SCORES.TXT** to anything else, we only need to change one line: the line containing the macro definition.

Tip *Before the qualifier* **const** *was officially introduced by ANSI C, programmers had the tendency to write all constants as macros. For example, the following macro may have been used in programs written for non-ANSI C compilers*

```
#define PI          3.1415
```

Numeric constants such as `PI`, *which will never be changed, are better declared using a* `const`, *as shown:*

```
const float pi = 3.1415; /* Not likely to change soon */
```

In summary, these are the two advantages of using simple macros:

- Macros make the code more readable: Using constants in programs makes the program hard to understand.
- Macros keep to a minimum the number of lines of code that needs to be changed due to upgrading the program. This point was illustrated in the math tutor example and will become even more apparent when you learn about arrays in Chapter 8.

Tip *Always try to assign symbolic names to the constants in your programs. It is hard to guess what significance the numbers have when you are trying to second-guess someone else's program — or even your own programs at a later date.*

The preprocessor defines a few macros of its own, which can be accessed from our programs. The names of these macros begin and end with two underscore characters. The macros and their use are given below:

Macro name	Purpose
__LINE__	To obtain the line number of the current statement in the program source file
__FILE__	To obtain the name of the current source file
__DATE__	To obtain the date the program file was preprocessed
__TIME__	To obtain the time the program file was preprocessed
__STDC__	To check if the compiler is ANSI conformant. Returns a 1 if compiler is ANSI

The use of these macros will be illustrated at the end of this section by writing a macro for debugging purposes.

Macro Substitution

6.3a Exercises

1. Modify the Mariana Trench conversion program, and get rid of all the constants by assigning them symbolic names using the **#define** directive. Compile and run the program.

2. It is possible to examine the preprocessed output of your source files before the actual compilation phase. A compiler switch controls the creation of a disk file with the preprocessed output. On most UNIX systems, the command **cc -E** *filename* runs the source file through the preprocessor only and sends the output to the terminal, or to a file named with the **-o** option. If you are not using a UNIX system, find the appropriate switch on your compiler. Compile the program in the previous exercise, create a preprocessed file and examine its contents to see the token replacements. We will use this technique to debug problems with more complicated macros.

6.3b Macros with arguments

So far, we have only seen simple token replacement macros, i.e., a macro name which is replaced by a string. In fact, one can write more complicated macros: macros that take arguments. The syntax of macros with arguments follows.

Syntax **Macros with arguments**

```
#define name(arg1, arg2, ...)    string
```

Notice that there are no blanks between the name of the macro and the opening parenthesis that follows it.

Example **Defining a macro to compute the square**

```
#define SQUARE(x)  x * x
```

Once the macro is defined, it can be used in the program to compute the square of its argument. The following program illustrates how the above macro may be used in a program:

Example Compute square of numbers from 1 to 25

```
#define  SQUARE(x)     x * x
#define LIMIT    25 int count = 1;
while(count <= LIMIT)
{
   printf("%d\t%d\n", count, SQUARE(count));
   count = count + 1;
}
```

During preprocessing, the macro `SQUARE(count)` gets replaced with `count * count`. Thus the above program, after preprocessing, will be as follows:

```
int count = 1;
while(count <= 25)
{
   printf("%d\t%d\n", count, count * count);
   count = count + 1;
}
```

But the macro has a problem. Consider what happens if we use a somewhat more complicated expression as the macro argument:

```
printf("%d\t%d\n", i+j, SQUARE(i+j));
```

The macro will be expanded to

```
printf("%d\t%d\n", i+j, i+j * i+j);
```

Remember the precedence of arithmetic operators? If we invoked the macro as `SQUARE(2+3)`, we expect to get the value 25 as the answer. However, the evaluation of `SQUARE(2+3)` proceeds as follows:

```
2+3 * 2+3          /* Macro expansion */
2+6+3              /* * has higher precedence than + */
11                 /* How's that for SQUARE(5)? */
```

We can fix the problem by writing the macro as

```
#define SQUARE(x)  (x) * (x)
```

Macro Substitution

In this case, the above example `(SQUARE(2+3))` would expand to

```
(2+3) * (2+3) = 5 * 5 = 25;
```

Note *In fact, even the above macro is not completely safe. When writing macros such as the one shown above, it is a good idea to enclose the whole string in parentheses, as shown below:*

```
#define SQUARE(x) ((x) * (x))
```

There is a very common problem that creeps up when you are getting accustomed to writing macros. Novice C programmers tend to write macros such as:

```
#define SQUARE (x) ((x) * (x))
```

If such a macro is used in a program, the program will generate a lot of nonsensical errors upon compilation. Have you spotted the error yet?

The error here is that the syntax of the macro is defined as

```
#define name string
```

The name of the macro (*name*) is the first word after the keyword **#define**, separated by a white space (blanks, tabs, etc.). The preprocessor will replace the name by the string that is to the right of the name, white spaces and all (but not including comments).

In the example shown above, the name of the macro is **SQUARE** and the string is `(x) ((x) * (x))`. If the program contained the following statement

```
printf("%d\n", SQUARE(3));
```

it will get transformed by the preprocessor to

```
printf("%d\n", (x) ((x) * (x))(3));   /* Syntax error */
```

The compiler is likely to issue an error indicating that an undeclared variable is used in the above statement.

The correct version does not have a blank between the macro name and the argument:

```
#define SQUARE(x)  ((x) * (x))
```

Macro definition can be split across many lines if each line is properly "escaped" using the \ (backslash) character.

Example **Macro to compute average of two numbers**

```
#define AVERAGE(a,b)  (((float)(a) + (float)(b)) / 2.0)
```

The above macro may be used in statements such as

```
mean = AVERAGE(value1, value2);
printf("Average of %d and %d is %f\n", 3, 5, AVERAGE(3,5));
```

Example **Macro to swap the values in two variables**

```
#define SWAP(a,b)   {            \
            int _temp;           \
            _temp = a;           \
            a = b;               \
            b = _temp;           \
        }
```

There is no requirement that the macro names should be in uppercase letters. We use this convention to distinguish between the macros with arguments used in a program and the function calls used. Both have a similar appearance. Also, note the declaration of the variable **_temp**. It is not a common practice to name variables to begin with an underscore (_) even though the variable declaration rules allow it. Here the intent is to choose a name for the temporary variable that will not clash with names the programmer may have used in the program. We are relying on the convention that variables that begin with underscores are reserved for special cases as shown here.

Notice that the definition of the macro is enclosed in a pair of curly braces. In C, an opening curly brace starts a *new block*. Any variable that you declare inside a block is deleted when the block is exited. Thus the declaration of a new variable inside the block will not clash with any other declaration. However, for temporary variables, it is a good idea to choose names the

Macro Substitution

programmer may not be using. You will learn more about properties and visibility of variables when we discuss *scope rules* in Chapter 12.

6.3c Converting tokens to strings using the # operator

The preprocessor recognizes the token **#** *appearing within a macro definition* as a *stringization* operator. The preprocessor stringization operator (do not confuse with C operators) converts its operand to a string. For example, if we use **#xyz** inside a macro definition, it will be converted to **"xyz"**. The stringization operator is mainly used as an aid to printing its argument in string form.

The following example uses the stringization operator to create a string that can be printed.

Example Using the stringization operator #

```
#include <stdio.h>
#define GREET(person) printf("Hello " #person "\n")

main()
{
   GREET(World);
   GREET(John);
}
```

When compiled and run, the program produces the following output:

```
Hello World
Hello John
```

Note *The stringization operator was officially introduced in ANSI C and may not be available on older C compilers.*

6.3d Exercise

This exercise involves designing a macro with arguments and using the stringization operator. In Chapter 5, we have been using the **perror** function as

```c
fhandle = fopen("SCORES.DAT", "r");
if (fhandle == NULL)
{
   perror("SCORES.TXT (fopen)");
   exit(EXIT_FAILURE);
}
/* Followed by statements such as*/
ret_value = fread((void *)&score,sizeof(int),
                    1, fhandle);
if (ret_value != 1)
{
   perror("SCORES.TXT (fread)");
   exit(EXIT_FAILURE);
}
```

Now, we wish to use a macro to define the filename, in order to minimize the number of changes if the file name is changed. If we use a macro to define the file name, the code shown above will be changed as

```c
#define INFILE "SCORES.DAT"

fhandle = fopen(INFILE, "r");
if (fhandle == NULL)
{
   perror(INFILE);
   exit(EXIT_FAILURE);
}
/* Followed by statements such as*/
ret_value = fread((void *)&score,sizeof(int),
                    1, fhandle);
if (ret_value != 1)
{
   perror(INFILE);
   exit(EXIT_FAILURE);
}
```

Notice that the information printed by **perror** has been limited in this case. **perror** can no longer tell us whether the error occurred during a

fopen or a **fread** function call. Notice that we cannot use perror as shown

```
perror("INFILE (fopen)");
```

We can fix this problem by using a macro with arguments and the stringization operator. Shown below is a scheme for using **perror**

```
perror(ERROR_STRING(SCORES.DAT, (fopen) ));
```

where **ERROR_STRING** is the name of a macro that takes two arguments, and using the stringization operator, converts the two arguments into one string and passes it to **perror**. Write the **ERROR_STRING** macro and test your program.

6.4 Debugging Aid: The `assert` Macro

A useful macro that can aid in the debugging of programs is the **assert** macro. The **assert** macro is used to ascertain that certain conditions that you would expect to be true in a program really hold true at run-time. In the case of "buggy" programs, simple assumptions that you make about the state of a program may not really be true. As an example, consider one of the programs in the previous chapter that deals with reading a file header to find the number of students in a class and the scores of all the students. We made an assumption in the program that if the file could be successfully opened, we could read the number of students from the top of the file. But what if the file had junk data? We need to check if the number of students is a valid number.

ANSI C provides a header file called **assert.h** which contains the definition of the macro **assert**. The syntax for the **assert** macro is as follows:

Syntax   **assert macro for debugging**

```
assert(expression); /* Assert that the expression is TRUE */
```

If the expression within the parentheses yields a true value (assertion succeeds), the **assert** macro has no effect. Otherwise (assertion fails), it prints a message containing the program file name, the line number in which the assertion failed and the expression that failed the assertion. The `assert` macro also terminates the program.

If we wanted to make sure that the number of students in the score file was within reasonable limits, we could have made the assertion as shown in the example below:

Example   **Using the `assert` macro**

```
/* Assert that the number of students in the
 * score file is a reasonable value */

#define MAX_LIMIT 35
assert((no_students >= 1) && (no_students <= MAX_LIMIT));
```

When the program is run, if the expression is satisfied, the assertion succeeds and the program proceeds. Otherwise, the program is terminated with an error message similar to the one shown below:

```
Assertion failed in file "my_prog.c", line 34.
```

If you have an older, non-ANSI compliant compiler that does not contain the header file **assert.h** (your compiler generates an error message if **assert.h** is included), you can write the `assert` macro easily by using the preprocessor defined macros __FILE__ and __LINE__. Edit a file called **my_defs.h**, and put the following macro definition in it.

```
/* Header file my_defs.h. Includes useful definitions.*/

/* Assert macro definition */

#define assert(cond)   {                                      \
   if (!(cond))                                               \
   {                                                          \
      fprintf(stderr,                                         \
       "Assertion (%s) failed in file %s line %d\n",          \
         #cond, __FILE__, __LINE__);                          \
      exit(EXIT_FAILURE);                                     \
   }                                                          \
}
```

Notice the use of the preprocessor stringization operator **#**.

Debugging Aid: The `assert` Macro

The following program uses the `assert` macro.

```
/* File mytest.c */
#include <stdio.h>
#include "my_defs.h"
main()
{
   int x = 5;
   assert(x > 5);  /* Will always fail */
}
```

When the program is run, you will get the following message:

```
Assertion (x > 5) failed in file mytest.c line 7
```

If your compiler does not support the stringization operator, simply modify the macro as

```
#define assert(cond)   {                                          \
      if (!(cond))                                                \
        {                                                         \
           fprintf(stderr,                                        \
           "Assertion failed in file (%s) line %d\n",             \
              __FILE__, __LINE__);                                \
          exit(EXIT_FAILURE);                                     \
         }                                                        \
     }
```

Even though the above macro does not generate as much information as the earlier macro, the file name and line number information is sufficient to realize where the program went wrong.

The `assert` macro can be used in a program as follows:

```
/* File fread.c   (Exercise from previous chapter)        */

#include <stdio.h>
#include "my_defs.h"
#define   MAX_LIMIT 35
```

```
main()
{
   open the score file, etc ...
   read the no_of_students
   assert((no_of_students = 1) &&
          (no_of_students <= MAX_LIMIT));
   rest of the statements
}
```

After the preprocessing stage, the assert macro will be expanded as

```
{
   if (!((no_of_students > 0) && (no_of_students < 35)))
   {
      fprintf(stderr,
         "Assertion (%s) failed in file %s line %d\n",
         "(no_of_students >= 1) &&
            (no_of_students <= 35)",
         "fbuild.c", 41);
      exit(EXIT_FAILURE);
   }
};
```

The source file passed to the compiler proper will contain the expansion as shown above. Note that the preprocessor has replaced the macros **MAX_LIMIT**, **__FILE__** and **__LINE__** with the appropriate replacements at compile time. Notice the extra semicolon appearing at the end of the block. The expression

```
assert(no_of_students > 0 && no_of_students < MAX_LIMIT)
```

is expanded to the set of statements as shown below, and the semicolon from the statement:

```
assert(no_of_students > 0 && no_of_students < MAX_LIMIT);
```

gets tagged on the end. It does not hurt anything, since a semicolon is a null statement.

Conditional compilation allows us to compile parts of a program under the preprocessor's control. This is useful if we are writing programs that depend on some system features which may not be standard across all platforms. We will discuss conditional compilation in detail in Chapter 12.

6.4a Conditional expressions: A digression

Macros may contain multiple lines of code, often employing `if` statements. The conditional expression operators `?` and `:` are a useful shortcut to writing lengthy `if` statements. The operator has the following syntax:

Syntax **Conditional expressions**

relational-expression ? *expression1* : *expression2*

The evaluation of the conditional expression proceeds as follows:
- The left operand of the `?` operator is evaluated.
- If the above evaluation yields a nonzero value (true), then the second operand (*expression1*) is evaluated and becomes the value of the whole conditional expression.
- If the first operand yields a zero value (false), then the third operand (*expression2*) is evaluated and becomes the value of the whole conditional expression.

Consider the `if` statement that computes the minimum of two values contained in variables `a` and `b` and assigns it to a variable called `min`:

```
if (a < b)
{
    min = a;
}
else
{
    min = b;
}
```

The above statements can be rewritten using the conditional expression:

```
min = (a < b ? a : b);
```

Let us analyze the evaluation of the conditional expression:

```
a < b ? a : b;
```

The first operand `a < b` is evaluated. If it yields a nonzero value (implying `a` is less than `b`), then the second operand (the expression `a`) is evaluated and is the result of the conditional expression. If the first operand `a < b` yields zero (implying `a` is not less than `b`), then the third operand (the expression `b`) is evaluated and becomes the value of the conditional expression. Note that the result of the conditional expression (either `a` or `b`) is assigned to the variable `min`.

Note that the second and third operands of the conditional expression (*expression1* and *expression2*) may themselves be conditional expressions. Here is a conditional expression that returns the minimum of three values in variables `a`, `b` and `c`

```
min = (a < b) ? ((a < c) ? a : c) : ((b < c) ? b : c);
```

Verify the evaluation of the above expression. The above expression is really hard to read, and its use should be avoided. It is best to limit the use of conditional expressions to simple cases, for the sake of clarity.

The precedence of conditional expressions, in relation to other operators introduced in Chapter 4, is shown below.

Operator	Meaning	Precedence	Associativity
!	Logical NOT	10 (high)	Right to left
-, +	Sign change	9	Left to right
*, /, %	Multiplicative	8	Left to right
-, +	Additive	7	Left to right
<, >, <=, >=	Relational	6	Left to right
==, !=	Equality	5	Left to right
&&	Logical AND	4	Left to right
||	Logical OR	3	Left to right

Debugging Aid: The assert Macro

Operator	Meaning	Precedence	Associativity
? :	Conditional	2	Right to left
=	Assignment	1 (low)	Right to left

Note that the conditional expressions are right associative with respect to their first and third operands. Thus an expression such as

```
r1 ? e1 : r2 ? e2: r3 ? e3 : e4
```

is evaluated as

```
(r1 ? e1 : (r2 ? e2: (r3 ? e3 : e4)))
```

6.4b   Exercises

1   Implement the following three macros:

  - A macro called MIN to compute minimum of two numbers
  - A macro called MAX to compute the maximum of two numbers
  - A macro called RANGE to compute the range (the absolute difference) between two numbers

  Use the conditional expression operators to implement the MIN and MAX macros. Include the above macros in the file **my_defs.h**. Use these macros in a program that prompts the user for 10 test scores and computes the minimum, the maximum and the range of the scores. Also, compute the mean (the average) of all the scores. Print the computed minimum, maximum, range and mean.

2   Modify the above program to compute the sum of the absolute deviation from mean of all the test scores. Begin by modifying the program to read all the scores from a text file and then compute the average. To compute the absolute deviation from the mean, compute the absolute value of the difference of each score from its mean. You may use the standard library function **abs** to compute the absolute value of the difference, as shown:

```
              abs(score - average)    /* Absolute value of
                                         difference from mean */
```

Compute the sum of all the differences. For this, you would need to rescan the scores from the file (use **rewind**, after you have computed the mean). Next, compute the standard deviation of the scores. The standard deviation can be computed by taking the mean of the square of the sum of all deviations and then taking its square root. In plain English, this translates to the following steps:

- Square the sum of all absolute differences computed above. Use a macro called SQUARE.
- Compute the mean of the square: Just divide the computed value from the previous step by the number of test scores.
- Take the square root of the value from the previous step (use the library function **sqrt**). This gives the standard deviation of the test scores.

Print the standard deviation. Next, use the computed standard deviation to assign letter grades. Scores within one standard deviation of the mean (i.e., mean ± standard deviation) should be assigned a B. Scores greater than one standard deviation of the mean (any score greater than or equal to the mean plus one standard deviation) should be assigned an A. Scores less than one standard deviation of the mean (any score less than the mean minus one standard deviation) should be assigned a C. Compute the number of A's, B's and C's assigned this way, and print these values.

6.5 Common Problems

Problems common at this stage of development are due to the incorrect specification of macros.

1. Extraneous characters in macros. Consider the following macro:

   ```
   #define   NO_STUDENTS         5;
   ```

   Do you spot anything obviously wrong with this macro? If not, consider using the above macro in a statement as shown:

   ```
   printf("Average score = %d\n", sum_of_scores/NO_STUDENTS);
   ```

   The preprocessor will expand the above macro as shown:

   ```
   printf("Average score = %d\n", sum_of_scores/5;);
   ```

   Obviously, the semicolon (;) at the end of the replacement string is in error. Correct as shown:

   ```
   #define   NO_STUDENTS         5
   ```

2. Space between macro name and argument list. The following macro is incorrect and will produce bizarre compilation problems:

   ```
   #define MAX (a, b)    ((a) < (b) ? (a) : (b))
   ```

   Fix the macro as shown below:

   ```
   #define MAX(a, b)    ((a) < (b) ? (a) : (b))
   ```

3. Token replacement does not take place within strings. This causes problems if you write code such as

   ```
   #define INFILE      "SCORES.DAT"
   ```

```
      fhandle = fopen(INFILE, "r");
      if (fhandle == NULL)
      {
         perror("INFILE (fopen));
         exit(EXIT_FAILURE);
      }
```

The string `"INFILE (fopen)"` will be displayed by `perror` as such, without any token replacement.

7

Case for do Loops

Chapter 4 covered the basic C constructs for conditional and iterative execution, namely, the `if` and the `while` statements. C supports additional constructs for performing these tasks: the `switch` statement for conditional execution and the `for` and `do` statements for iterative execution. In this chapter, we finish covering conditional and iterative execution, before moving on to newer topics. We also examine a few operators commonly used along with the `for` loop: The increment operator (++), the decrement operator (--) and the comma operator (,). In addition, we discuss problems that may arise when mixing formatted and unformatted input, using `scanf`.

7.1 Multiway Branching Using the `switch` Statement

The `switch` statement is used for multiway branching based on the value of a *branch control expression*. The `switch` statement is a more appealing version of the nested `if` statement. The syntax for the `switch` statement is as shown below:

Syntax `switch` **statement for multiway decision making**

```
switch (branch-control-expression)
{
    case constant-expression1:
        statement-list
    case constant-expression2:
        statement-list
    case constant-expression3:
        statement-list
```

```
        any number of case statements as shown above...
        default:  /* Optional */
            statement-list
}
```

To use the `switch` statement, the following two requirements must be met:

- The branch control expression must evaluate to an integer value.
- The constant expressions following the keyword `case` must be constant integer values, i.e., integer constants or character constants. Recall that character constants have integral values.

The evaluation of the `switch` statement proceeds as follows:

1 The branch control expression is evaluated.

2 The integral result of the evaluation is matched against the integral values of the constant expressions following the `case` labels.

3 If a match is found, the statements following that `case` label are executed.

4 If no match is found and there is a `default` label, the statements following the `default` label are executed.

5 If no match is found and no `default` label is found, no further action is taken and the control transfers to the statement after the `switch` statement.

The following example shows how the `switch` statement can be used to implement a menu selection program:

Example `switch` **statement for multiway branching**

```
int selection;
printf("\t\tMenu Selection\n");
printf("1. Display Options\n");
printf("2. Return to Previous Menu\n");
printf("3. Exit the Program\n");
printf("\n\tEnter your choice ==> ");
scanf("%d", &selection);
```

Multiway Branching Using the `switch` Statement

```
switch (selection)
{
   /* Body of the switch statement */
   case 1: statement-list
   case 2: statement-list
   case 3: statement-list
   default: printf("Invalid Selection: Returning \
to Main Menu\n");
            statement list
} /* End of switch statement */
```

In the above example, the integer value input by the user is stored in the variable `selection` and is used as the branch control expression. The user's input is matched against the constant expressions (the values `1`, `2` or `3`) following the case labels. If a match is found, the statement list following the corresponding `case` label is executed. Otherwise (for all other values), the statements following the `default` label are executed. Note that the `default` label is optional.

7.1a   `switch` statement and "falling through effect"

The `switch` statement has an apparent problem: Once the statement list following a `case` label has been executed, control simply "falls through" to the statement list below until the end of the `switch` statement is encountered. For example, in the program shown above, if the user enters the number `1`, the statement list following `case 1:` will be executed and then control falls through, executing the statements corresponding to the labels `case 2:`, `case 3:` and the label `default`. Verify this by running the following small program:

```
main()
{
   int number;
   printf("Enter a number between 1 and 3: ");
   scanf("%d", &number);
   switch (number)
   {
     case 1: printf("You entered a one");
     case 2: printf("You entered a two");
     case 3: printf("You entered a three");
```

```
       default: printf("You did not enter a number \
between one and three\n");
    }
}
```

Compiling and running the program will yield surprising results:

```
Enter a number between 1 and 3: 1
You entered a one
You entered a two
You entered a three
You did not enter a number between one and three
```

Falling through can be avoided by using the `break` statement. Recall that the `break` statement is used to transfer control out of a loop. The `break` statement can also be used to transfer control out of a `switch` statement. In a `switch` statement, as in a loop, when the execution encounters the `break` statement, control is transferred out to the statement following the `break` statement.

The example modified with appropriate `break` statements is shown below.

```
/* Corrected to fix the falling through problem */
main()
{
    int number;
    printf("Enter a number between 1 and 3: ");
    scanf("%d", &number);
    switch (number)
    {
      case 1: printf("You entered a one\n");
            break;
      case 2: printf("You entered a two\n");
            break;
      case 3: printf("You entered a three\n");
            break;
      default: printf("You did not enter a number \
between one and three\n");
            break;
    }
}
```

7.1b   <u>case values</u>

As mentioned before, the branch control expression and the constant expressions following the `case` labels must be *integer-valued*. The data type `enum` provided by C allows the programmer to specify a list of names, with the compiler assigning integer values to the names. We will make a short detour here and examine the data type `enum`.

❑ **Data type `enum`**

The data type `enum` is used to represent a list of similar items. For example, the colors (red, blue, green), days of the week, boolean (true, false), etc. Each item of the list will be assigned an integer value.

Syntax   **Declaring enumeration constants**

```
enum name {list-of-values};
```

The above declaration creates a new enumerated type with the given name *name*, whose values are as given by the comma separated list of values in *list-of-values*.

Example   **Declaring enumeration constants**

```
enum boolean { FALSE, TRUE };
enum days { Sun, Mon, Tue, Wed, Thr, Fri, Sat };
```

In the above example, `enum boolean` is a new type with values FALSE and TRUE. When a name is declared as an enumerated data type, the list of values (within the curly braces) takes on distinct integral values, starting with 0. Thus FALSE will be assigned the value 0 and TRUE will be assigned the value 1 by the compiler. The enumerated data type can be used in declarations the same way as the other data types seen so far. Using the examples above, one can write programs as

```
enum boolean value; /* Value is of type enum boolean */
enum days Today;    /* Today is of type enum days;

Today = Mon;     /* Assigns 1 (value of Mon) to Today */
value = FALSE;
```

Here's another example that uses enumerated data types.

Example **Using integer-valued enumerated names**

```
enum choices { NO, YES };

enum choices answer;
printf ("Enter 0 to QUIT and 1 to CONTINUE ->");
scanf("%d", &answer));
if (answer == NO)
{
   /* Quit the program */
   ...
}
else
{
   /* Continue */
   ...
}
```

It is possible to override the compiler's default assignment of values starting with 0 to the enumerated list of names:

Example **Overriding the default initialization**

```
enum escape_chars { BELL = '\a', BACKSPACE = '\b',
                    TAB = '\t', NEWLINE = '\n',
                    VTAB = '\v', RETURN = '\r'
};
```

If only a few names are assigned initial values by the programmer, the compiler will assign default incremental values to the remaining names.

Example **Overriding default starting value**

```
enum months { JAN = 1, FEB, MAR, APR, MAY, JUNE,
              JULY, AUG, SEP, OCT, NOV, DEC
};
```

In the above example, JAN is assigned the value 1 explicitly by the programmer. The names FEB through DEC will be assigned the values 2 through 12, respectively, by the compiler.

❑ Integer-valued branch and control expressions

Back to the `switch` statement again. Since enumerated types are integer values, it is a common practice to use enumerated types as the `case` values in `switch` statements. Here's an example:

Example Using `enum` as integer-valued expressions

```
enum DAYS {Sun, Mon, Tue, Wed, Thr, Fri, Sat};

enum DAYS today;

statement list
switch (today)
{
   case Sun:
      statement-list
      break;
   case Mon:
      statement-list
      break;
   case Tue:
      statement-list
      break;
   /* Similar code for all valid days */

   default:
      printf ("Invalid day code: Error\n");
      break;
}
```

Since character constants (single characters enclosed within a pair of single quotes) also have integer values, they can be used as constant expressions following the `case` labels. We will illustrate this by adding a front end to our math tutor program to give the user a choice for the type of test. The front end will be as shown below:

```
****Arithmetic Tutor Tests ****

Addition Tests:            +
Subtraction Tests:         -
```

```
Multiplication Tests:    X
Division Tests:          /

Enter your choice: [+, -, X, /]
```

Depending on the input by the user, the math tutor will perform only tests of the selected type. The code below implements the front end of the tutor program. Completing the program is left as an exercise.

```c
/* File mtutor.c: Modified math tutor
 * with a menu-driven front end
 */
#include <stdio.h>

main()
{
   enum TestTypes {ADD, SUBTRACT, MULTIPLY, DIVIDE};
   enum TestTypes testtype;
   char selection;
   printf("****Arithmetic Tutor Tests ****\n\n");
   printf("Addition Tests:       +\n");
   printf("Subtraction Tests:    -\n");
   printf("Multiplication Tests: X\n");
   printf("Division Tests:       /\n");
   printf("Enter your choice:    [+, -, X or /] ");
   scanf("%c", &selection); /* Note: %c format */

   switch(selection)
   {
      case '+': testtype = ADD;
            printf("Addition Tests\n");
            break;
      case '-': testtype = SUBTRACT;
            printf("Subtraction Tests\n");
            break;
      case 'X': testtype = MULTIPLY;
            printf("Multiplication Tests\n");
            break;
      case '/': testtype = DIVIDE;
            printf("Division Tests\n");
```

```
                break;
    default:    printf("Invalid test selection. Exiting\n");
                exit(EXIT_FAILURE);
    }
    /* Rest of the program */
}
```

Note *Reading one character using `scanf` may cause problems if the program tries to perform any further input operations. Please read Section 7.5 for a discussion of problems with input operations.*

Let us modify the program further to prompt for the student name, prior to testing, so that we can print the name along with the test results. This will illustrate how to read input from the keyboard and store it as a string. You can also use the technique developed in this example to complete the parking permit program presented in the exercise at the end of this section.

The program will prompt the student for his/her name. The name is a string of the form

```
first-name last-name
```

To store the name in a program variable, we need to declare a buffer that can hold a string. Even though we have used string constants such as `"hello world\n"`, we have never read such a string into a program variable and we have not seen a data type to represent such a variable. The problem is that we have not seen *arrays* yet.

Arrays are a *derived data type* used to represent a collection of other basic data types. Arrays are discussed in detail in Chapter 8. The syntax for an array declaration is as shown:

```
data-type variable-name[size]
```

To represent a sequence of 25 characters, we can declare an array as follows:

```
char name[25];      /* Buffer for name */
```

We can read the name into the array by using the `fgets` function, which has the following form:

```
fgets(buffer, no_of_chars, file-handle);
```

Since we are reading from the keyboard, the file handle is simply the variable **stdin**. The function **fgets** reads from the file represented by *file-handle* until a new line is seen, or the end of file is reached, or *no_of_chars* − 1 characters have been read without encountering the end-of-file or a new line character. The function **fgets** copies the new line character and appends the null character (`'\0'`) to the end of the array. For our program, we can use

```
fgets(name, 25, stdin);
```

Note that we cannot use the **scanf** or the **fscanf** function to read the name, as shown above. Since **scanf** and **fscanf** consider a blank as a valid input separator, both functions will only read the first part of the name string (the first name). Also, if an unfriendly student types a carriage return when we prompt for the name, **scanf** will simply ignore the carriage return and wait for more input.

To print a string, we will use the **printf** or the **fprintf** functions, with the format control sequence **%s**.

```
#include <stdio.h>
#define NAME_SIZE        25

main()
{
    char name[NAME_SIZE];

    printf("Please enter your name: ");
    fgets(name, NAME_SIZE, stdin);
    printf("Hello %s\n", name);
}
```

7.1c Exercise

1 Implement the selective testing code in the math tutor program as follows:

Using the variable **testtype** as the branch control expression, implement a **switch** statement. Use the enumerated test types as the control expression in the individual **case** labels. In the body of the individual `case` labels, generate two random numbers appropriate for the test (remember that for division the numerator should be an integral multiple of the denominator and for subtraction the first number in the pair should be larger than the second number).

After administering the selected test 10 times and displaying the scores at the end of the test, return to the main menu and prompt the user for further tests. One way to implement this is to use an outer infinite `while` loop (exiting the loop if an invalid choice is made) and an inner counting `while` loop inside the individual `case` labels.

2. In this exercise, we provide detailed instructions on developing a program to print a parking permit for students, staff and faculty members at Georgia Tech. The exercise is designed to make you familiar with declaring and using enumerated data types, the `switch` statement and techniques for reading input from the keyboard and storing it as strings. It is important that you attempt this program.

   A sample permit for the faculty is shown below.

   ```
   ------------------------------------------------------------
   |      Parking Permit for GT Faculty                       |
   |      Name: John Jollyfellow                              |
   |      Fee Paid: $70                                       |
   ------------------------------------------------------------
   ```

   The word "Faculty" should be replaced by "Staff" or "Student" for staff and student permits. Also, the fee paid should be according to the following schedule: $70/faculty, $60/staff and $50/student.

   Use an enumerated type to represent faculty, staff and students. The program should prompt the user for his/her name and a classification code that matches the value of the enumerated types. The name is a string of the form

   ```
   first-name last-name
   ```

To print a string, you may use the `printf` or the `fprintf` functions. For strings, the format specifier `%-50s` will print a string, left-justified, with a width of 50 (padding with blanks if the length is less than 50). To produce the box effect, you may use:

```
printf("| ");
printf("%-50s", "Parking Permit for GT Staff");
printf("|\n");
```

This will print the following:

```
| Parking Permit for GT Staff                        |
```

At this point, you may be tempted to perform an array assignment as shown:

```
char type[16];
type = "Faculty";
```

Unfortunately, the above assignment is not going to work: You cannot assign a string to a variable by using an assignment operator. You will realize why this is so when you learn how arrays are implemented in C. For now, you will have to write the program the old-fashioned way (similar to the three `printf` statements above). If you are adventurous, you may use a function such as `strcpy` (for string copy), as follows:

```
strcpy(to, from);
```

For example, the following will do the trick:

```
strcpy(type, "Faculty");
```

If you use the `strcpy` function, include the header file **string.h** at the beginning of your program.

7.2 Increment and Decrement Operators

Before we discuss the next major topic (namely the `for` loop), let us digress a bit here and introduce two operators unique to C, the ++ (increment) and the -- (decrement) operators. These operators provide a shorthand notation for an often-used operation inside loops: incrementing or decrementing a variable's value by 1.

Operator	Purpose
++	Increments the value of its operand by 1
--	Decrements the value of its operand by 1

Example Increment operator

```
/* Increment the value in variable i by 1 */
i++;    /* Means i = i + 1 */
```

Example Using the decrement operator

```
/* Count down using while loop */
int i = 365;
while(i)
{
   printf("%d days left till XMAS\n", i);
   i--;  /* Decrement i by 1 */
   /* Sleep for a day */
}
```

7.2a Prefix and postfix application of ++ and --

The increment and decrement operators can be applied as a prefix (operator before the operand) or a postfix (operator after the operand) operator.

```
         ++i;    /* Prefix increment operator */
         i--;    /* Postfix decrement operator */
```

- When applied as a prefix operator, the increment or decrement (by 1) operation is applied to the operand and the result of the expression is the modified value of the operand.
- When applied as a postfix operator, the increment or decrement (by 1) operation is applied to the operand, but the result of the expression is the previous value (the value before modification) of the operand.

To illustrate the difference between prefix and postfix applications of these operators, consider the following examples:

Example **Prefix evaluation**

```
i = 36;
x = ++i; /* x is assigned the modified value of i */
printf("x = %d, i = %d\n", x , i);
```

If the above statements were compiled and run, they would produce the following result:

```
x = 37, i = 37
```

Note that the statement

```
x = ++i;
```

is equivalent to

```
x = (i = i + 1);
```

Example **Postfix evaluation**

```
i = 36;
x = i++; /* x is assigned the value of i and
         *  then i is incremented         */
printf("x = %d, i = %d\n", x , i);
```

The above statements will produce the following result:

```
x = 36, i = 37
```

Note that the statement

```
x = i++;
```

is equivalent to

```
x = i;
i = i + 1;
```

Note *It is a very bad idea to build expressions containing these operators that operate on the same variables. The evaluation of a statement such as*

```
x = x++ - ++x;
```

is totally compiler-dependent and may not produce the same results if tried on different compilers. You may verify this by writing a small program containing this statement, assigning some value to **x** *and displaying the value of* **x**, *after the operation shown above.*

Note *Be careful about using the increment and decrement operations in loops, such as:* `while(i--)` *or* `while(--i)`. *If the postfix and prefix nature of the increment operators is not taken into account while designing the loop, the loop statements may be executed one more time or one less time than expected.*

7.3 Looping Using the `for` Statement

Next, we will examine a versatile looping construct known as the `for` loop. The `for` loop is an *everything-in-one-line loop*, since it combines many loop control operations into one line.

Syntax **`for` statement**

```
for (expression1; expression2; expression3)
   statement;
```

or

```
for (expression1; expression2; expression3)
{
   statement-list
}
```

Example **Print numbers and their square using the `for` loop**

Before we explain the evaluation of the `for` statement, here is a simple example that prints the number and the square of the numbers from 1 to 25.

```
int count;
for (count = 1; count <= 25; count++)
{
   /* Loop body */
   printf("%d\t%d\n", count, count * count);
}
```

In the above example, the three expressions that control the evaluation of the `for loop` are

expression1	count = 1
expression2	count <= 25
expression3	count++

The evaluation of the `for` loop proceeds as follows:

1. If *expression1* is present, it is evaluated. Usually, *expression1* is used to assign initial values to variables that may be used within the loop body. In the example above, the variable `count` is assigned the initial value `1`.

2. If present, *expression2* is used as the loop control expression (similar to the loop control expression used in the `while` statement). If *expression2* evaluates to nonzero (true), then the body of the `for` loop is executed. If *expression2* evaluates to zero (false), then the execution of the `for` loop is complete and control passes to the statement after the `for` loop.

3. If *expression3* is present, it is evaluated at the end of the loop. Evaluation then proceeds according to step 2. Usually, *expression3* is used to modify the value of the variables in the loop control expression (*expression2*), so that the loop may eventually terminate.

Thus, according to the intended usage, the loop can be rewritten as

Looping Using the for Statement

```
for (initialization;loop-control;loop-variable-modification)
{
    statement-list
}
```

The `for` statement to print numbers and their squares will be evaluated as given below.

Step ❶ The `count` is initialized to `1`.

Step ❷ The conditional expression `count <= 25` is evaluated, and if it yields a 1 (true), the loop body is entered and the `printf` statement is executed. If the condition no longer holds, the loop is terminated.

Step ❸ The `count` is incremented by `1` and control goes to step ❷.

Here are some more examples:

Example `for` loop to compute the factorial of a number

```
/* The number is in a variable called n */
factorial = 1;
for (i = 1; i <= n; i++)
{
    factorial = factorial * i;
}
```

One or more of the expressions can be omitted in the loop construct. For example, if no initialization needs to be performed, the first expression (*expression1*) can be omitted. However, if either of the first two expressions is omitted, the null statement (`;`) must be employed as a place holder. Omitting the second expression is equivalent to using 1; i.e., C assumes that the expression is always true.

The example below shows a `for` loop with all three expressions omitted. The result is an infinite loop: nothing to initialize, no check to perform, no modification of the loop control expression.

Example A never-ending loop using the `for` loop

```
for ( ; ; )
{
   /* Infinite loop */    statement list
}
```

or

```
for (;;)
   ;
```

Of course, it is possible to terminate the loop by using a **break** statement.

Note *The `for` statement is semantically equivalent to the following `while` statement:*

```
expression1;   /* Initialization */
while (expression2)   /* Loop control expression */
{
   statement-list /* Loop body */
   expression3; /* Control expression modification */
}
```

7.3a Nested loops

Loops can be nested; i.e., it is possible to enclose loops within other loops. An example of two-level nesting is shown below:

```
for (outer = 0; outer < OUTER_LIMIT; outer++)
{
   statement-list
   for (inner = 0; inner < INNER_LIMIT; inner++)
   {
      statement-list
   } /* End inner loop */
   statement-list
} /* End outer loop */
```

7.3b Combining expressions using the comma operator

We can specify more than one expression in any of the three expression place holders in the `for` loop by using the *comma operator* `,`. The syntax of the comma expression (expression containing a comma operator) is as shown below.

Syntax **Comma expression:**

```
expression1, expression2
```

The comma operator evaluates its left and right operands sequentially. The value and type of the comma expression is the value and type of the right operand (*expression2*). The comma operator is often used in `for` loops to specify more than one expression in any of the three expression place holders.

The next example is our factorial program, modified slightly to include more than one initialization in the first expression of the `for` loop:

Example `for` **loop to compute the factorial of a number**

```
/* The number is in a variable n */
for (factorial = 1, i = 1; i <= n; i++)
{
    factorial = factorial * i;
}
```

Notice that the first expression place holder contains two expressions. The next example computes the sum of integers from 1 to *n*. The variables `sum` and `i` need to be initialized before the loop body is entered:

Example **Sum of numbers 1 through n**

```
for (sum = 0, i = 1; i <= n; i++)
{
    sum = sum + i;
}
printf ("%d\n", sum);
```

The comma operator may be used in *expression3* as well. The next example shows the factorial program rewritten to do all the work in the loop construction itself.

Example **Cryptic `for` loop to compute the factorial**

```
/* The number is in a variable n */
for (factorial = 1, i = 1; i <= n;
     factorial = factorial * i, i++);
```

Notice that the `for` loop is terminated by the semicolon at the end of the statement. This example is presented for illustration only: We do not recommend such overloading of the loop control expressions.

7.3c Exercises

1 Modify Exercise 5.3b to use a `for` loop instead of the `while` loop.

2 Write a program to compute the minimum, maximum, the sum and the average of a set of numbers input by a user. The program should prompt the user for the count of the numbers that will be entered. After reading the count, prompt the user for the numbers, one by one. Each time the user enters a number, compute the minimum, the maximum, the sum and the average of all values seen. Shown below is a sample run:

```
Enter the number of items: 5
Enter item 1: 4
min = 4, max = 4, sum = 4, average = 4.00
Enter item 2: 7
min = 4, max = 7, sum = 11, average = 5.50
Enter item 3: 2
min = 2, max = 7, sum = 13, average = 4.33
...
```

7.4 Iteration Using the do Statement

Another variant of the `while` construct is called the `do` statement (`do while`). The loop control expression for the `do` statement is evaluated *after* the body of the loop has been executed (contrast this with the `while` loop, for which the loop control expression is evaluated before the loop body is entered). As a consequence, the body of the `do` loop is executed at least once regardless of the true and false evaluation of its loop control expression. In this regard, the `do` loop is a *do-it-at-least-once* loop.ido loop

Syntax

```
do  statement
do
    statement
while (loop-control-expression);
```

or

```
do
{
    statement-list
} while (loop-control-expression);
```

The statement list in the body of the `do` loop will be repeatedly executed until the loop control expression becomes false. Notice that the statement list will be executed at least once before the loop control expression is evaluated. Many other programming languages provide a *repeat-until* construct which also does the loop control test *after* the loop body.

The next example shows an excerpt from a menu-driven front end of a program. The program displays a menu and prompts the user for a choice. If the user makes an invalid choice, the program loops again, until a valid choice is made. This is a good candidate for writing as a `do` loop: The body of the loop displays the menu and inputs the selection. After the selection is made, the input value is tested for conformance.

Example Menu selection using `do` loop

```
do
{ /* Body of the loop */
    error = 0; /* Initialize to no error */
```

```
            printf("****Arithmetic Tutor Tests ****\n\n");
            printf("Addition Tests:        +\n");
            printf("Subtraction Tests:     -\n");
            printf("Multiplication Tests: X\n");
            printf("Division Tests:        /\n");
            printf("Enter your choice:     [+, -, X or /] ");
            scanf("%c", &selection); /* Note: %c format */
            if (selection != '+' && selection != '-' &&
                selection!= 'X' && selection != '/')
            {
               error = 1;
               printf("Invalid selection: Try again\n");
            }
    } while (error);
```

In the above example, if the user makes a valid selection, the body of the **if** statement will not be entered and the variable **error** will have its initial value **0**. Thus the loop control expression will evaluate to false, and the loop will be terminated. On the other hand, if the user makes an invalid selection, **error** will be set to **1**, the loop control expression will evaluate to true, and the loop body will be entered again. The iteration will continue until the user makes a valid selection.

Note   *If you compile and run the a program using the do statement shown above, you might notice an unexpected behavior. If you type an invalid character as input followed by the carriage return, the program will complain twice about invalid characters. This is a very common problem with input operations and will be explained in section 7.5.*

C programmers often use the side effect of conditional expression evaluation to set variables, such as **error** in the above program. Don't be surprised if you see statements such as

```
if (error = (selection != '+' && selection != '-' &&
             selection!= 'X' && selection != '/'))
{
     printf("Invalid selection: Try again\n");

}
```

In the above `if` statement, if all of the inequality tests succeed, the evaluation yields the value `1`, which is assigned to `error`. If any of the inequalities fail (the user has made a valid choice), the evaluation yields a `0`, which is assigned to `error`.

As another example of using the `do` statement, consider one of the examples in Chapter 4, where we learned about the `while` loop. In that example (shown below), we used the `while` loop to ensure that the denominator, for the division test in the math tutor program, will always be greater than zero:

Example Using a `while` loop to iterate

```
/* Test the user's skill in division */
random1 = rand() % 20;   /* Numerator */
random2 = rand() % 20;   /* Denominator */
while (random2 == 0)
{
    random2 = rand() % 20;
}
```

The above example can be more naturally implemented by using the `do` statement, as shown below:

Example Using a `do` loop to iterate

```
/* Test the user's skill in division */
random1 = rand() % 20;   /* Numerator */
do
{
    random2 = rand() % 20;   /* Denominator */
} while (random2 == 0);
```

7.4a Exercise

It's time to add a configuration option to our math tutor program, so that the teacher administering the test may customize it to the individual student's capability. For the individual tests, it should be possible to customize the upper bound of the random numbers. For example, the upper bound of the random numbers for multiplication should be lower than the upper bound of the random numbers for addition (it is easy to add 18 + 19, but not easy to multiply). Enhance the menu interface to the math tutor program by adding a customizing option. The menu should appear as shown below:

```
****Arithmetic Tutor Tests ****

Addition Tests:         +
Subtraction Tests:      -
Multiplication Tests:   X
Division Tests:         /
Customize the Tests:    C


Enter your choice: [+, -, X, /, C]: C

****Welcome to the Test Customization Menu ****

Enter the upper bound for addition [default 20]:<CR>
Enter the upper bound for multiplication [default 20]:10
Enter the upper bound for division [default 20]:50
Enter the upper bound for subtraction [default 20]:<CR>
```

After the customization is complete, the program should display the main menu again.

Implement the program using an infinite **for** loop to cycle through the menu, a **do** statement to loop until valid choices are made and **switch** statements to implement individual selections. If you notice the input operations behaving incorrectly, read the next section.

7.5 Understanding Input Operations

All through this chapter we have been dropping hints about problems with input using functions such as `scanf`. Most of the problems with input operations stem from a lack of understanding about the nature of the input data and how functions such as `scanf` view data. Compile and run the following program for a firsthand look at one of the problems discussed here:

```c
#include <stdio.h>

main()
{
    int selection;
    int error;

    do
    { /* Body of the loop */
        error = 0; /* Initialize to no error */
        printf("****Arithmetic Tutor Tests ****\n\n");
        printf("Addition Tests:         +\n");
        printf("Subtraction Tests:      -\n");
        printf("Enter your choice:      [+ or -] ");

        scanf("%c", &selection); /* Note: %c format */
        if (selection != '+' && selection != '-')
        {
            error = 1;
            printf("\n*****Invalid selection: Try again \
*****\n\n");
        }
    } while (error);
    printf("Valid selection made\n");
}
```

The program seems to runs correctly if a valid selection is made. However, entering an invalid selection causes the program to complain twice, as shown in a sample execution:

```
****Arithmetic Tutor Tests ****

Addition Tests:        +
Subtraction Tests:     -
Enter your choice:     [+ or -] 2          ← Invalid selection

*****Invalid selection: Try again*****     ← First complaint

****Arithmetic Tutor Tests ****

Addition Tests:        +
Subtraction Tests:     -
Enter your choice:     [+ or -]
*****Invalid selection: Try again****      ← Second complaint

****Arithmetic Tutor Tests ****

Addition Tests:        +
Subtraction Tests:     -
Enter your choice:     [+ or -]
```

The second complaint from the program seems to be without any input at all. How does this happen?

The problem here is that we didn't account for all the data that we typed at the keyboard. In the example shown above, when we typed the input 2 followed by the carriage return, the input stream contains 2 characters: the character 2 followed by the carriage return character. Next, the first time through the loop, scanf reads one character (due to the %c conversion specification). This causes the character 2 to be removed from the stream and the carriage return remains. After checking the character 2, the program posts a complaint and proceeds with the next iteration of the loop. In this iteration, scanf reads the second character (the carriage return) and returns. The carriage return is checked against valid input, and a complaint is posted again. Meanwhile the stream is now empty, and further input operations will wait for more data to be typed at the keyboard.

Problems such as the one discussed above are very common and baffle the novice programmer. These problems can be avoided if all input data is accounted for.

Understanding Input Operations

Note *Certain menu selection programs require input to be satisfied with the user typing only one character, without a carriage return. This can be accomplished by using functions provided by the operating system to support nonblocking input operations.*

To correct the above problem, we will avoid `scanf` altogether, use `getchar` to read one character at a time and use a `while` to skip over data that we want to discard. The corrected program segment is shown below.

```
do
{ /* Body of the loop */
    error = 0; /* Initialize to no error */
    printf("****Arithmetic Tutor Tests ****\n\n");
    printf("Addition Tests:        +\n");
    printf("Subtraction Tests:     -\n");
    printf("Enter your choice:     [+ or -] ");
    /* Loop, till a non new line character is read */
    while ( (selection = getchar()) == '\n');
    if (selection == EOF) /*  If the user wants out */
    {
        exit(EXIT_SUCCESS);
    }
    if (selection != '+' && selection != '-')
    {
        error = 1;
        printf("\n*****Invalid selection: Try again \
*****\n\n");
    }
} while (error);
```

If `getchar` returns a new line, the `while` loop continues until any another character is input.

If you attempted to solve the previous exercise, a similar problem may have occurred. If you tried to use `scanf` to read the input in the customization menu, the program may not have worked, due to the following reason.

If the default value does not need be changed, the user simply types a carriage return (shown as <CR>). The `scanf` function considers the carriage return a valid input separator. Since no input has been entered, `scanf` will simply ignore the carriage return and wait for valid input. In this case, you would need to apply an often-used technique: Read the input in string form and convert the string to a numeric value. We already know how to read a string by using the `gets` function. The function `gets` has the advantage that a carriage return typed as input gets converted to a null string and stored in the buffer, thus satisfying the input. To convert the string to a numeric form, we can use the library function `atoi` (*ascii-to-integer*). Compile and run the following short program, and incorporate it into your exercise:

```c
#include <stdio.h>
#include <stdlib.h>
/* Test program to read input in string
 * form and convert to int
 */
main()
{
   int answer;
   char buffer[8];   /* Buffer to hold the string */

   printf("Enter the upper bound for + [default 20]: ");
   gets(buffer);/* Read the response in string form */
   answer = atoi(buffer); /* Convert the contents
       * of the buffer into integer and store in answer */
   answer = (answer == 0) ? 20: answer;
   printf("Answer now contains %d\n", answer);
}
```

Compiling and running the above program with sample data produces the following output:

```
Enter the upper bound for + [default 20]: 50
Answer now contains 50

Enter the upper bound for + [default 20]: <CR>
answer now contains 20
```

7.6 Skipping the Execution in a Loop: `continue` Statement

Another useful statement that may be used inside a loop (`do`, `for` and `while`) to alter the flow of control is the `continue` statement. The `continue` statement is similar to the `break` statement except that it does not cause the loop to terminate. When a `continue` statement is encountered inside a loop, execution skips over the remaining statements below the `continue` statement, and the loop control expression of the nearest enclosing loop is evaluated again to test whether the loop should continue.

Syntax Continue statement

```
continue;
```

Note that the loop is not started all over again with the initial value. The `continue` statement just skips over the execution of the remaining statements in the loop body and starts at the top of the loop again. In the case of the `for` loop, *expression3* is evaluated before entering the loop body again. In the case of the `do` statement, the loop control expression is evaluated, and the loop is reentered.

The following example illustrates yet another way of getting a good random number for the division test of the math tutor.

Example Using the `continue` statement

```
/* Test the user's skill in division */
random1 = rand() % 20;   /* Numerator */
for( ; ; )   /* Forever */
{
    random2 = rand() % 20;   /* Denominator */

    if (random2 == 0)
        continue;   /* Go back to the loop top */

    /* Have a non zero random number here */
    break;   /* Get out of the loop */
}
```

In the above example, inside the infinite `for` loop, if the random number generated is a zero, the loop is restarted. Otherwise, the loop is executed.

Note that in the case of a `for` loop, the `continue` statement restarts the loop, reevaluating *expression3*, before testing the loop control expression (*expression2*).

7.6a `for` loops: A complete example

It's time to work on our test scores program again. This time, we will modify the program to incorporate names of the students as well. Prof. Jollyfellow has a new format for his scores file, and he needs a new, simplified output file. Here is how the new input file format looks:

```
Thomas Hardy:     88  74  96 100  87 100  78  95  85 90
John Smith:       66  88  93 100  99  76  77  90  72 79
Mary Davis:       93  92  91  98 100  99  89  88  91 99
Mark Pearson:     89  94  93  88 100  99  86  93  91 95
Cathy Dickerson:  90  88  76  78  85  87  74  82  90 99
```

Each line in the input file (named **SCORES.TXT**) contains the name of a student, followed by a colon and 10 test scores. The output file needs to be in the following format:

```
Thomas Hardy              B
John Smith                B
Mary Davis                A
Mark Pearson              A
Cathy Dickerson           B
```

The assignment of letter grades is done according to the following rule:

```
90 to 100  - A
80 to  89  - B
70 to  79  - C
Below 70   - D
```

Here is how we will tackle this problem. Note that each input line is in the following form:

```
Thomas Hardy:     88  74  96 100  87 100  78  95  85 90
```

Skipping the Execution in a Loop: continue Statement

Starting at the beginning of a line, we will read each character (using `getc`), until the colon is seen. Each character read will simply be written to the output file. After the colon has been read, the line contains 10 test scores. The scores will be read, in a loop, using `fscanf`. After the scores have been read, we will compute the sum, the average and the letter grade, which will be written to the output file.

The above step will be done in an infinite loop. How do we terminate the program? Upon reaching the end of the file, `getc` will return an EOF. We will test for EOF, and break out of the loop when EOF is encountered. Since the `break` only transfers control out of the nearest enclosing loop, we have to use some extra logic to get out of all the loops.

The program is given below:

```
#include <stdio.h>

#define INPUT_FILE      "SCORES.TXT"
#define OUT_FILE        "GRADES.TXT"

#define NUM_SCORES      10

#define FALSE           0
#define TRUE            1

main()
{
   FILE *ifhandle, *ofhandle; /* Input and output
                               * file handles */
   int ch;       /* To read one character at a time */
   int score, score_count, sum, average
   int end_flag = FALSE;   /* Flag used to break
                            * out of loops */

   if ((ifhandle = fopen(INPUT_FILE, "r")) == NULL)
   {
      perror(INPUT_FILE);
      exit(EXIT_FAILURE);
   }
```

```c
   if ((ofhandle = fopen(OUT_FILE, "w")) == NULL)
   {
      perror(OUT_FILE);
      exit(EXIT_FAILURE);
   }
   for ( ; ; )  /* Forever */
   {
      /* Read the name until : is seen */
      while((ch = fgetc(ifhandle)) != ':')
      {
         /* If EOF flag was seen, set a flag to indicate
          * end of input and get out of the loop we are in */
         if (ch == EOF)
         {
            end_flag = TRUE;
            break; /* Gets out of the while loop */
         }
         putchar(ch);           /* For debugging */
         fputc(ch, ofhandle); /* Simply, write to output */
      } /* End while */
      /* Check for end_flag to see if we got here due to
       * the break statement
       */
      if (end_flag == TRUE)
      {
         /* Got here because of end-of-input */
         break; /* Gets out the enclosing infinite for loop */
      }
      /* End of input was not seen: Read the 10 scores */
      putchar('\n');      /* For debugging */
      fprintf(ofhandle,"\t");   /* Put a tab after the name */
      sum = 0; /* Initialize sum to zero for this student */

      for (score_count = 0; score_count < NUM_SCORES;
                                          score_count++)
      {
         /* Read one score at a time */
         fscanf(ifhandle, "%d", &score);
         /* Output score for debugging */
         fprintf(stderr, "Score read is %d\n", score);
```

```
            sum = sum + score;
        } /* End for loop */
        /* 10 scores have been read. Next compute the average */
        average = sum / NUM_SCORES; /* Note: We truncate the
                                     * fractional part */
        /* Next, compute the letter grade */
        if (average >= 90)
        {
            fprintf(ofhandle, "A\n");
        }
        else if (average >= 80)
        {
            fprintf(ofhandle, "B\n");
        }
        else if (average >= 70)
        {
            fprintf(ofhandle, "C\n");
        }
        else /* Must be below 70 */
        {
            fprintf(ofhandle, "D\n");
        }
    } /* End for loop */
    /* Will get here upon seeing end of file */
    /* Close all files */
    fclose(ifhandle); /* Check for return values */
    fclose(ofhandle);
    exit(EXIT_SUCCESS);
}
```

7.6b Exercises

1 Write a program that reads a file containing lines of addresses in the following form:

```
M. Person, P.O. Box 12345, Atlanta, GA 30067
A. Hitchcock, Vertigo Lane, Mount Rushmore, SD 50678
```

and produce an output file containing addresses in the form

```
    M. Person
    P.O. Box 12345
    Atlanta
    GA 30067

    A. Hitchcock
    Vertigo Lane
    Mount Rushmore
    SD 50678
```

2. Modify the above program to accept input of the form

```
    M. Person, P.O. Box 12345, %Atlanta, GA 30067%
    A. Hitchcock, Vertigo Lane, %Mount Rushmore, SD 50678%
```

to produce the following output:

```
    M. Person
    P.O. Box 12345
    Atlanta, GA 30067

    A. Hitchcock
    Vertigo Lane
    Mount Rushmore, SD 50678
```

7.7 The goto Statement

The `goto` statement is used for unconditional branching to an arbitrary label within the same function.

Syntax   **Unconditional branching using `goto` statement**

```
    goto  label;
    statements
label:
    statements
```

The rule for naming a label is the same as the rule for naming variables.

A possible use of the `goto` statement is to transfer control from a nested loop if an error condition has been detected. Since the **break** statement only gets out of the *nearest* enclosing loop, getting out of a deeply nested loop will require a lot of extra logic. In such cases, the `goto` statement is an alternative to the **break** statement.

Consider the following example of a nested loop. If you wish to transfer control from the innermost loop (possibly due to an error condition), the **break** statement is woefully inadequate:

```
for(...)
{
   statements
   while (...)
   {
      more statements
      for (...)
      {
         even more statements
         if (error)
         {
            break;
         }
         statements
      } /* End inner loop. Break gets out of this loop */
```

```
    } /* End while loop */
} /* End outer for loop */
```

When control transfers out of the inner `for` loop using the **break** statement, it will still be within the outer `while` loop. If our intent was to get out of all the loops we will have to use a flag variable (as shown in the previous test score program) at the end of each loop statement, to test whether the loop should be continued or terminated.

Under these circumstances (and mostly limited to these situations), the `goto` statement is actually useful. We can rewrite the above program as

```
for(...)
{
    statements
    while (...)
    {
        more statements
        for (...)
        {
            even more statements
            if (error)
            {
                goto cleanup;
            }
            statements
        } /* End for. break gets out of this loop */
    } /* End while */
} /* End outer for */

cleanup:
    statement-list
```

Tip   *Avoid using `goto` statements as much as possible. If you have to use a `goto` statement, limit its use to cases as shown above. Also, make sure that you transfer control to a label which is placed close to the `goto` statement.*

7.7a   Updated precedence table

The precedence table, updated to include the increment, decrement and comma operators, is shown below. The table also includes the precedence for function call evaluation (operator ()). As before, each operator has been assigned a number indicative of its precedence. The larger the number, the higher the precedence. Operators of the same precedence have been assigned the same number.

Operator	Meaning	Precedence	Associativity
( )	Function call	13 (high)	Left to right
++, --	Increment, decrement	12	Right to left
!	Logical NOT	11	Right to left
-, +	Sign change	10	Left to right
*, /, %	Multiplicative	9	Left to right
-, +	Additive	8	Left to right
<, >, <=, >=	Relational	7	Left to right
==, !=	Equality, inequality	6	Left to right
&&	Logical AND	5	Left to right
||	Logical OR	4	Left to right
? :	Conditional	3	Right to left
=	Assignment	2	Right to left
,	Comma	1 (low)	Left to right

7.7b   Exercise

Prof. Jollyfellow wants to incorporate into his test scores the Olympics procedure of scoring on platform diving: He wants to throw away the highest and the lowest test scores in the list of 10 test scores, compute the average and then assign the letter grade. Modify the test score program to incorporate this change.

7.8 Common Problems

1 Trying to use a *nonconstant expression* in `case` labels always causes problems. For example, the following is invalid:

```
int x, y, z;

switch (x)
{
   case x: statement-list
           break;
   case y: statement-list
           break;
}
```

The expression following the `case` statement must be a constant expression. Note that the following, even though legal, will not fix the above problem:

```
int x, y, z;

switch (x)
{
   case 'x': statement-list
           break;
   case 'y': statement-list
           break;
}
```

2 If your program that contains a `for` statement does not terminate when you expect it to, it may be due to the inadvertent placement of a semicolon at the end of the line containing the `for` statement. The following example shows an infinite `for` loop:

3

```
for (i = 1; a   100; i++);
{
    a = a * i;
}
```

The problem here is that the semicolon at the end of the line containing the **for** statement terminates the **for** statement. But the **for** loop cannot terminate until the variable **a** becomes equal to or greater than 100. But **a** is only modified in the next statement: One that will not be reached!

To fix the problem, remove the semicolon at the end of the line containing the **for** statement.

8
Grouping Data, Using Arrays

Arrays in C are an extension of the basic data types (such as `int`, `char`, `float`) that is used to represent a collection of identical data types. In programs that use a large number of identical data that has the same type and a "common purpose," arrays are an extremely convenient abstraction.

In this chapter, you will learn about *one-dimensional* and *two-dimensional* arrays. You will also learn how to sort the *elements* of an array by using two different sorting techniques.

8.1   Arrays

Consider Prof. Jollyfellow's new and improved grading program. To maintain anonymity each student has picked an identification number to be used when the grades are openly posted on Prof. Jollyfellow's office door. Prof. Jollyfellow also wants to post the scores in sorted order, from the highest to the lowest. From our knowledge of data types and assuming that there are six students in the class, here's how the declaration may look:

```
int id1, id2, id3, id4, id5, id6;
int grade1, grade2, grade3, grade4, grade5, grade6;
```

Obviously, the above declaration is cumbersome if the number of students is high. We need a better way to represent these sets of identical data values, and that's where arrays fit in.

8.1a Declaring arrays and accessing elements

The syntax for declaring arrays is as shown:

Syntax **Array declaration**

```
datatype  array_name[size];
```

The name of the array, *array-name*, follows the rules for variable declarations. The *size* indicates the number of *elements* (individual data-items) of the array, and has to be a positive integer constant.

Example **Array declaration**

```
/* The above data-items can be declared as shown */
int id[6], grade[6];
```

In C, the subscript of the first element in the array is *always zero*. Thus, if you have an array of *n* elements, the valid range of subscripts is *0* through $n - 1$. Figure 8.1 shows the depiction of an array.

The elements of the array `grade[6]`, in the example given above, are

```
grade[0], grade[1], grade[2], grade[3], grade[4], grade[5]
```

Arrays can be of any data type. For example, we can represent an array to

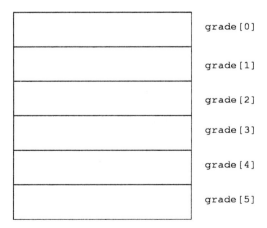

Figure 8.1 Representation of array `grade`.

Arrays

store lowercase letters as

```
char alphabet[26];
```

❑ **Accessing elements of an array**

Individual elements of the array can be accessed through the array *subscripting* operator []. The syntax for the array subscripting operator is as shown:

Syntax **Accessing elements using subscripting operation**

array_name[*index-expression*]

The *index-expression* must evaluate to an integer value (called the *index*). The index specifies the position of the array element from the beginning of the array.

Example **Accessing array elements**

```
/* Assigning values to array elements */
int grade[6];
grade[0] = 100;
grade[1] = 90;
grade[2] = 95;
grade[3] = 89;
grade[4] = 78;
grade[5] = 99;
```

Example **Printing individual elements**

```
int index;
printf("Grades are ");
for (index = 0; index < 6; index++)
{
   printf("%d ", grade[i])
}
printf("\n");
```

When the statements shown above are executed, the following will be the result:

```
Grades are 100 90 95 89 78 99
```

Note that the array subscript goes from 0 to 5. Here's another example of accessing individual elements of an array:

Example Accessing elements of a character array

```
char alphabet[26];
alphabet[0]  = 'a';
alphabet[2]  = 'b';
alphabet[13] = 'n';
alphabet[25] = 'z';
```

Since array subscripts start at 0, the set of valid indices for the above example is from 0 to 25. Unfortunately, when we use the array subscript operator, C does not check for the validity of the index at all. Thus, even if you performed

```
alphabet[26] = 'z';
```

it would not be an error as far as C is concerned. It is up to the programmer to ensure that the index value does not go out of bounds. This has the potential to cause many problems.

The next example shows how to search for a value in an array, using *linear search*. Assuming that the elements of the array `grade` have been assigned as shown in the earlier example, here's how you traverse the array:

Example Searching for a value in an array (linear search)

```
#include <stdio.h>

main()
{
   int search_value;

   /* Prompt the user for the search value */
   printf("Enter the search key ");
   scanf("%d", &search_value);
   for (index = 0; index < 6; index++)
   {
      if (grade[index] == search_value)
      {
         printf("Key found at index %d\n", index);
```

```
        exit(EXIT_SUCCESS);
      }
   }
   printf("Key not found\n");
   exit(EXIT_FAILURE);
}
```

The program shown below prompts the user to enter the test scores for six students. The test scores entered are stored in an array of size 6. After all the scores have been entered, the program prints out the highest score, the lowest score and the average.

```
/* File scores.c:   Compute the average and the
 * high and low scores for sample test scores
 */
#include <stdio.h>

#define         NO_STUDENTS        6
/* Macro to compute maximum */
#define MAX(a, b) ((a) > (b) ? (a) : (b))
/* Macro to compute minimum */
#define MIN(a, b) ((a) < (b) ? (a) : (b))

main()
{
   int grade[NO_STUDENTS];
   int index, sum, high, low, average;

   /* Initialize variables */
   sum = high = 0;
   low = 100;
   for (index = 0; index < NO_STUDENTS; index++)
   {
      /* Note that array index starts with zero */
      printf("Enter grade for student %d: ", index + 1);
      scanf("%d", &grade[index]);
      sum = sum + grade[index];/* Add to sum */
      /* Check if the score entered is a new
       * high or new low */
      high = MAX(grade[index], high);
```

```
        low = MIN(grade[index], low);
    }
    average = sum/NO_STUDENTS; /* Note: truncation */
    printf("The average score is %d\n", average);
    printf("The high score is %d and the low score is %d\n",
            high, low);
}
```

When the program is compiled and run with some sample scores, it produces the following result:

```
Enter the grade for student 1: 88
Enter the grade for student 2: 96
Enter the grade for student 3: 78
Enter the grade for student 4: 100
Enter the grade for student 5: 92
Enter the grade for student 6: 75
The average score is 88
The high score is 100 and the low score is 75
```

Note that initializing **sum** to zero is necessary. Otherwise, the first time through the loop, when we execute **sum + &grades[index]** and assign it to **sum**, it will have a garbage value. Also, note the initialization of the variable **high** to 0 and **low** to **100**.

Note *Forgetting to initialize variables before they are used is a common mistake that novice C programmers often make.*

Tip *Notice the declaration of the macro* **NO_STUDENTS** *and its subsequent use in the program. If we were to change the number of students from six to any other number, the only line we would have to modify is the macro definition directive. The preprocessor will take care of the rest.*

Remember the report generator that you built in Chapter 5 for Prof. Jollyfellow's introduction to file processing class? In that program, we used **fread** and **fwrite** to read and write individual data-items. Even though **fread** and **fwrite** are capable of operating on multiple data-items at a time, we only used these functions to read or write one data-item at a time. We mentioned in Chapter 5 that reading or writing multiple data-items requires the knowledge of arrays. Well, it's time to rewrite the program with our newly acquired knowledge.

The file format is shown below:

```
no. of students
score1
score2
score3
...
average
no. of A's
no. of B's
no. of C's
no. of D's
```

But before we start, there is a potential snag to be cleared. We will not know the size of the array to hold the grades until we read the file. But the array needs to be declared in our program before we can compile it. How do we deal with this?

The problem here is that the we only know how to allocate the memory to hold all program variables *statically*, or at *compile time*. In Chapter 13, you will learn to allocate memory to hold program variables *dynamically*, or at *run-time*. For now, we will just assume that the number of students in a class cannot be larger than a preset limit. We may be wasting some space if the actual number of students is much less than the maximum allowed. But we will not worry about it here.

```c
/* File report.c: Reads a binary file containing test
 * scores and produces a report.
 */

#include <stdio.h>
#include <assert.h>        /* Or use my_defs.h */

#define MAX_STUDENTS      30
#define NO_LETTER_GRADES  4    /* For A's, B's, C's and D's */
#define INPUT_FILE        "SCORES.DAT"
```

```c
main()
{
   FILE *fhandle;
   int grade[MAX_STUDENTS]; /* Array to hold all scores */
   float average;
   int no_of_students;
   int lgrades[NO_LETTER_GRADES]; /* To hold number of
                                   * letter grades */

   char letter_grades[NO_LETTER_GRADES] =
                            {'A', 'B', 'C', 'D'};
   int ret_value, index;

   if ((fhandle = fopen(INPUT_FILE, "r")) == NULL)
   {
      perror(INPUT_FILE);
      exit(EXIT_FAILURE);
   }
   /* Read the number of students from the file */
   fread((void *)&no_of_students, sizeof(int), 1, fhandle);

   /* Make sure that the value read is a sane one */
   assert((no_of_students > 0) &&
          (no_of_students < MAX_STUDENTS));
   /* Read the scores for no_of_students in to array */
   ret_val = fread((void *)grade, sizeof(int),
                   no_of_students, fhandle);
   /* fread returns the number of items read.
    * Make sure that it is sane */
   assert(ret_val == no_of_students);
   /* Next, read the average score */
   ret_val = fread((void *)&average, sizeof(float),
                   1, fhandle);
   assert(ret_val == 1); /* Make sure that the
                          * return value is 1 */
   /* Next read the list of letter grades */
   ret_val = fread((void *)lgrades, sizeof(int),
                   NO_LETTER_GRADES, fhandle);
   assert(ret_val == NO_LETTER_GRADES);
```

```
    /* The file has been read completely. Now print */
    printf("*******************************************\n");
    printf("* Midterm Grades for Intro to File \
Processing\n");
    printf("* Instructor: John Jollyfellow\n");
    printf("* Number of students: %d\n", no_of_students);
    printf("* Scores:\n");

    for (index = 0; index < no_of_students; index++)
    {
       printf("* Student %d: %d\n", index + 1,
              grade[index]);
    }
    printf("* Average Score = %4.2f\n, average);
    /* Now print the no. of A's, B's. etc */
    for (index = 0; index < NO_LETTER_GRADES; index++)
    {
       printf(" No of %c's = %d\n",
              letter_grades[index], lgrades[index]);
    }
    printf("*******************************************\n");
    exit(EXIT_SUCCESS);
}
```

Observe the following two **fread** statements:

```
ret_val = fread((void *)grade, sizeof(int),
                          no_of_students, fhandle);
ret_val = fread((void *)lgrades, sizeof(int),
                          NO_LETTER_GRADES, fhandle);
```

Compare it with the following **fread** statement:

```
ret_val = fread((void *)&average, sizeof(float),
                          1, fhandle);
```

Notice the omission of the **&** in front of the buffer in the case of the arrays **scores** and **lgrades**. This is not a typographic error. Due to reasons too complicated to explain here (oh, there goes that line again!), the **&** need not be placed before the array if an array is used as the buffer. In the next chapter you will learn why the **&** (*address-of-operator*) is omitted from when the variable is an array. Meanwhile, if you don't like this form, you may use the following equivalent statement:

```
fread((void *)&scores[0], sizeof(int),
                no_of_students, fhandle);
fread((void *)&lgrades[0], sizeof(int),
                NO_LETTER_GRADES, fhandle);
```

The reason behind all this black magic will become clear when you learn about pointers in the next chapter.

The following statement declares a character array and also assigns initial values to the individual elements:

```
char letter_grades[NO_LETTER_GRADES] = {'A', 'B', 'C', 'D'};
```

Array initialization rules are covered in detail in the next section.

8.1b Exercises

1. Modify the file **scores.c**, shown earlier in this chapter, to also count the number of students who scored over 90 on the test. At the end of the program, display the number of students who scored over 90.

2. Redo the second problem in Exercise 5.5a. Create an array to hold 20 random numbers. Create all the necessary random numbers before starting the testing. Use the numbers stored in the array to perform the tests.

8.1c Sorting the elements of an array

The next example illustrates sorting by using arrays. In the program, we will sort a list of test scores from the lowest to the highest. To sort the numbers, we will use a simple algorithm known as *bubble sort*. The idea behind bubble sort is very simple: The program makes several passes through the array containing the scores, compares adjacent scores and swaps them if they are out of order. Thus smaller values *bubble* to the top.

During the initial pass through the array, the first element is compared with the rest of the elements If the first element is the largest, it drops down to the end of the array and the remaining elements bubble up by one position. During the second pass, since the largest element will be at the bottom from the previous pass, the complete length of array need not be traversed: The pass length can be decremented by 1. Thus, during each pass, the pass length is decremented. The algorithm is terminated when a pass through the array does not lead to any more values to swap (indicating that all the elements are in order).

Figure 8.2 illustrates the execution of the bubble-sort algorithm. .

We assume that the file **my_defs.h** contains macro definitions for **FALSE**, **TRUE** and **SWAP(a,b)**. The program contains extra `printf` statements that will help you visualize what is going on in the program when you compile and run it.

```
#include <stdio.h>
#include "my_defs.h"

#define NO_STUDENTS       6

main()
{
   int grades[NO_STUDENTS];
   int index;   /* Generic loop variable */
   int pass_length; /* Number of items to look at,
                     * at each pass */
   int swapped_flag = TRUE; /* To check if we need
                             * any more passes */

   /* First, read all the scores into the array */
   for (index = 0; index < NO_STUDENTS; index++)
   {
      printf("Enter grade for student %d ", index + 1);
      scanf("%d", &grades[index]);
   }

   /* Debug: print all scores input */
   printf("Original scores are ");
   for (index = 0; index < NO_STUDENTS; index++)
```

```c
      {
         printf("%d ", grades[index]);
      }
      printf("\n");

      /* All scores have been input. Now sort */
      pass_length = NO_STUDENTS;
      /* Length of the pass.
       * This is the number of array elements to look at
       * during each pass through the loop
       */
      while(swapped_flag == TRUE)
      {
         pass_length = pass_length - 1;
         /* Decrement the pass length,
          * each time through the loop. */
         swapped_flag = FALSE; /* Assume that everything
                                * was in order */
         for (index = 0; index < pass_length; index++)
         {
            /* Debug statement */
            fprintf(stderr, "Comparing %d vs %d\n",
                         grades[index], grades[index + 1]);
            if (grades[index] > grades[index + 1])
            {
               /* Debug statement */
               fprintf(stderr, "Swapping: %d and %d\n",
                         grades[index],grades[index + 1]);
               SWAP(grades[index], grades[index +1]);
               fprintf(stderr, "After swapping: %d and %d\n",
                         grades[index], grades[index + 1]);
               swapped_flag = TRUE;
            } /* End if */
         } /* End for */
      } /* End while */
      printf("The sorted array is ");
      for (index = 0; index  NO_STUDENTS; index++)
         printf("%d ", grades[index]);
      printf("\n");
   }
```

Arrays

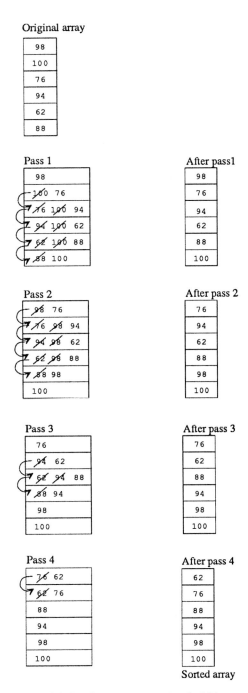

Figure 8.2 Sorting an array using bubble sort.

Compile and run the bubble-sort program, and study its behavior.

8.1d Exercises

1. Modify the file **scores.c** in Section 8.1 to print the number of students above the average and the number below the average.

2. In its worst case, the bubble-sort algorithm makes n^2 passes through the array. The worst case occurs if the original array elements are sorted in the reverse order. Verify this by introducing a counter in the program to count the number of passes made. Use a presorted array, sorted in the reverse order as the input.

3. If the array is already sorted correctly, how many passes does the bubble-sort algorithm make?

8.1e Array initialization

It is possible to assign initial values to each array element at the time of declaration. The syntax for initializing array elements at the time of declaration is shown below:

Syntax   **Initializing arrays elements at time of declaration**

```
datatype   array_name[size] = {list-of-values};
```

or

```
datatype   array_name[] = {list-of-values};
```

or (for character arrays only)

```
char   array_name[] = string;
```

The *list-of-values* is a comma-separated list of values to be assigned to each element of the array, from the first to the last, respectively. In the first form of the initialization shown above, the array size is given inside the subscript. C allows us to omit the size in the declaration if the list of initial values is

Arrays

supplied with the declaration (the size is taken to be the number of initial values supplied). This is shown in the second form above. The last form of declaring and initializing arrays is allowed only for character arrays. Note that the *string* is a sequence of characters enclosed in double quotes. The array will include the null character at the end of the string.

Example **Initializing an integer array**

```
/* Declaring and initializing the grades array */
int grade[6] = { 91, 88, 67, 78, 63, 70 };
```

The above declaration is equivalent to:

```
int grade[6];
grade[0] = 91;
grade[1] = 88;
grade[2] = 67;
grade[3] = 78;
grade[4] = 63;
grade[5] = 70;
```

Example **Declaring an array without the size**

```
int grade[] = { 91, 88, 67, 78, 63, 70 };
```

In the case of the above example, the compiler will recognize that the array is being initialized with six items and set the size to 6. Automatic setting of size is very useful in the case of character arrays (since we don't have to count the number of characters). The example below initializes a character array:

Example **Initializing a character array**

```
char student[] = "Alfred E. Neumann";
```

Note that strings are always null-terminated by the compiler. Thus the size of the above array will be one more than the length of the string shown above. The above declaration is equivalent to the following alternate declaration:

Example **Initializing a character array**

```
char student[] = { 'A', 'l', 'f', 'r', 'e', 'd', ' ',
                   'E', '.', ' ', 'N', 'e', 'u', 'm', 'a',
                   'n', 'n', '\0' };
```

Grouping Data, Using Arrays   *Chapter 8*

8.1f Problem with arrays: Lack of bounds checking

Array implementation in C is quite unsafe: *C does not perform any compile-time or run-time bounds checking on arrays*. For example, given the declaration

```
int grades[5];
```

C does not complain at compile-time or at run-time if we index the array as

```
grades[6];    /* Valid indices are 0 to 4 */
```

or even

```
grades[12984];
```

Compile and run the following program to verify that C does not perform run-time bounds checking:

```
#include <stdio.h>

main()
{
   int test_array[5] = { 1, 2, 3, 4, 5 };
   int index;

   for (index = 0; index <= 5; index++)
   {
      printf("Array index [%d] has value %d\n",
             index, test_array[index]);
   }
}
```

The problem with the example shown above is that the array index should go from 0 to 4, but instead goes from 0 to 5. Unfortunately, C doesn't notice that anything is amiss.

Since C does not perform bounds checking, it is left up to the programmer to make sure that the array indices generated at run-time are correct.

Arrays 217

Tip *Use the `assert` macro during program development stages to check if the indices are within valid ranges. After the program has been successfully tested and debugged, you may remove the macro.*

On the other hand, if the array index grows way out of bounds, at some point, your program will be terminated by the system. The following exercise will verify this:

8.1g <u>Exercise</u>

Access the array in the above program using invalid indices. For example, in an infinite loop, access the array using a counter that is constantly incremented. At what index does your program die (crash, dump core, choke, etc.)?

8.1h <u>Compile-time memory allocation</u>

When using arrays, the programmer must predefine the maximum size of the array. Declaring the size of an array cannot be delayed until run-time. For example, in the student grades program, it would be really convenient to prompt the user for the number of students and then determine the size of the array. If it were possible, we could write the program as

```
int no_students;
printf("Enter the number of students: ");
scanf("%d", &no_students);

int student[no_students], grades[no_students];
rest of the program
```

But, unfortunately, C does not allow the determination of array size at run-time. To be able to handle arbitrary sizes during run-time, one needs to use the *dynamic memory allocation* routines provided with the standard library. This will be discussed in Chapter 13.

8.1i <u>Sorting an array without shuffling the elements</u>

Prof. Jollyfellow has yielded to student pressure and has agreed to use student IDs, rather than names, while posting test scores on his door for the whole world to see. The students have chosen the IDs (a nine-digit number). Prof. Jollyfellow's score file now appears as shown:

```
338303565         98
148428312        100
356658871         76
194340065         94
298425912         62
668316617         88
```

Prof. Jollyfellow wants to sort the scores from highest to lowest and print them. He wants the output to appear as follows:

```
148428312        100
338303565         98
194340065         94
668316617         88
356658871         76
298425912         62
```

The program calls for sorting the test scores, possibly using the bubble-sort algorithm presented before. But there's a problem: When we sort the grades and rearrange them, we also need to rearrange the IDs accordingly. This could get somewhat messy!

Instead of sorting and rearranging the scores as well as IDs, we will try a different approach: finding the sorted index of each test score and storing that index in a different array. This is shown in Figure 8.3. In the figure, note that the newly created array contains the sorted index of each element in the original score array. Once we have created the new array, all we need to do is use the indices in the array to print the grades and the IDs from the original arrays.

The algorithm to build the new arrays is quite simple: We will scan the score array and find the highest score. The index of the array that contains the highest score will be stored in the first position of the new array. Next, we need to eliminate this high score from further contention. For this, after finding the high score, we will set it to zero (thereby eliminating that score from further competition). We will repeat the scanning until the positions of all scores have been computed. This technique is known as *index sorting*.

Arrays

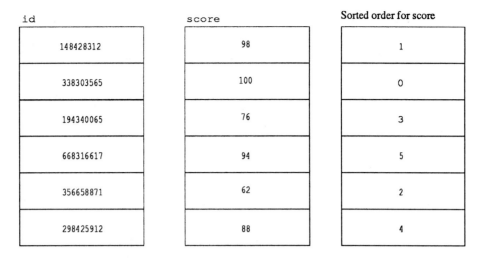

Figure 8.3 Sorting by storing a sorted index.

Since we don't want to destroy the original scores before doing any manipulation, we will copy the original score to a temporary array and manipulate the temporary array.

The complete program is given below:

```
/* File indsort.c: Creates an array which contains
 * the sorted index for another array */

#include <stdio.h>
#include <assert.h>

#define MAX_LIMIT  32   /* Allowed maximum students */
#define INPUT_FILE "scoresfile"

main()
{
   long id[MAX_LIMIT]; /* For storing IDs */
   int scores[MAX_LIMIT], temp_scores[MAX_LIMIT];
   char sort_position[MAX_LIMIT]; /* Array to hold
                                   * sorted position */
   int index;                     /* Loop variable */
```

```c
   int no_students;  /* Actual number of students in
                      *  the file */
   int ret_val;      /* To check return values */
   int max, max_position, array_length;
   int position;
   FILE *fhandle;

   if ( (fhandle = fopen(INPUT_FILE, "r")) == NULL)
   {
      perror(INPUT_FILE);
      exit(EXIT_FAILURE);
   }
   no_students = 0;       /* Initialize */
   for (index = 0; index < MAX_LIMIT; index++)
   {
      ret_val = fscanf(fhandle, "%ld %d",
                       &id[index], &scores[index]);
      /* Note the format specifier l for long integer */
      if (ret_val == EOF)
         break;   /* No more lines in the file */

      no_students++;
      assert(no_students < MAX_LIMIT);
   } /* End reading the scores */
   /* Verify (for debugging) that original scores and IDs
    * have been read  correctly. Also, create a temporary
    * array for manipulating scores
    */
   fprintf(stderr, "Original Scores\n");
   for (index = 0; index < no_students; index++)
   {
      fprintf(stderr, "%ld\t%d\n", id[index],
              scores[index]);
      temp_scores[index] = scores[index];
   }

   for (array_length = 0; array_length < no_students;
        array_length++)
   {
      max = 0; /* Initialize */
```

```c
      /* Make a pass through all elements
       * and find maximum */
      for (index = 0; index < no_students; index++)
      {
         if (temp_scores[index] > max)
         {
            max_position = index;
            max = temp_scores[index];
         }
      } /* End inner for loop.
         * One pass has been completed */
      /* max_position contains the index of the
       * largest score in the original array.
       * Take the current max out of the competition
       */       temp_scores[max_position] = 0;
      /* Store the position of the score in the new array */
      sort_position[array_length] = max_position;
   } /* End outer for. All positions have been determined */
   /* Print the sorted scores and IDs */
   printf("\nSorted Scores\n");

   for (index = 0; index < no_students; index++)
   {
      position = sort_position[index]; /* Correct position
                                        * of each score */
      printf("%ld\t%d\n", id[position], scores[position]);
   }
   exit(EXIT_SUCCESS);
}
```

Compiling and running the above program (with the test scores shown above) produces the following results:

```
Original Scores
338303565       98
148428312       100
356658871       76
194340065       94
298425912       62
668316617       88
```

```
Sorted Scores
148428312       100
338303565        98
194340065        94
668316617        88
356658871        76
298425912        62
```

8.1j Binary search: Program development

In this section, we outline the algorithm to implement binary search using pseudo code. The actual code to implement the algorithm is left as an exercise.

Linear search is very inefficient, especially if the array size is very large. In the worst case, you will have to search all the elements in the array to determine if an item is present in the array or not.

The search can be speeded up considerably, if the elements of the array are already ordered (sorted). In this case, we can examine the element at the middle point of the array and decide if the item to be searched for may be in the first half or the second half of the array. Once we determine which half the item may be in, the other half can be eliminated from contention. Repeatedly performing this process will lead to finding the item or realizing that the item is not present. This technique is known as *binary search*. Binary search is faster, since we don't have to examine all the elements in the array: if we have an array of size N, we only need $\log_2 N$ steps to determine if the item is present in the array or not (as opposed to N steps in the case of linear search).

The algorithm to perform binary search is presented in the form of pseudo code, below. The names of the variables used in the algorithm are:
- `sarray` — Presorted array
- `first` — Beginning index of the unexamined portion of the array
- `last` — Ending index of the unexamined portion of the array
- `mid_point` — Current middle point of the unexamined portion of the array
- `N` — Number of elements in the array

- **item** — The item being searched for

```
first = 0;
last = N - 1;
Do
    mid_point = (first + last) / 2;
    If item is larger than  sarray[mid_point]
        first = mid_point + 1;
    Else
        last = mid_point - 1;
While (sarray[midpoint] ≠ item AND first ≤ last)
```

8.1k Exercises

1 Implement the binary search algorithm discussed above. To test the program, use an the following array:

```
int my_array[] = { 0, 2, 7, 34, 47, 94, 99, 213,
                   873, 4000 };
```

Note that the array is already sorted (as required by the algorithm).

2 Modify the program **indsort.c** to sort and print the scores from the lowest to the highest.

8.2 Multidimensional Arrays

What if Prof. Jollyfellow has asked us to keep track of multiple test scores for each student? In other words, he has given us a sample file that looks like

```
338303565      98  99  67  78  87
148428312     100 100  97  89  88
356658871      76  67  84  82  86
194340065      94  93  88  79  80
298425912      62  60  72  78  81
668316617      88  90  96  89  97
```

To represent all the test scores in program memory, we need an *array of arrays*, or a *two-dimensional* array.

The number of indices used to access an element of the array is called its *dimension*. So far, we have only been dealing with *one-dimensional* arrays. Arrays with more than one dimension are known as *multidimensional* arrays. C places no restriction on the number of dimensions allowed for arrays.

A two-dimensional array for the student scores shown above can be declared as follows:

```
#define MAX_LIMIT       32   /* Maximum number of
                              * students allowed */
#define NO_OF_SCORES     5   /* Number of test scores */

int scores[MAX_LIMIT][NO_OF_SCORES]; /* Array declaration */
```

To access a student's test score for a specific exam, we need to specify both indices. For example, to print the second test score for a student with the ID **298425912**, the following statement can be used.

Example Accessing an individual element of a multidimensional array

```
/* To print the second test score
 * for student 298425912 */
printf("score = %d\n", scores[4][1]);
/* Remember that arrays have 0 origin */
```

For a two-dimensional array, the array declaration has the following form:

Syntax **Two-dimensional array declaration**

```
data-type array-name[row][column];
```

The two-dimensional array `scores` can be visualized as shown in the following table:

98	99	67	78	87
100	100	97	89	88
76	67	84	82	86
94	93	88	79	80
62	60	72	78	81
88	90	96	89	97

The array is traversed in *row-major* order; i.e., the scores in each row are traversed before moving to the next row. As a consequence, the second subscript grows more rapidly than the first subscript, as shown below:

```
scores[0][0], scores[0][1], scores[0][2], scores[0][3],
scores[0][4], scores[0][5]

scores[1][0], scores[1][1], scores[1][2], scores[1][3],
scores[1][4], scores[1][5]

scores[2][0], scores[2][1], scores[2][2], scores[2][3],
scores[2][4], scores[2][5]

etc.
```

Thus, according to intended usage, the array can be visualized as

```
scores[STUDENT0][TEST0], scores[STUDENT0][TEST1],
scores[STUDENT0][TEST2], scores[STUDENT0][TEST3],
scores[STUDENT0][TEST4], scores[STUDENT0][TEST5]
```

```
scores[STUDENT1][TEST0], scores[STUDENT1][TEST1],
scores[STUDENT1][TEST2], ...

scores[STUDENT2][TEST0], scores[STUDENT2][TEST1],
scores[STUDENT2][TEST2], ...
etc.
```

Let us modify the program for Prof. Jollyfellow to read in all the test scores, compute the average and the letter grade for each student and create a report file that contains the IDs, scores and the final letter grades.

```
/* File 2darray.c: Generate a
 * report file test scores */
#include <stdio.h>
#include <assert.h>

#define INPUT_FILE    "SCORES.TXT"
#define OUTPUT_FILE   "REPORT.TXT"

#define MAX_LIMIT   32   /* Maximum number of students
                          * allowed */
#define NO_OF_TESTS 5    /* Number of test scores
                          * per student */
main()
{
   long id[MAX_LIMIT]; /* For storing IDs */
   int scores[MAX_LIMIT][NO_OF_TESTS];
   int student, test; /* Loop variables */
   int no_students;   /* Actual number of
                       * students in the file */
   int ret_val;       /* To check return values */
   int sum, average;
   char grade[MAX_LIMIT];
   FILE *ifhandle, *ofhandle;

   if ( (ifhandle = fopen(INPUT_FILE, "r")) == NULL)
   {
      perror(INPUT_FILE);
      exit(EXIT_FAILURE);
   }
```

```
            if ( (ofhandle = fopen(OUTPUT_FILE, "w")) == NULL)
            {
               perror(OUTPUT_FILE);
               fclose(ifhandle);
               exit(EXIT_FAILURE);
            }

            /* Read all the scores */
            no_students = 0;      /* Initialize */
            for (student = 0; student < MAX_LIMIT; student++)
            {  /* Index student controls the number of students */
               /* First read the ID */
               ret_val = fscanf(ifhandle, "%ld", &id[student]);
               if (ret_val == EOF)
                  break;  /* Out of the for loop */
               /* Valid ID read */
               no_students++;
               assert(no_students < MAX_LIMIT);

               /* Next read the individual scores for the student */
               for (test = 0; test < NO_OF_TESTS; test++)
               { /* Index test controls the test scores/student */
                  ret_val = fscanf(ifhandle, "%d",
                                   &scores[student][test]);
                  assert(ret_val != EOF); /* Not expecting EOF */
               } /* End reading all scores */
            } /* End reading the file */

            /* Print the number of students, for debugging */
            fprintf(stderr, "no_of_students = %d\n", no_students);

            /* Verify (for debugging) that original scores and IDs
             * have been read correctly
             */
            fprintf(stderr, "Original Scores\n");
            for (student = 0; student < no_students; student++)
            {
               /* Print the ID */
               fprintf(stderr, "%ld\t", id[student]);
               /* Print the scores corresponding to the ID */
```

```
            for (test = 0; test < NO_OF_TESTS; test++)
                fprintf(stderr, "%3d ", scores[student][test]);
            fprintf(stderr,"\n");
        }
        /* Next compute the average for each student and
         * assign a grade */
        for (student = 0; student < no_students; student++)
        {
            sum = 0;
            for (test = 0; test < NO_OF_TESTS; test++)
                sum = sum + scores[student][test];

            average = sum/NO_OF_TESTS;
            if (average >= 90)
                grade[student] = 'A';
            else if (average >= 80)
                grade[student] = 'B';
            else if (average >= 70)
                grade[student] = 'C';
            else
                grade[student] = 'D';
        }
        /* Now prepare the output file */
        for (student = 0; student < no_students; student++)
        {
            /* Print the ID */
            fprintf(ofhandle, "%ld\t", id[student]);
            /* Print the scores for the ID */
            for (test = 0; test < NO_OF_TESTS; test++)
                fprintf(ofhandle, "%3d ", scores[student][test]);

            fprintf(ofhandle, "............... %c\n",
                    grade[student]);
        }
        /* Close the input and output files, check for error */
        fclose(ifhandle);
        fclose(ofhandle);
        exit(EXIT_SUCCESS);
    }
```

Multidimensional Arrays 229

Compiling and running the program produces a report file called
REPORT.TXT, with the following contents (on sample data shown above):

```
338303565      98  99  67  78  87  .............. B
148428312     100 100  97  89  88  .............. A
356658871      76  67  84  82  86  .............. C
194340065      94  93  88  79  80  .............. B
298425912      62  60  72  78  81  .............. C
668316617      88  90  96  89  97  .............. A
```

Since strings are character arrays, arrays of strings are two-dimensional arrays. Strings and associated topics are covered separately, in Chapter 9.

8.2a Exercises

1 Modify the program shown above to compute and print the size of the newly created data type **NAME**. Also, modify the program to read input in lowercase and print it out uppercase.

2 Modify the program **2darray.c** to include the average test scores as well as the letter grades in the final report.

3 Discard the lowest test score from the set of scores for each student (do this without sorting the array). Produce the report with the remaining test scores, the averages and the letter grades.

4 Two-dimensional arrays are a useful abstraction for drawing graphs, charts, etc. The two dimensions of the arrays can be used as the x coordinate and the y coordinate in the Cartesian system. For example, to draw a graph illustrating a student's progress through the various tests, we can create a two-dimensional character array and then insert markers in the array (such as the * character), corresponding to the x and y coordinates (in our case, corresponding to test score and student number). After the markers have been placed, all we need to do is scan the array and print the markers. A sample character array for the the student **148428312** is shown below:

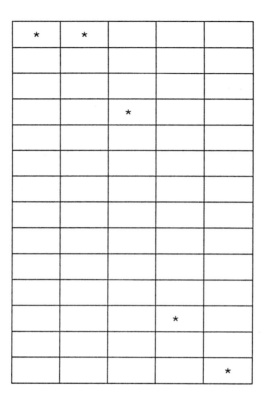

Write a program that prompts the user for a student ID. Search the ID array for a match, and if found, build a two-dimensional character array. Next, print the graph, which should be similar to Figure 8.4.

To simplify printing, initialize all the elements of the array with the space character (' ') before you place the markers. You can then print each element of the character array by using the function **putchar**:

```
putchar(graph[i][j]);   /* Assuming the character
                         * array is called graph */
```

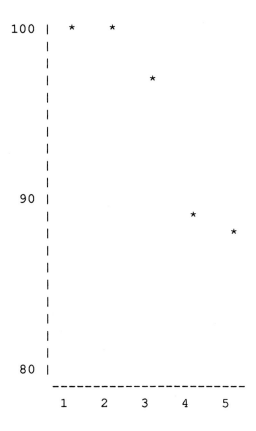

Figure 8.4 A student's progress.

8.3 Common Problems

1. The most common problems at this stage are due to array indices going out of bounds. If you are lucky, this may result in the program terminating abnormally (with messages such as "memory fault", "segmentation violation", "bus error", etc.). If you are not so lucky, the program may run to completion, but with incorrect results. The latter type of bugs is hard to catch: Without checking all the data ourselves, we will not be able to tell whether the results are correct or not!

   Using **assert** macros and **printf** statements to verify results at intermediate steps may alleviate some of the program development blues. This is also a good point to begin using your system's symbolic debugger, if you have one.

2. Another mistake that novice C programmers make is in indexing a two-dimensional array using the comma operator, as shown:

   ```
   sum = sum + scores[i, j];
   ```

   The statement shown above is valid C syntax. Evaluation of the comma operator returns the value of its right operand. Thus, the statement is similar to:

   ```
   sum = sum + scores[j];
   ```

   Even though **scores** has been declared a two-dimensional array, C does not complain! Correct the above statement as:

   ```
   sum = sum + scores[i][j];
   ```

9
Accessing Memory Directly: Pointers

In this chapter, you will learn about a derived data type called *pointers*. Pointers allow unrestricted access to memory locations in a program. So far, we have been accessing variables by using their *names*. Pointers allow us to access the actual memory locations designated to hold these variables.

If we can access the variables by their names, why would we want to access them by using pointers to their memory locations? There are many advantages to accessing memory directly:

- Once we know the memory location where a certain data-item such as an array is loaded, accessing individual elements can be done faster by using pointers to the memory locations.
- If we need to exchange data between functions (which you will study in detail in the next chapter), it is more efficient to tell the function where the data is, rather than copying all the data to the function.
- Requesting memory to hold data-items at run-time (dynamic memory allocation) requires us to access these locations directly. You will study dynamic memory allocation in Chapter 13.

On the flip side, unrestricted access to memory has the potential to cause severe problems if programs are not written carefully. C provides very little checking, in terms of telling us if we are accessing memory correctly or not.

In spite of all their pitfalls, pointers are a powerful data type and are one of the principal reasons behind C's acceptance as the chosen language of systems programmers.

9.1 Pointers

Until now, when we were using a program variable (such as `scores`), we were only concerned about its *type* (such as `int, float`). Now we will introduce one more attribute: its *location,* or *address.* Inside the computer, a running programs memory locations are referred to by its address (a number).

Computer memory is *addressable*: Each byte in the memory has a distinct number. We can refer to the memory by its number, called its *address,* or *location.* Inside the computer, a running program's memory locations are referred to by its address, not by its name. In fact, a variable's name is just a shorthand notation for its address. We deal with names in our programs because it is somewhat inconvenient to deal with numbers.

Figure 9.1 shows a conceptual view of the computer's memory. Each row shown is called a *word* of memory, and the size of the word depends on your machine's architecture. In our examples here, we will assume a word size of 2 bytes.

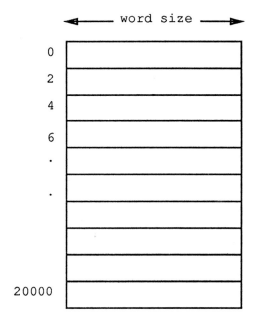

Figure 9.1 Memory layout.

Pointers

Figure 9.1 shows the memory starting at address 0 and ending at address 20000. We will use the following convention to describe memory locations and contents: The number on the left side of the box represents addresses, and a name (if shown) on the right side of the box indicates variable names. Inside the box will be the contents of the variables: the value that you put into the variable.

Prior to running, the entire program is loaded into memory. Thus your program code, as well as the data, is in memory and is addressable. So far, we have been accessing the data by its name, which is the name of the variable that contains the data.

9.1a Variables and address locations

Consider what happens to the following declaration:

```
int a;
```

Let us assume that **a** is loaded into memory at location 1004. This is shown in Figure 9.2. In the figure, the location or address of **a** is 1004.

When we assign a value to the variable **a**, it goes into this memory location. For example, when we perform the assignment

```
a = 25;
```

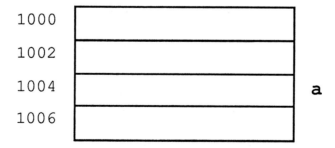

Figure 9.2 Location of a variable in memory.

the resulting picture of memory is as shown in Figure 9.3 According to the figure, the address of `a` is 1004 and the content of address 1004 is 25, which is also the value of the variable `a`.

Note *Note that computers differ in which byte they consider as the first one, in a variable storage location which occupies more than one byte (such as the `int` in our example, which occupies 2 bytes). If a left to right or big endian architecture, the address of an integer is the high-order byte (the leftmost byte) of the integer. In a right to left or little endian architecture, the address of an integer is the address of the low-order byte (the rightmost byte) of the integer.*

How do we find the address of any variable (i.e., which location in memory does the variable occupy)? The *address operator* (`&`) provides the address (an integer value) of any variable.

Example **Printing the address of a variable**

```
printf ("%lu\n", &a);
```

If we executed the above statement in a program, `1004` will be printed.

Note *Notice the format specifier `lu`, in the first `printf` statement. Since addresses are always positive values and can be very large, we instruct the `printf` function that the value passed to it is `unsigned` and `long`. ANSI C provides the `%p` format specifier for printing pointers, but most C compilers do not support it yet.*

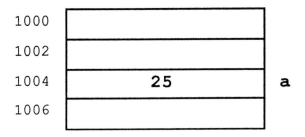

Figure 9.3 Assigning a value to a variable.

Now there are two ways to get to the contents of the variable **a**:

- Accessing the contents of the variable directly by its name (as we have done so far).

    ```
    printf ("%d\n", a);          /* Will print 25 */
    ```

- Accessing the contents at the memory location indirectly, by using its address. C provides the *indirection operator* (*) for accessing the contents of a memory location by its address.*

Applying the * operator to a memory address yields the contents at that address. The syntax for the indirection operator is shown below:

Syntax   **Indirection operator for accessing contents of memory**

* *expression*

The operand for the indirection operator is an expression that evaluates to an integer value. The type of the value need not be **int**: it could be larger than an **int**, such as a **long**. The integer value is intended to refer to a valid memory location.

Using the indirection operator, the contents at any valid memory location can be accessed. The following example shows how we can indirectly access the contents at the address location 1004.

Example   **Accessing the contents at a memory location**

```
/* Print the contents at address 1004 */
printf("%d\n", *(1004));
```

Note   *The above statement is not complete and may not compile on most compilers until you instruct the compiler as to the type of data stored at location 1004. To do so, we need to use the cast operator on the address 1004. In reality, we will not be dealing with numbers, such as 1004, directly, and the cast is omitted here in order to simplify the explanation.*

---

* This is not to be confused with the multiplication operator. The *indirection operator* * is a unary operator.

If the above statement was compiled and executed, it would print the value at the memory location 1004, which is **25**.

What would happen if we execute the following statement?

```
printf("%d\n", *(1006));
```

In this case, the contents at memory location 1006 will be printed. What is in address location 1006? We don't know!

In summary, a pointer, as the name indicates, tells you *where* an item of interest (the data) is, rather than *what* the item is. For example, a pointer to an **int** variable tells you where the variable is located in memory rather than what value the variable contains. For a variable named **a**, the following table shows you how to get to the contents of **a**, directly and indirectly. Assume that for the first row of the table, we have declared **a** as

```
int a = 25;
```

and, for the second row, the declaration is

```
int b = 25;
int *a;
a = &b;
```

The table shows how to access the value **25** using direct and indirect means and where the value **25** is stored.

Declaration	How to get the value	How to get the address
int a;	a	&a
int *a	*a	a

❑ **Finding the address of variables**

Dealing with numbers like 1004 is messy and impossible, as we will never know, *a priori*, where the variable **a** will be loaded into memory. Hence we will use the address operator (&) to get the address of the variable and get its contents by using the indirection operator (*):

```
printf("%d\n", *(&a)); /* Will print 25 */.
```

Notice that the & operator and the * operator cancel each other! Thus we are left with the equivalent statement

```
printf("%d\n", (a)); /* Will print 25 */.
```

Let's verify all this by writing a simple program. Compile and run the following program:

```c
#include <stdio.h>

main()
{
   int a = 25;
   printf("Address of a = %lu\n", &a);
   printf("Contents of a, direct method = %d\n", a);
   printf("Contents of a, indirect method = %d\n", *(&a));
   /* Now modify a indirectly */
   *(&a) = 50;
   printf("Contents of a, direct method = %d\n", a);
}
```

When compiled and run using the C compiler on a Sun SPARCstation 1 running UNIX, the program displays the following:

```
Address of a = 4160747060
Contents of a, direct method = 25
Contents of a, indirect method = 25
Contents of a, direct method =  50
```

9.1b What is an address?

Since addresses are integer values, how do we distinguish between integer values that represent memory addresses and normal integer values in a program? For example, how can we tell whether the number 1004 is an address or just a plain integer value with no meaning attached to it?

Do we even have to worry about the distinction? We do! Consider the following operations:

```
25 * 2;     /* Yields the value 50 */
1004 * 2;   /* Yields the value 2008 */
```

Both the above operations are legal. But does the second multiplication make any sense? It doesn't, because 1004 is an integer that represents an address value and we don't know what it means to multiply that. We definitely get an integer value, but we don't know if it is a valid address.

To make this distinction, what we need is another data type that indicates to the compiler that variables of this type are meant to hold address values. C provides such a derived data type, which is called a *pointer*.

9.1c Declaring pointer variables

Pointer variables are variables that contain memory addresses. Since memory addresses are effectively integral values, pointers contain integer values that represent memory locations of *other* variables.

The syntax for declaring a pointer variable is shown below:

Syntax   **Declaring a pointer variable**

```
data-type *pointer-variable-name;
```

The *data-type* in the above declaration is the type of the variable, whose location will be stored in the variable *pointer-variable-name*. For example, in the case of the declaration

```
int a;
```

we can declare a pointer variable as

```
int *ptr_to_a;      /* Meant to contain the address
                     * of an integer variable */
```

For the declaration

```
char ch;
```

Pointers

a pointer variable can be declared as

```
char *ch_ptr;       /* Meant to contain the address
                     * of a character variable */
```

Tip *Read the above declaration from right to left. That is, starting with the variable name* `ptr_to_a` *(which is our abbreviation for pointer-to-a), read the declaration as* `ptr_to_a` *is a pointer to an* `int`.

Note *C uses* `*` *in the declaration of a pointer variable, which is to be read as a pointer. Don't confuse this with the indirection operator* `*`, *which is an operator, whereas as the* `*` *in the declarative statement is just a declaration to the compiler, not an operator.*

Note that in the declaration

```
int *ptr_to_a;
```

the name `ptr_to_a` is also a variable. The variable `ptr_to_a` is allocated just like any other variable. Its size will usually be the size of `int` or `long`, as it has to contain addresses which are integers and which may be very large. Figure 9.4 shows the memory allocation for these two declarations:

```
int a;
int *ptr_to_a;
```

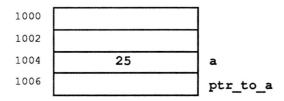

Figure 9.4 Memory location for a pointer.

A few more examples of pointer declarations are shown below:

Example **Declaring a pointer to a `float` variable**

```
float value;
float *pval; /* pval is a pointer to a float */
```

Example **Declaring a pointer to a `char` variable**

```
char ch;
char *pch;   /* pch is a pointer to a character */
```

Example **Declaring a pointer to a character array**

```
char name[25];
char *pname; /* pname is a pointer to a character */
```

In the last example, `pname` is a pointer to a character. We will use `pname` to point to an array of characters. We will examine how this is done later in this chapter.

9.1d Initializing pointer variables

So far we only declared pointer variables, but such a variable will not contain anything useful until we initialize it by placing an address value into it. Initializing involves putting a value into the variable — a value which is the address of another variable. Examples are given below:

Example **Initializing a pointer variable**

```
int a;
int *ptr_a;
ptr_to_a = &a; /* ptr_a contains the address of a */
```

Using the address values in the earlier example, the statement

```
        ptr_to_a = &a;
```

is equivalent to

```
        ptr_to_a = 1004;
```

After the initialization is done, the resulting memory structure is as shown in Figure 9.5. We indicate that a pointer variable is initialized to the address of another variable by placing an arrow with its tail starting in the pointer variable's memory location and its head ending in the variable it *points to*.

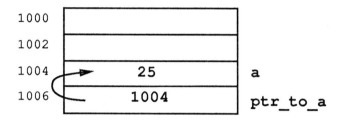

Figure 9.5 Using a pointer to point to a location.

There are two ways to get to the value of **a**: directly, by using the name **a** or indirectly, using **ptr_to_a** and the indirection operator *****.

Example Accessing a variable value through its pointer

```
int a;
int *ptr_to_a;
a = 25;  /* Initialize a */

ptr_to_a = &a; /* Initialize the pointer variable */
printf("Variable a contains (direct method) %d\n", a);
printf("Variable a contains (indirect method) %d\n",
       *ptr_to_a);
```

To help visualize the operation ***ptr_to_a**, compile and run the following program:

```
#include <stdio.h>
main()
{
    int a = 25;
    int *ptr_to_a;
```

```
    ptr_to_a = &a; /* Initialize the pointer variable */

    printf("a is loaded at address %lu\n", &a);
    printf("ptr_to_a is loaded at address %lu\n", &ptr_to_a);

    printf("\na contains the value %d\n", a);
    printf("ptr_to_a contains the value %lu\n", ptr_to_a);

    printf("Following the pointer ptr_to_a, we get %d\n",
        *ptr_to_a);
}
```

Compiling and running the above program produces the following output:

```
a is loaded at address 4160747076
ptr_to_a is loaded at address 4160747072

a contains the value 25
ptr_to_a contains the value 4160747076

Following the pointer ptr_to_a, we get 25
```

Note that the variable **ptr_to_a** is a memory location, just like the variable **a**. Also note that **ptr_to_a** contains just a number. When we use the indirection operation * on the address indicated by the number, we get the contents at that address.

A few more examples of initializing pointer variables follow.

Example   **Initializing a floating point pointer variable**

```
float value, *valp;
valp = &value; /* valp contains the address of value */
```

Example   **Initializing a character pointer variable**

```
char *greet = "Hello World";
```

In the above declaration, we are initializing the pointer variable **greet** to point to the memory location at the beginning of the character array. We will examine this again at the end of this chapter.

9.1e Exercises

1 Draw the memory locations corresponding to the program statements shown below. Trace the execution of the statements and write the output below without actually compiling and running the program. Next, compile and run the program to verify the output with your answers.

```
int a, b;
int *ptr_to_a;

ptr_to_a = &a;
a = 41;
printf("%d\n", *ptr_to_a);   /* What will be printed? */

b = *ptr_to_a;
printf("%d\n", b);   /* What will be printed? */

*ptr_to_a = 36;

printf("%d\n", a);   /* What will be printed? */
printf("%d\n", b);   /* What will be printed? */
```

2 Next, add these statements to the above list; then compile and run the program:

```
ptr_to_a = b;
printf("%d\n", *ptr_to_a);
```

9.1f Invalid addresses

By now, you know that preceding Exercise 2 did not work too well. Let us examine the reason for this. When we execute the assignment statement

```
ptr_to_a = b;
```

the variable **ptr_to_a** is assigned the the number **41** (the last value of **b**). When the expression

```
*ptr_to_a
```

is evaluated, we will be accessing the contents of memory location `41`. Is `41` a valid memory location? Who knows! When we put a value into a pointer variable, we have to make sure that the value is a legal address.

9.1g The null pointer

What are the legal values that you can store in the variable `ptr_to_a`? Obviously, `&a` is a valid value. Since addresses are integer values, any integer is a legal value. But since addresses represent memory, values from 0 to the highest memory value that can be generated on your machine are valid values. However, the number 0 gets special treatment. The number 0 is used to represent an invalid memory address.

If a pointer variable contains the address 0, it is said to be a *null* pointer, or a pointer that does not point to anything. The macro `NULL`, defined to be 0 in the header file **stddef.h**, is used to represent null pointer values.

Null pointers are useful as end-of-memory markers, and we will be using them when we deal with dynamic memory allocation. Many functions that return pointer values use the null pointer to indicate errors.

Example Creating a null pointer

```
#include <stddef.h> /* Or stdio.h, in old C */
ptr_to_a = NULL; /* Null pointer */
```

9.1h Exercises

1 Compile and run the following program, and write its output in the space below.

```
/* Program to illustrate the difference between a
 * pointer value and its dereferenced (indirect) value
 */
main()
{
   int i = 100, *ptr_to_i;
   ptr_to_i = &i;
```

```
    printf ("Value of i is %d\n", i);
    printf ("Address of i is %lu\n", &i);
    printf ("Contents at ptr_to_i is %d\n", *ptr_to_i);
    printf ("Value of ptr_to_i is %lu\n", ptr_to_i);
    printf ("Address of ptr_to_i is %lu\n", &ptr_to_i);
}
```

Value of i is
Address of i is
Contents at ptr_to_i is
Value of ptr_to_i is
Address of ptr_to_i is

2 Draw the memory layout for the previous example, and show all the values.

3 In the previous example, if you change the statement

```
ptr_to_i = &i;
```

to

```
ptr_to_i = 0;
```

what will happen when you compile and execute the program again? Guess the output of the program, and then verify it by running it.

4 What will the output of the following program be?

```
main()
{
    int a = 25;
    int b = 40;
    int *ptr_var; /* ptr_var is a pointer to an int */
    ptr_var = &a;
    printf("a = %d, b = %d, *ptr_var = %d\n", a, b,
           *ptr_var);
    *ptr_var = 36;
    printf("a = %d, b = %d, *ptr_var = %d\n", a, b,
           *ptr_var);
    ptr_var = &b;
```

```
        printf("a = %d, b = %d, *ptr_var = %d\n", a, b,
                *ptr_var);
        *ptr_var = 64;
        printf("a = %d, b = %d, *ptr_var = %d\n", a, b,
                *ptr_var);
        b = 128;
        printf("a = %d, b = %d, *ptr_var = %d\n", a, b,
                *ptr_var);
}
```

9.2 Pointers and Arrays

There is a very strong relationship between pointers and arrays in C. In fact, arrays are implemented by using pointers. Any operation that you perform on array elements by using the subscript operator can be performed just as easily, and perhaps more efficiently, by using pointers.

To understand the similarity between pointers and arrays, let us examine how arrays are implemented. The declaration

```
    int a[8];
```

will be represented in memory as shown in Figure 9.6. You can see from the figure that the memory cells holding the elements of the array are contiguous.

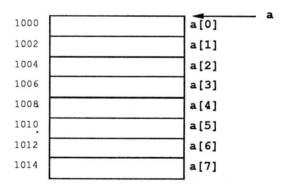

Figure 9.6 Layout of array in memory.

Pointers and Arrays

In this case, the declaration allocates memory to hold 8 `ints`. When we access the array element `a[0]`, we are instructing the compiler to access the integer value stored at the location assigned to `a`.

Next, we will declare a pointer to the array as

```
int *ptr_a;
```

Now, we will initialize the pointer variable to point to the beginning of the array.

```
ptr_a = &a[0];
```

The above statement sets `ptr_a` to point to element 0 of `a`, which is shown in Figure 9.7.

Now for a very interesting and important fact: The *name of the array really contains the address of the beginning of the array* (the position of the first element). Thus, in our example above, the name of the array `a` is the same as `&a[0]`, the position of the first element. Thus the statement shown above could have been written as:

```
ptr_a = a;  /* Same as ptr_a = &a[0] */
```

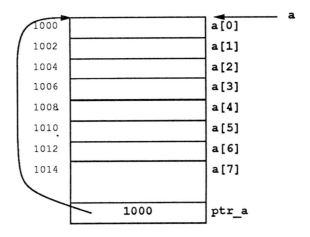

Figure 9.7 Using a pointer to point to an array.

After the initialization, we have two choices for stepping through the elements of the array: to use subscripts as we have been doing (such as `a[0]`, `a[1]`) or the pointer variable `ptr_a`. Since `ptr_a` has been initialized to point to the beginning of the array, if we *increment* the value in `ptr_a` by 1, it will effectively point to the next element and so forth.

But wait a minute. How much should we increment? By 1? 2? If the array's beginning address (which is the first element) was at 1004, where will the second element be? 1005? 1006?

The answer lies in the size of the element. In our example, since the elements are all `int`s, we have to increment the pointer variable `ptr_a` by the size of `int`. In general, we can step through the array by incrementing the pointer variable that points to the beginning of the array by the size of its element. Thus,

```
a[0]      is equivalent to ptr_a;
a[1]      is equivalent to ptr_a + 1*sizeof(int);
a[2]      is equivalent to ptr_a + 2*sizeof(int);
etc.
```

❑ **Pointer arithmetic is different from integer arithmetic**

Isn't it inconvenient to be computing `ptr_a + n * sizeof (int)` every time you access the *n*th element? Well, don't worry. You just increment the pointer variable `ptr_a` by 1 and the compiler will take care of adding the right amount to the pointer variable. Adding or subtracting the right size to the pointer variable, when you just increment or decrement the pointer variable, is known as *pointer arithmetic*. This explains why we needed another data type for pointers, even though pointer values are integers: Pointer arithmetic is different from integer arithmetic.ipointers;arithmetic

Thus, if `ptr_a` points to the first element,

   `ptr_a+1` points to the next element

   `ptr_a+2` points to the element after that

   `ptr_a+i` points to the *i*th element after `ptr_a`

`ptr_a-i` points to the *i*th element before `ptr_a`.

This is shown in Figure 9.8.

But why go through all this pain when we can access the elements by good old subscripts? There are two reasons:
- Any operation on arrays by using pointers will be faster than using array subscripts.
- Along with dynamic memory allocation and user-defined data types such as *structures* (which you will learn about in Chapter 10), pointers provide a powerful tool to build *data structures* such as *lists, queues,* etc.

Let us look at some example declarations:

```
#define NO_STUDENTS      12
int grades[NO_STUDENTS], *grades_p;

grades_p = grades; /* Same as grades_p = &grades[0] */

*grades_p = 98;    /* Same as grades[0] = 98 */
*grades_p++;       /* grades_p now points to grades[1] */
*grades_p = 100;   /* Same as grades[1] = 100 */
```

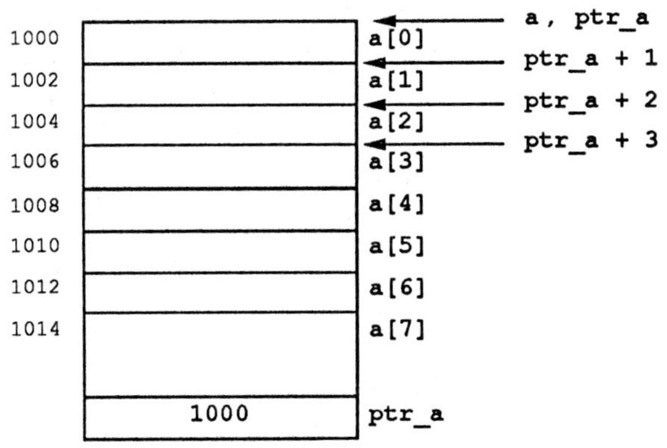

Figure 9.8 Using a pointer to access array elements.

Note that even though the name of the array itself is a pointer to the beginning of the array, the name of the array cannot be modified to point to each element in turn. Thus, the following operation cannot be performed:

```
grades++; /* Wrong: cannot modify array name */
```

Note *The reason for this is obvious. If we are allowed to modify the array name that contains the beginning address of the array, we will lose track of where the beginning of the array is. Hence we need to declare another pointer variable and initialize it to point to the beginning of the array and modify the pointer variable.*

The example shown below uses a pointer variable to input student grade point averages (`float` values) into an array.

Example Using the pointer variable to input an array

```
#define NO_STUDENTS    12

float gpa[NO_STUDENTS], *gpa_p;
int index;

gpa_p = gpa; /* Initialize the pointer to
              * the beginning of the array */
for (index = 0; index < NO_STUDENTS; index++)
{
   printf("Enter the grade for student %d\n", index);
   scanf("%f", gpa_p); /* Read the score into array */
   gpa_p++; /* Increment the pointer so that gpa_p
             * points to the next element */
}
/* Now print the GPA's. Note that gpa_p now points
 * past the end of the array. We will have to set it
 * back to the beginning of the array, before we print
 */
gpa_p = gpa; /* Reset gpa_p to beginning of array */
for (index = 0; index < NO_STUDENTS; index++)
   printf(" %3.2f ", *gpa_p++); /* Print the score */

printf("\n");
```

Examine the following statement closely:

```
scanf("%f", gpa_p)  /* Read the score into array */
```

Notice the omission of the address operator & from the variable name **gpa_p**. Can you reason why this is so?

The address-of operator & returns the address of a variable. The variable **grades_p** already contains an address: the address of the array element. Thus there is no need to take the address of **gpa_p** again, in the **scanf** function. On the other hand, what would happen if we applied the address-of operator to **gpa_p** again, in the **scanf** function?

Modify the program to include the address-of operator in front of the variable **gpa_p** and then compile and run the program. Can you explain why the program does not produce correct results?

In the next example, we will write a complete program that computes the average student grade by using pointer variables to step through an array of student grades.

Example **Using pointers to traverse an array**

```
#include <stdio.h>
#define NO_STUDENTS 12

main()
{
   int grades[NO_STUDENTS], *student_p;
   int index, sum, average;

   student_p = grades;   /* Point to the first element */
   for (index = 0; index < NO_STUDENTS; index++)
   {
      printf ("Enter grade for student %d ",index);
      scanf ("%d", student_p++);
   }
   /* Student_p now points past the end of the array.
    * Reset it again in the for loop (notice the multiple
    * initialization expressions)
    */
```

```
        for (index = 0, student_p = grades, sum = 0;
             index < NO_STUDENTS; index++, student_p++)
        {
            sum = sum + *student_p;
        }

        average = sum / NO_STUDENTS;
        printf ("Average Score is %d\n", average);
}
```

Notice the statement

```
        scanf ("%d", student_p++);
```

Since **student_p** has been initialized to point to the first element, we will read the first grade value to **grades[0]**. After we use the value of **student_p++**, we will increment it by one, pointing it to the next element, and read a value into it. After we finish inputting all the values, **student_p** points past the end of the array and it needs to be reset to the beginning. This is done as part of the initialization in the **for** loop.

Now go back and read Section 5.3 in Chapter 5. For the **fread** and **fwrite** functions, we used a buffer to read and write binary data. It was mentioned in 5.3 that the buffer is not just a variable name but an actual memory location. We applied the address-of operator to a variable to get its address and then cast it to type **void *** to prepare the buffer. Is it all starting to make sense? The reason for casting the variable and the actual reason why a memory location is needed in some functions (such as **scanf, fread, fwrite**) and not in some other functions (such as **printf, rand**) will become clear when you learn about functions and *call-by-value* semantics in Chapter 11.

9.2a Exercises

1 Modify the above example to include an **int** array of student IDs as well as grades. Input the ID into the array, along with the grades. When the input is complete, print the array backwards (i.e., the last element to the first element) by using pointers to traverse the array. Print the ID and the grades.

2 Using a pointer to traverse the array, find the highest and lowest grades in the array, and print the values, along with the student IDs.

3 Redo Exercise 1, with the array of student IDs stored in a unsigned character array. Thus the IDs cannot be larger than 255.

9.3 Strings

Even though strings are simply arrays of characters, they are treated as a separate topic here due to the following reasons:
- The C standard library provides a variety of special-purpose functions to deal with strings.
- Strings are always terminated by the null character (`'\0'`). The compiler automatically places a null character at the end of the character sequences enclosed in double quotes. If you construct a string in your program (by writing characters into a character array), it is your responsibility to ensure that the null character is placed at the end of the string.

To understand why it is necessary to place a null character at the end of every string, consider the declaration

```
char my_string[10];
```

The declaration allocates 10 bytes of memory for the string. If we allocate a pointer to point to the beginning of the string and repeatedly increment the string, at some point the pointer will point to a memory location past the end of the string. C stores the beginning address of **my_string** in the variable **my_string**. But the ending address or the length of the string is not stored anywhere! As a result, if we traverse past the end of the array by advancing a pointer to the beginning of the array, or simply by using an invalid index, there is no way to check if we are within the legal bounds of the array. As "a work around", the compiler (or the programmer) places a null character (which has the ASCII value 0) at the end of the array. When the array is accessed, we need to check whether the end of the array has been reached by testing for the null character.

A string constant (such as `"hello world"`) is treated by the compiler as a pointer. For example, in the declaration

```
char *mascot ="whatizit";
```

the character array `"whatizit"` is stored in memory, at some location, and `mascot` points to the first element in the array. If we execute the statements

```
printf ("%s\n", mascot);
printf ("%s\n", mascot+1);
```

the following output will be printed

```
whatizit
hatizit
```

To illustrate working with strings, let us write a few simple programs. The first program takes a string of lowercase letters and converts it to uppercase. We will use the library routine `toupper` to convert from a lowercase character to its corresponding uppercase equivalent.

Example **Working with strings**

```
main()
{
    char alpha[] = "abcdefghijklmnopqrstuvwxyz";
    int index;

    printf("Size of string alpha is %d\n",
            sizeof(alpha));
    for (index = 0; index < 26; index++)
    {
        printf("%c", toupper(alpha[index]));
    }
    printf("\n");
}
```

The size of the string `"abcdefghijklmnopqrstuvwxyz"` is 27, not 26. This is due to the extra null character that the compiler has placed at the end of the string.

The above program, rewritten to use pointers instead of arrays, is shown below. We will also use the null character at the end of the string to terminate the conversion.

Example **Using pointers and the null character**

```
#include <stddef.h> /* Or stdio.h */
#include <ctype.h>
main()
{
   char alpha[] = "abcdefghijklmnopqrstuvwxyz";
   char *str_ptr;

   str_ptr = alpha;

   while(*str_ptr != '\0')
   {
      printf("%c", toupper(*str_ptr++));
   }
   printf("\n");
}
```

Note *If you have an older, non-ANSI C compiler, the program shown above may not compile on your machine. Some non-ANSI C compilers do not allow arrays to be initialized within blocks (such as the* **main** *block shown above). On such systems, you will have to initialize the array, outside of any block, as shown below:*

```
#include <stddef.h>

char alpha[] = "abcdefghijklmnopqrstuvwxyz";

main()
{
   char *str_ptr;

   str_ptr = alpha;

   while(*str_ptr != '\0')
   {
      printf("%c", toupper(*str_ptr++));
   }
   printf("\n");
}
```

Let us modify the program to convert the input string into uppercase and copy it to another array.

```c
#include <stdio.h>
#include <stddef.h>

main()
{
   char lower_alpha[] = "abcdefghijklmnopqrstuvwxyz";
   char upper_alpha[27]; /* Space for converted string
                          * including null and all*/
   char *in_p, *out_p;   /* Pointer variables */
   in_p = lower_alpha;   /* in_p points to array
                          * lower_alpha */
   out_p = upper_alpha;  /* out_p points to array
                          * upper alpha */
   while (*in_p != '\0')
   {
     fprintf(stderr, "Copying %c \n", *in_p); /* Debug */
     *out_p++ = toupper(*in_p++);
   }
   /* All characters, except the null character, have been
    * converted and copied to the array upper_alpha.
    * Now copy the null character
    */
   out_p = '\0';   /* Note that out_p is already pointing
                    * to the end of the array */
   /* Verify that the new array contains the
    * converted characters */
   printf("Converted array contains: %s", upper_alpha);
}
```

Tip *When dealing with strings, always make sure that the string is null-terminated. If you declare a string constant, the compiler places the null character at the end. If you declare a character array and use it to store character sequences, it is your responsibility to place the null character at the end of the array.*

9.3a String-handling functions

A variety of string-handling functions are available in the standard library. To access the functions, include the header file **string.h**, which contains the necessary declarations, at the beginning of the program:

```
#include <string.h>
```

Some of the commonly used string-handling functions are listed in the table below. All of the functions listed below assume that strings used as arguments to the functions are null-terminated. Also, the arguments *s1* and *s2* indicate strings: string constants such as `"hello"` or variables of type `char *` (or `char []`).

Function name	Purpose
strcat(s1, s2)	Appends string *s2* to string *s1* and returns *s1*.
strcmp(s1, s2)	Compares *s1* with *s2* lexicographically and returns an integer greater than, equal to or less than zero, according to whether *s1* is greater than, equal to or less than *s2*.
strncmp(s1, s2, n)	Same as above, except comparison stops after *n* characters of *s1* have been tested.
strcpy(s1, s2)	Copies the contents of string *s2* to *s1*, overwriting the contents of *s1*. String *s1* is returned.
strncpy(s1, s2, n)	Same as above, except *n* characters are copied (or fewer if null character is encountered in *s2*).
strlen(s1)	Returns the length of the string *s1*, not including the null character.
strchr(s1, ch)	Searches the string *s1* for the first occurrence of the character in *ch*. Returns a pointer to the occurrence or NULL if not found.

A complete description of these and other string-handling routines is outside the scope of this workbook. Please refer to the documentation on the standard library available with your system.

The next example illustrates the use of the string-handling routine `strcat`. In the example, we will prompt the user for his/her first name, last name and middle initial. We will concatenate the strings using the `strcat` routine and print the user's full name.

```
#include <stdio.h>
#include <string.h>
main()
{
    char fullname[80], last[40], middle[10];
    printf("Enter your first name: ");
    gets(fullname);
    printf("Last name: ");
    gets(last);
    printf("Middle Initial: ");
    gets(middle);
    /* Construct the full name */
    strcat(fullname, " ");
    strcat(fullname, middle);
    strcat(fullname, " ");
    strcat(fullname, last);
    printf ("Hello! %s\n", fullname);
}
```

9.3b Exercises

1 Write a program that encrypts the user's input by using the "rot 13" (rotate by 13) formula. That is, for each character in the user's input, rotate the alphabet by 13 (add 13 to the ASCII value for letters 'a' through 'm' and 'A' through 'M' and subtract 13 from the ASCII values for letters 'n' through 'z' and 'N' through 'Z'). Read a line from the user, apply rot 13 to it and print the resulting line. For example, the input line "Hi there" should be transformed into "Uv gurer" and "Uv gurer" should be transformed back to "Hi there".

9.4 Pointer Arrays

Pointer arrays are arrays, the elements of which are pointers. Pointer arrays are very convenient for representing a list of character strings. For example, consider the following list of names, which are string constants:

```
"Oxford Ox"
"Karen Kangaroo"
"Audry Owl"
```

Since each of the names is a character array, we can assign pointer variables to the names as shown:

```
char *name1 = "Oxford Ox";
char *name2 = "Karen Kangaroo";
char *name2 = "Audry Owl";
```

By now, you have learned that if we need to represent a list of similar data types, it is probably more convenient to declare an array to do this. Thus we will declare and initialize an array to hold the above string constants:

```
char *name[3] = {"Oxford Ox","Karen Kangaroo","Audry Owl"};
```

Or:

```
name[0] = "Oxford Ox";
name[1] = "Karen Kangaroo";
name[2] = "Audry Owl";
```

The above array is shown in Figure 9.9.

A declaration such as `char *name[3]` should be read from right to left, starting from the name of the variable. Thus we should read the above declaration as

```
    name                /* Start at the name & move right */
is an array of 3        /* After the array, nothing more on
                         * the right */
    pointers            /* To the left is pointer symbol */
    to chars            /* Data type comes last */
```

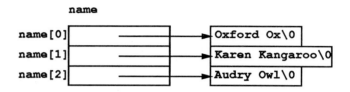

Figure 9.9 An array of names.

The above English description of the declaration matches the pictorial representation as well:

`name is an array that contains 3 pointers to characters`

The following program creates an array containing names. Next, it prompts the user to enter a name. Once a name is input, the array is searched for a matching name, and if a match is found, the index at which the name occurred is output.

One of the main considerations in declaring a pointer array (or a two-dimensional array) for holding the list of names is in understanding the layout of the array. Recall that (from Chapter 8) arrays are stored in *row-major* order: Thus an array of names can be visualized as shown in Figure 9.10.

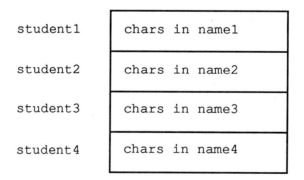

Figure 9.10 Declaration for an array of names.

From Figure 9.10, we arrive at the following declaration:

```
#define NO_OF_STUDENTS   5
#define NAMESIZE         25

char namelist[NO_OF_STUDENTS][NAMESIZE];
```

The complete program is shown below:

❏ **Sample program: Pointer arrays**

```
#include <stdio.h>

#define NO_OF_STUDENTS   5
#define NAMESIZE         25

main()
{
  char namelist[NO_OF_STUDENTS][NAMESIZE];
  int index; /* Loop variable */
  char search[NAMESIZE]; /* Array to hold
                          * name to search */

  for (index = 0; index < NO_OF_STUDENTS; index++)
  {
     printf("Enter the student name: ");
     fgets(namelist[index], NAMESIZE, stdin);
  }

  /* Debug: Verify that names have been read correctly */
  fprintf(stderr, "Names are \n");
  for (index = 0; index < NO_OF_STUDENTS; index++)
  {
     fprintf(stderr, "%s\n", namelist[index]);
  }

  printf("Enter a name to search for ");
  fgets(search, NAMESIZE, stdin);
```

```
    for (index = 0; index < NO_OF_STUDENTS; index++)
    {
       if (strcmp(search, namelist[index]) == 0)
       {
        printf("Name %s was found at position %d\n",
                search, index);
        exit(EXIT_SUCCESS);
       }
    }
    printf("Name %s was not found\n", search);
    exit(EXIT_FAILURE);
}
```

Observe the following statement closely:

```
fgets(namelist[index], NAMESIZE, stdin);
```

Notice that only one subscript is used to access the array. To understand why, visualize the layout of the array, as shown in Figure 9.11.

Inside the first index lies the address corresponding to the location for the name. Think of the duality between addresses and arrays: the address inside the first index is the array to hold the name.

If dealing with pointer arrays is not too intuitive to you yet, let's try a new approach. We can simplify things a bit, using the **typedef** facility provided by C. The **typedef** mechanism is used to provide an alternate name for an existing data type, or to define new data types. Let us digress a bit here and examine the **typedef** facility. Later we will use the **typedef** mechanism to simplify the explanation of two-dimensional arrays.

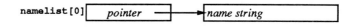

Figure 9.11 Pointer array.

9.4a Defining data types using `typedef`

Using the `typedef` declaration, it is possible to provide an alternate name for an existing data type or create new data types. Alternate names used in place of the data type names make the program easier to read if the names are chosen carefully. Alternate names are also used to abbreviate long declarations. The syntax for using `typedef`s is shown below:

Syntax **Declaring a name as a type using `typedef`**

```
typedef existing-data-type new-name;
```

The `typedef` declaration tells the compiler that we want to define a new data type called *new-name*, which is of the same type as *existing-data-type*. In short, we are providing an alternate name for the *existing-data-type*.

Example **Using `typedef` to provide alternate names**

```
typedef unsigned char uchar;
typedef unsigned short ushort; /* Name unsigned short as
                                           ushort */
typedef unsigned int uint; /* Name unsigned int as uint */
typedef unsigned long ulong; /* Name unsigned long as
                                           ulong */
typedef int distance /* Name int as distance */;
```

Once the name has been declared as a type, it may appear in the program anywhere a type declaration is permitted. For example, the following is valid:

```
/* First example */
main()
{
   distance miles, kilometers; /* distance is a
                                       name for int */
   miles = 26;
   ...
}
```

Think of the the `typedef` declaration as a `#define` preprocessor command. Wherever the new type appears, the compiler (not the preprocessor) replaces the new type with the appropriate substitution. However, there are some significant differences between a **typedef** and the **#define** command. We will outline the differences after showing some more examples.

The next example uses **typedef** along with enumerated types.

Example **Using `typedef` to create a boolean data type**

```
typedef enum { FALSE, TRUE } boolean;
boolean value;
statements
if (value == FALSE)
{
    statements
}
```

The **typedef** mechanism can also be used to name new data types. The example below creates a new data type.

Example **Creating a data type using `typedef`**

```
typedef char NAME[25];
```

The above declaration creates a new data type called **NAME**, which is an array of **25** characters. Once the data type has been created, variables of the type can be declared and used, as shown.

```
/* Second Example */
#include <stdio.h>
typedef char NAME[25]; /* Define a type called NAME */

main()
{
   NAME my_name;           /* my_name is of type NAME */
   gets(my_name);          /* Input to my_name */
   puts(my_name);          /* Output my_name */
}
```

❑ **typedef vs. #define**

From the usage of **typedef** shown here you may think that the **#define** preprocessor command will perform essentially what the **typedef** declaration does. For example, you may be tempted to rewrite the first program in this section as

```
#define distance int
main()
{
    distance miles, kilometers;
    miles = 26;
    ...
}
```

This works nicely, as the preprocessor replaces the name **distance** with the type **int**, in the declaration

```
distance miles, kilometers;
```

Now consider the case of the second example (type **NAME**). If we define a preprocessor macro as

```
#define   NAME   char[25]
```

the declaration

```
NAME my_name;
```

will be preprocessed as

```
char[25] my_name;
```

whereas the correct declaration is

```
char my_name[25];
```

As another example, consider the following declaration of a data type called **String**. We know now that a string is of type **char ***. Using **typedef**, we can define a string as

```
typedef char * STRING;
```

Now we can define strings in our program as

```
    STRING dots, dashes;

    dots = "................................";
    dashes = "--------------------------------";
    printf("%s", dots);
```

If we were to use the #define command to declare a STRING type, we would write the program as

```
    #define   STRING char *

    STRING dots, dashes;
```

After preprocessing, the declaration shown above will be expanded as

```
    char * dots, dashes;
```

Clearly, the variable `dashes` is not a string.

Back to our main topic. We will use the **typedef** mechanism to simplify the declaration and use of a two-dimensional array.

9.4b Arrays and typedef

Using the **typedef** mechanism, we can define a new type for a name, which is an array of characters, as shown:

```
    typedef char NAME[25];
```

The above declaration creates a new type called **NAME**, which is an array of **25** characters. Now we can declare variables of type **NAME**, as follows:

```
    NAME  my_name; /* my_name is of type NAME */
    NAME  name_list[10]; /* name_list is an array
                                of names */
```

Using the new type called **NAME**, we can rewrite the program shown above:

```
#include <stdio.h>
#define NAMESIZE 25
#define NO_OF_STUDENTS 5
```

```c
typedef char NAME[NAMESIZE];

main()
{
  NAME namelist[NO_OF_STUDENTS]; /* An array of NAMES */
  NAME search;  /* Name to search for */
  int index;


  for (index = 0; index < NO_OF_STUDENTS; index++)
  {
     printf("Enter the student name: ");
     fgets(namelist[index], NAMESIZE, stdin);
  }
  /* Debug */
  printf("names are \n");
  for (index = 0; index < NO_OF_STUDENTS; index++)
  {
     printf("%s\n",namelist[index]);
  }
  printf("Enter a name to search for ");
  fgets(search, NAMESIZE, stdin);
  for (index = 0; index < NO_OF_STUDENTS; index++)
  {
     if (strcmp(search, namelist[index]) == 0)
     {
         printf("name %s was found at position %d\n",
               search, index);
         exit(EXIT_SUCCESS);
     }
  }
  printf("name %s was not found\n", search);
  exit(EXIT_FAILURE);
}
```

As you may have observed, giving a new name to the character array makes it easier to visualize and deal with pointer arrays.

Let's incorporate what we have learned so far into our infamous score files. We will now create a report file containing student names and scores in sorted order (using the index sort algorithm discussed in Chapter 8). The format for the file containing the original scores is shown below. The names of the students below have been changed to protect their identity (Ha ha!).

```
Oxford Ox                98
Karen Kangaroo           100
Dennis Dinosaur          76
Audry Owl                94
Lionel Lion              62
Cat Stevens              88
```

Each line in the scores file is of the form

firstname lastname spaces or tabs   integer-score

We will use the function `fscanf` to read a line of input and partition it into a first name, a last name and an integer score. Next, we will alter the names to the form

last-name, firstnames

and write it to into an array of names. Next, we will sort the scores and print the sorted scores and the names.

```
#include <stdio.h>
#include <assert.h>
#include <string.h>
#define MAX_LIMIT       32    /* Max no. of students */
#define NAMESIZE        25
#define FNAME_LEN       10
#define LNAME_LEN       14
#define INPUT_FILE      "NAMES.TXT"

typedef char NAME[NAMESIZE]; /* Define a new type */

main()
{
   NAME namelist[MAX_LIMIT]; /* For storing names */
   int scores[MAX_LIMIT], temp_scores[MAX_LIMIT];
   char sort_position[MAX_LIMIT]; /* Array to hold
                                   * sorted position */
```

```c
   int student;     /* Loop variable */
   int no_students; /* Number of students in the file */
   int ret_val;     /* To hold return values */
   int max, max_position, array_length;
   int position;
   char fname[FNAME_LEN], lname[LNAME_LEN];
   NAME temp; /* Temporary array */

   FILE *fhandle;

   if ( (fhandle = fopen(INPUT_FILE, "r")) == NULL)
   {
      fprintf(stderr,"Could not open file %s\n",
              INPUT_FILE);
      exit(EXIT_FAILURE);
   }

   no_students = 0;    /* Initialize */
   for (student = 0; student < MAX_LIMIT; student++)
   {
      ret_val = fscanf(fhandle, "%s%s%d", fname,
                       lname, &scores[student]);
      if (ret_val == EOF)
         break; /* Out of the for loop */
      no_students++;
      assert(no_students < MAX_LIMIT);
      strcpy(temp, lname); /* Copy last name into temp */
      strcat(temp, ", ",); /* Concatenate ", " at end */
      strcat(temp, fname); /* Copy first name at end */
      fprintf(stderr, "Name is %s\n", temp); /* Debug */
      /* Now copy the modified name into names array */
      strcpy(namelist[student], temp);
   } /* End of reading score */

   /* Print number of students, for debugging */
   fprintf(stderr, "no_of_students = %d\n", no_students);
   /* Create a temporary array with scores */
   printf("Original Scores\n");
```

```
for (student = 0; student < no_students; student++)
{
   /* Verify (for debugging) that original scores
    * and names have been stored correctly
    */
   printf("%-25s\t%d\n", namelist[student],
          scores[student]);
   temp_scores[student] = scores[student];
}

for (array_length = 0; array_length < no_students;
     array_length++)
{
   max = 0;  /* Initialize */
   /* Make a pass through array and find maximum */
   for (student = 0; student < no_students; student++)
   {
      if (temp_scores[student] > max)
      {
         max_position = student;
         max = temp_scores[student];
      }
   } /* End of inner for loop */
   /* max_position contains the student having the
    * largest score in the original array
    */

   /* Take the current max out of the competition */
   temp_scores[max_position] = 0;

   /* Store the position of the score in the new array */
   sort_position[array_length] = max_position;
} /* End outer for. All positions have been determined */

/* Print the sorted scores and IDs */
printf("Sorted Scores\n");
for (student = 0; student < no_students; student++)
{
   position = sort_position[student]; /* Correct
                         position of each score */
```

```
            printf("%-25s\t%d\n", namelist[position],
                    scores[position]);
        }
    }
```

9.4c   **Exercises**

1   Read a list of addresses in a text file of the following form and print them in three columns, as shown below:

Input file format:

```
Oxford Ox, 123 Meadow Land, E. Rutherford, New Jersey 10049
Karen Kangaroo, 78 Down Under Blvd, Augusta, Georgia 33344
Lionel Lion, Bronx Zoo, Bronx, NY 10010
Audry Owl, Perch Pl, Redwood Forest, San Francisco, CA 34578
```

Output file format:

```
Oxford Ox                Karen Kangaroo           Lionel Lion
123 Meadow Land          78 Down Under Blvd       Bronx Zoo
E. Rutherford            Augusta                  Bronx
New Jersey 10049         Georgia 33344            NY 10010


Audry Owl
Perch Pl,
Redwood Forest
San Francisco, CA 34578
```

9.5 Common Problems

Most of the common problems in dealing with pointers arise due to incorrect understanding of pointer arithmetic. Most of these problems occur in programs terminating with messages such as "memory fault," "segmentation violation," etc.

1. Since pointers (and arrays) allow unrestricted memory access, incorrect pointer increment/decrement has the potential for corrupting memory elsewhere in the program. The following seemingly harmless program has a dangerous bug. Can you spot the bug by reading the code?

```
#include <stdio.h>
main()
{
   int unrelated_variable;
   int array[5], i;

   unrelated_variable = 24;
   for (i = 0; i <= 5; i++)
   {
      array[i] = i * i;
   }
   /* Now print all the values */
   for (i = 0; i <= 5; i++)
   {
      printf("i = %d\n", array[i]);
   }
   printf("unrelated_variable has %d\n"
          unrelated_variable);
}
```

Execution of the above program on a Sun SPARCstation 1 produces the following result:

```
i = 0
i = 1
i = 4
i = 9
```

```
i = 16
i = 25
unrelated_variable has 25
```

Notice that the value in the `unrelated_variable` has changed even though no explicit assignment is performed to that variable. Since arrays are implemented using pointers, and due to the lack of bounds checking on array subscripts, it is possible to corrupt memory by generating incorrect pointer values. These type of bugs are extremely hard to catch.

2   Most of the problems in dealing with character arrays are due to omitting the null character at the end of the string being manipulated.

10
Reusing Code by Using Functions

You may have realized that our programs are getting longer and somewhat unmanageable. Some of the programs that we have written contain some functionality that is duplicated throughout the program. Consider our simple math tutor program. The four types of arithmetic testing that we administer have an identical form, except for some minor differences. For all four types, we implement the following functionality:

> Generate two random numbers.
> Prompt the user.
> Read the user's input.
> Compare the input with the actual result.
> Print a response.

The functionality described above is duplicated in all four types of testing implemented by our program. It would have been better if we could *encapsulate* (capture) this functionality in a *module* and then reuse the module. In C, modules that encapsulate some given functionality that can be reused in a program are called *functions*.

If we could create a function with the functionality shown above and name it **test**, our tutor program would appear as follows:

```
main()
{
   test();
   test();
   test();
```

```
    test();
}

test()
{
    generate two random numbers
    prompt the user
    read the user's input
    compare the input with the actual result
    print a response
}
```

Note that the function named **test** is reused, and there is no longer a duplication of functionality. However, there are some more details to work out: Even though the functionality is encapsulated by the function, its behavior must be more precisely controlled. For the four arithmetic tests implemented by the function, the prompt string and the results differ according to the type of test performed. For example, the prompt string for the addition test has the form

```
printf("%d + %d? ", random1, random2);
```

whereas the prompt string for the multiplication test appears as

```
printf("%d * %d? ", random1, random2);
```

Also, the computed result will be different in each case. Thus it is obvious that the code inside the function should be controlled through external means. The mechanism used to control the execution of the function is the function's *arguments*. If we introduce arguments to our program shown above, it will have the following form:

```
main()
{
    test(addition);
    test(subtraction);
    test(multiplication);
    test(division);
}
```

```
            test(type-of-test)
            {
              generate two random numbers
              prompt the user for type-of-test
              read the user's input
              compare the input with the result for
                  the type-of-test
              print a response
            }
```

Another rationale for using functions has to do with the complexity of large applications. It is extremely difficult to manage source code that is more than one or two pages long. Code that is split into multiple source files with each file implementing a small set of functions is more maintainable, readable and easier to debug. These files can be compiled separately and linked together to make an executable program.

In the rest of this chapter, you will learn the C mechanisms that implement functions.

10.1   Functions

C programs typically consist of numerous small functions. Functions are nothing new to us. Each C program has at least one function: the `main` function. We have also used functions such as `printf`, `scanf`, and `getchar`.

When we execute the program by typing the file name of the executable program, execution begins at the `main` function. The `main` function can then *call* other functions, such as the functions available in libraries and functions that you have written. When a statement containing a function call is executed, control transfers to the function named in the call. After the code in the function is executed, control transfers back to the caller. Calling the function named `test` from the tutor program and returning back to the `main` function is shown in Figure 10.1.

The caller of a function will be referred to simply as the "caller," and the function that it calls will be referred to as the "callee."

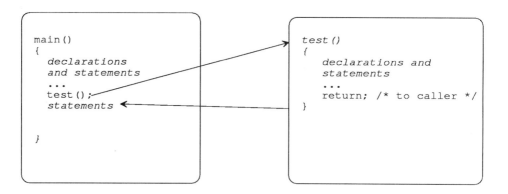

Figure 10.1 Function call and return.

When we call a function, we can pass it a set of data values to control the execution of the function. As we mentioned above, the values that we pass to a function are called the arguments to the function. After the function finishes executing, it can pass a value (only one value) back to the caller of the function. This value is called the *return value*.

Example **Function call with return value**

```
int ch;
ch = getchar();
```

In the example shown above, we call the function `getchar`. Notice that `getchar` needs no arguments. When the function `getchar` finishes execution, it returns to the caller an integer value (ASCII code corresponding to the character the user typed at the keyboard), which is assigned to the integer variable `ch`. The code that implements the function `getchar` is not shown. In this case, the precompiled code for `getchar` is in the standard library that we link with.

Example **Function call with arguments**

```
int v1, v2, max;
assign values to v1 and v2
max = maximum(v1, v2);
```

Here, we call the function **maximum** (which presumably computes the maximum of two numbers) that takes two arguments **v1** and **v2**. The arguments are comma-separated expressions. The comma used as the argument separator in the argument list is not the same as the comma operator that we have used in the **for** statement. The function returns a value (presumably an integer), which we assign to the variable **max**.

In the above example, we haven't shown the actual code in the function **maximum**. Soon, we will write the code that implements the function.

There are three components to implementing functions in C:
- Function declaration: Announcing the type of the function before it is actually used. Just as with variables, functions also need to declared before they are used (called).
- Function call: The actual act of calling the function, with the necessary arguments.
- Function definition: The actual set of statements that makes up the function.

The three components are shown in Figure 10.2.

In the next three sections, we examine these three components in detail.

10.1a **Function declaration: Function prototypes**

Declaring the function before its use enables the compiler to check the number and the types of the arguments used at the point of call against the number and types of the arguments specified in the declaration.

In our previous example, we made a call to the function **maximum**:

```
max = maximum(v1, v2);
```

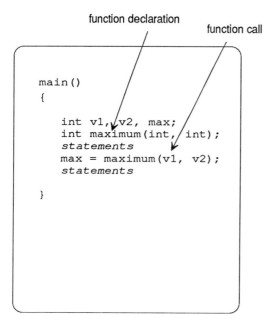

Figure 10.2 Function declaration, definition and call.

The variables **max**, **v1** and **v2** are all of type **int**. The compiler needs to check whether the function named **maximum** is compatible with the call made in the above statement. Specifically, it needs to verify that the function named maximum takes two integer arguments and returns an integer value. But the function **maximum** may not be in in the same file as the file containing the **main** function, or the function **maximum** may be placed after the **main** function. Thus to ensure that we are making the call properly, we need to show the *prototype* of the actual function.

The act of instructing the compiler about the number and type of arguments and type of the return value is called the *declaration* of, or *prototyping*, the function. The function prototype has to appear before the function call.

We will modify our example to include the function prototype:

```
int maximum(int, int);   /* The prototype */
int v1, v2, max;
assign values to v1 and v2
max = maximum(v1, v2)
```

The line

```
int maximum(int, int);
```

signifies that the function **maximum** takes two arguments, both of which are of type **int**, and that it returns a value, which is also of type **int**.

The arguments need not be named, as the compiler is only interested in the number and types of the arguments. It uses the information in the declaration to check that when you actually call the function, the arguments to the call and the return value are consistent with the function prototype.

Let us look at the formal syntax of the function prototype:

Syntax **Function prototype**

```
return-type function-name(argument-type-list);
```

The *argument-type-list* is a comma-separated list of data types.

Example **Prototype for a function that does not take an argument**

```
int print_heading(void);       /* No argument list */
```

Example **Prototype for a function that takes two integer arguments**

```
int maximum(int, int);
```

If the function does not return a value, the return type should be specified as **void**.

Example **Prototype for a function that does not return a value**

```
/* Declaration for a function
 * that prints an error message depending
 * on an integer type passed as the argument */
void print_error(int);
```

10.1b Function call

Function call is the act of calling the function with the desired arguments. When the statement containing the function call is executed, control transfers to the function named in the statement.

Syntax **Function call**

```
function-name(argument-list);
```

Example **Calling a function**

```
int maximum(int, int);    /* Prototype */
max = maximum(v1, v2);    /* Call a function named maximum */
```

The *argument-list* can be expressions: Each expression is evaluated before the call and the value is passed to the function.

Example **Calling a function with expressions as arguments**

```
int maximum(int, int);         /* Prototype */
value = maximum(b*b, 4*a*c);   /* Function call */
```

10.1c Function definition

So far we have left out a minor detail: the actual code that implements the function. The code that composes the function is called the *function definition*. The function definition consists of a header, which contains the return type, a list of *formal parameters* that receive the value(s) passed on by the function call and a body composed of the statements that implement the function.

Syntax **Function definition**

```
return_type function-name(formal-parameter-list)
{
   local declarations if any
   statement-list
   return(return value if any); /* Optional */
}
```

Everything before the first brace comprises the header, and everything between the braces comprises the body of the definition.

The definition of the function **maximum** is shown below:

Example **Function that returns the maximum of 2 integers**
```
/* Function that returns the maximum of 2 int's */
int maximum(int first, int second)   /* Header. Note:
                                      * no semicolon */
{ /* Function body */
   if (first >= second)
   {
        return(first);
   }
   return(second); /* Otherwise return second */
}
```

Here's the complete code with a **main** and the function:

```
main()
{
   int v1, v2, max;
   int maximum(int, int);            /* The prototype */

   printf("Enter two values: ");
   scanf("%d %d", &v1, &v2);

   max = maximum(v1, v2); /* The function call */
   printf("The larger value is %d\n", max);
}

/* Function definition begins here */
int maximum(int first, int second)
{
   if (first >= second)
   {
      return(first);
   }
   return(second);
}
```

Here is what happens when you call a function.

- At the point of calling the function, the argument list is evaluated. In the example shown above (`max = maximum(v1, v2);`) the evaluation yields the values of the variables **v1** and **v2**. In a function call such as

   ```
   value = maximum(b*b, 4*a*c);
   ```

   the expressions **b*b** and **4*a*c** are evaluated before the function is called.
- The values of the arguments are converted to the type specified in the prototype (if necessary).
- The function is called, and the parameters named in the function receive the values in the arguments at the point of call.
- The statements that make up the function body are executed.
- If the execution of the function encounters a **return** statement, the expression following the **return** statement (if any) is evaluated and used as the return value. The execution control is then passed back to the caller. The return value (if any) is converted to the type *return-type* declared in the function header. If no **return** statement is present, then control is passed back to the caller when the end of the body of the function is reached.
- The value returned by the function is the result of evaluation of the function call by the caller. This value is available for assignment, printing, etc.

Example Using a return value from a function

```
printf("The larger of 3 and 5 is %d\n", maximum(3, 5));
```

In the above example, the return value from the function **maximum** is the result of the evaluation of the function. This value is used in the **printf** statement.

❏ **Argument names vs. parameter names**

Notice that the names of the arguments in a function call need not correspond to the names of the formal parameters in the function header. In the function call

```
max = maximum(v1, v2);
```

and the function header

```
           int maximum(int first, int second)
```

the argument names **v1** and **v2** do not correspond with the names of the formal parameters **first, second**. The reason is that argument passing in C is achieved by *call by value*.

In call by value, the values in the arguments are passed into the variables in the formal parameter list. Thus it is the order of the arguments and the formal parameter list that matter in the function call, not the names. We will take up this issue in a lot more detail in a subsequent section.

10.1d   Returning from a function: `return` statement

When the function returns, a value is returned to the caller by using the **return** statement. Only one value can be returned by the function.

Syntax   **return** statement

```
return expression;
```

The expression following the **return** statement is evaluated. The type of the result is converted to the type of the function declared in the function header and returned to the caller.

Example   Function to compute the sum of two numbers

```
/* Function to compute the sum */
int sum (int a, int b)
{
    return a + b;
}
```

The next example shows our function **maximum** with a somewhat more complicated **return** statement: one that does all the work!

Example   Function to compute the maximum of two numbers

```
int maximum(int first, int second)
{
    return (first > second ? first : second);
}
```

If no return type is specified in the function definition, it is assumed to be `int` by default. Thus the function

```
sum(int a, int b)
{
    return a + b;
}
```

is equivalent to

```
int sum (int a, int b)
{
    return a + b;
}
```

Tip *It is good practice to always show the return type.*

If a function is declared as one which returns a value and if we are not interested in the return value, we can choose to ignore the return value by casting it as type `void`. For example, the function `printf` always returns a value (the number of items output) which is seldom of interest to us. The right way to deal with this is as shown below:

```
(void) printf("Enter your personal ID number\n");
```

However, since we use far too many `printf`s, we find ourselves omitting the `void` cast most of the time.

Here is a function called `rectangle` which takes two arguments (a length and a width) and returns the area:

```
int rectangle(int length, int width)
{
    int area;    /* Local declaration */

    if (length <= 0 || width <= 0)
    {
       return(0); /* Return 0 as the area if length or
                   * width was entered as negative */
    }
```

```
        area = length * width;
        return(area);
}
```

Given the function above, the following examples show some correct and incorrect calls to it from another function.

Example   **Invoking the function with same number and type of arguments**
```
int a, b, c;
initialize a and b
c = rectangle(a, b);  /* CORRECT: Argument types and
                       *          return values all match */
```

Example   **Invoking the function with a constant as an argument**
```
int a, x;
initialize a
x = rectangle(12, a);  /* CORRECT: Types match     */
```

The function call shown above is valid because the first argument to the function call is an integer constant (**12**) and is the same type as the first parameter of the function **rectangle** (which is an **int**). The value **12** gets passed into the variable **length**, and the second value (the value contained in the variable **a**) gets passed into the variable **width**.

Example   **Using automatic type conversion to call a function**
```
int a;
float y;
initialize a and y
printf("Area of rectangle = %d\n", rectangle(a, y));
```

In the example shown above, the function **rectangle** is called from within the function **printf**. The type of the second argument does not match the declared type of the first parameter of the function call. However, the compiler will convert the type of the argument to the type of the parameter and then copy the value into the parameter.

Example   **Incorrect call to a function**
```
printf("Area = %d\n", rectangle(12));/* INCORRECT */
```

In the above example, the number of arguments does not match the number of parameters in the function definition.

10.1e   Function prototyping and non-ANSI C

Before you start writing functions, let us explain function prototyping in ANSI C. The style of declaring functions and writing the function header that we have seen so far was introduced in ANSI C. If the C compiler that you are using on your machine is an older compiler and is not ANSI-compliant, you will see syntax errors when you compile your programs with functions.

Type in the following program (exactly as shown), and compile it. If you get any compilation errors, it may be because your compiler is not ANSI-compliant. We will show you how to modify the program to get it compiled successfully on your compiler. However, the rest of the examples in this workbook follow the ANSI standard, and you will have to modify the programs, as appropriate, to run them on your compiler.

```
/* Program to test if you have an ANSI
 * compliant C compiler */
#include <stdio.h>
main()
{
   int square(int); /* Prototype */
   printf("The square of 3 is %d\n", square(3));
}
int square(int val)
{
   return val * val;
}
```

If you have typed this program correctly and it does not compile due to syntax errors on the line

```
   int square(int); /* Prototype */
```

then you don't have an ANSI C compiler. Here is the above program modified to run on old C compilers:

```
/* Program modified to on old C compiler */
#include <stdio.h>
main()
{
   int square(); /* Note the omission of argument
                  * type in the prototype */
   printf("The square of 3 is %d\n", square(3));
}

int square(val) /* Note the omission of parameter type */
int val;        /* Note the addition of the declaration */
{
   return val * val;
}
```

❏ Functions: A complete example

Let us rewrite the math tutor program and use functions to implement the four basic tests. We will write the **main** function and a **function** named **test** to implement most of the work. We will also use a function called **my_random**, which takes an argument corresponding to the largest random number that you want generated. The implementation of the function **my_random** will be left as an exercise.

We will generate a random number to decide the type of testing to be performed. If the generated number is 0, addition is to be tested. Numbers 1, 2 and 3 indicate that subtraction, multiplication and division testing are to be performed, respectively.

```
#include <stdio.h>

#define NO_OF_TESTS      20

main()
{
   char test_symbols[] = { '+', '-', '*', '/' };
   int test(char);    /* Prototype for test function */
   int my_random(int); /* Prototype for our generator */
   int index, type_of_test, count = 0;
```

```c
        for(index = 0; index < NO_OF_TESTS; index++)
        {
            /* Generate a number from 0 to 3 */
            type_of_test = my_random(3);
            /* Call the function and use its return value
             * as a counter to update the score. Pass the
             * character symbol corresponding to the random
             * number generated
             */
            count = count + test(test_symbols[type_of_test]);
        }
        printf("You scored %d out of %d\n", count, NO_OF_TESTS);
        exit(EXIT_SUCCESS);
    } /* End of main */

    /* Function test: Implements arithmetic testing.
     * The parameter of the function is a character symbol
     * corresponding to the type of testing to be performed.
     * The function returns an integer value 1 if the user's
     * response was correct and 0 if otherwise.
     */

    int test(char testtype)
    {
        int random1, random2;
        int temp, answer;

        random1 = my_random(20);
        random2 = my_random(20);

        high = random1 >=  random2 ? random1 : random2;
        low = random1 <= random2 ? random1 : random2;

        if (testtype == '/') /* Division */
        {
          /* Make sure that numerator will be an
           * integral multiple of the denominator */
          high = high * low;
        }
```

```
        switch (testtype)
        {
           case '+':
              result = high + low;
              break;
           case '-':
              result = high - low;
              break;
           case '*':
              result = high * low;
              break;
           case '/':
              result = high / low;
              break;
        }
        printf("%d %c %d ? ", high, testtype, low);
        scanf("%d", &answer);
        if (answer == result)
        {
          printf("Correct!\n");
          return(1);
        }
        else
        {
          printf("Incorrect: The correct answer is %d\n",
                  result);
          return(0);
        }
}
```

Note *The* `rand` *function (which you will be using to implement the function* `my_random` *on some UNIX systems does not generate very good random numbers. The* `random` *function, if available, may be a better choice. However, realize that* `random` *is not an official ANSI C standard library function. If you choose to use* `random`, *seed the generator by using* `srandom`.

10.1f Exercises

1. Implement the function `my_random` that returns an integer random number between 0 and its integer argument.

2. While a random value of 0 may be acceptable to generate the type of test (0 means '+', 1 means '-', etc.), the value 0 cannot be used for the actual testing. Modify the function `my_random` to take an addition argument which indicates whether a 0 can be returned or not. Call the function as shown below:

   ```
   my_random(3, ZERO);  /* generate from 0 to 3 */
   my_random(20, ONE);  /* generate from 1 to 20 */
   ```

3. Write a function that interchanges the values contained in a pair of variables. The program should prompt the user to enter two values. After the values have been input, display the initial values. Next, interchange the two values by calling a function called `swap`. After the interchange, display values of the variable in the `main` function. The program should run as follows:

   ```
   Enter two values: 24 46
   The exchanged values are: 46 25
   ```

   Compile and run the program. And by the way, lots of luck! If you find yourself spending too much time trying to get this program working correctly, take a break and read the next section, but not before trying this exercise first.

10.2 Function Arguments: Call by Value

By now, you have probably realized that the last exercise did not work as expected (if you cheated and skipped the exercise, go back and do it now!). No matter how you write the function `swap`, when the function call returns, you still have the old values in the variables in the `main` function.

You probably wrote the function `swap` as shown below:

```
void swap(int first, int second)
{
   int temp; /* A local variable */
   temp = first;
   first = second;
   second = temp;
}
```

The program shown above will not work as intended. This is due to the fact that the passing of arguments from the call to the formal parameters of a function takes place by *value*. That is, values in the variables (and not the variables themselves) are *copied* to the formal parameters of the function when the function is called. The formal parameters declared in the function header are variables, private to the function. The function may manipulate these variables within the function body. But when the function returns to the caller, the variables that were used as arguments to the function have not been modified at all!

Figure 10.3 shows what really happens when we attempt to swap the values of two variables `v1` and `v2` from the `main` function by making a call to function `swap`. For illustration purposes, we will assume that the variables `v1` and `v2` contain the values `24` and `46`, respectively, before the call.

As you can see from the illustration, the function `swap` receives the values `24` and `46` in its private variables `first` and `second`. It then proceeds to interchange the values in these variables. However, when `swap` returns, `v1` and `v2` have not been modified at all. Note that the memory allocated for holding `v1` and `v2` is not the same as the memory for holding `first` and `second`.

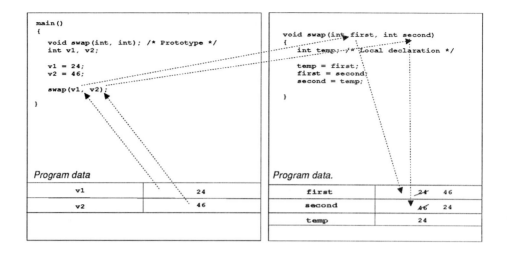

Figure 10.3 Function call and call by value.

In C, call by value is the only mechanism by which arguments are passed to functions. The main characteristics of the call-by-value mechanism are:

1 All arguments are *copied* from caller to the callee.

2 The callee cannot modify any variable in the caller.

Call by value is a simple mechanism that works for most simple functions. However, the characteristics of call by value mentioned above makes it somewhat inefficient and restrictive in the following cases:

- Due to **1**, passing large arrays as arguments to functions becomes very inefficient, since each element of the array will have to be copied from the caller to the callee. Consider a function called `sort` that uses an array as a formal parameter. If the size of the array is fairly large, call by value is very inefficient.

- Due to **2** above, we cannot implement functions such as the `swap` function that we attempted to write. Coupled with the fact that functions can only return one value, this makes exchanging information from the callee to the callee nearly impossible. Consider the `sort` program again: If the caller wishes to receive the sorted array from the function `sort`, the call-by-value mechanism will not suffice.

What is required is the ability to pass the arguments by *reference* and not by value. Programming languages such as Pascal implement both call by value and *call by reference*. In call by reference, rather than passing the value in a variable, the variable's *location* is passed to the callee. This allows the callee to directly modify the caller's memory.

Unfortunately, C only supports call-by-value semantics for functions. But we can *fake* call by reference by using the addresses of variables rather than the values of variables. Passing addresses of variables allows the callee to directly access the caller's memory.

10.2a Implementing call by reference by using pointers

In call by reference, rather than passing the contents of the variable (the value), the variable itself (its location, or address) is passed to the function.

To change the values of variables in the calling environment, rather than passing the value of a variable, the address of the variable can be passed to the function. The function can modify the variable in the caller, since the memory locations of the caller's variable(s) have been passed to it. Of course, the function can access the values in these variables by using the indirection operator *.

From the main program, rather than passing the values to be exchanged, we pass the addresses of the variables that contain them. The main program is shown below:

```
/* Program that exchanges two values by using pointers */
main()
{
   void swap(int *, int *); /* Arguments are addresses */
   int v1, v2;
   printf("Enter two values: ");
   scanf("%d%d", &v1, &v2);
   printf("Before: v1 contains %d and v2 contains %d\n",
          v1, v2);
```

```
        swap(&v1, &v2);  /* Pass the addresses,
                          * not the contents */
        printf("After: v1 contains %d and v2 contains %d\n",
               v1, v2);
}
```

The function **swap** now expects the incoming arguments to be pointers to the variables, rather than the values. Thus the function **swap** can be rewritten as shown below:

```
swap(int *firstp, int *secondp)
{
    int temp; /* A local variable */
    temp = *firstp; /* Get the contents from address
                     * in firstp and store in temp */
    *firstp = *secondp; /* Get the contents from address in
                         * secondp, and store it in location
                         * in firstp */
    *secondp = temp; /* Get the value stored in variable
                      * temp, and store it in location
                      * in secondp */
}
```

Figure 10.4 illustrates how call by reference is implemented by using pointer variables. We will assume that in the **main** function the variables **v1** and **v2** are loaded in memory at locations 1000 and 1002, respectively, and contain the initial values **24** and **46**. In function **swap**, we will assume that the formal parameters occupy memory locations 4000 and 4002.

The function call

```
        swap(&v1, &v2);
```

passes the address values as arguments. Thus the call is equivalent to

```
        swap(1000, 1002);
```

The values **1000** and **1002** are copied into the formal parameters. Thus, inside the function **swap**, we have access to the caller's memory location. All we need to do is exchange the values in these locations by accessing them through the indirection operator *****. Since the formal parameters **firstp** and **secondp**

Function Arguments: Call by Value

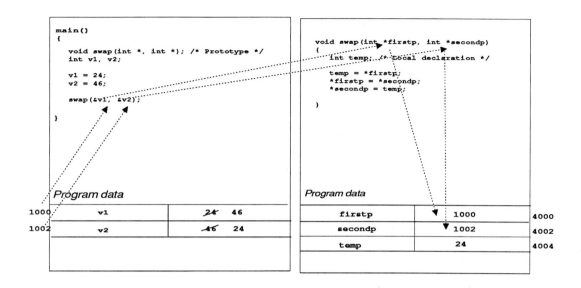

Figure 10.4 Implementing call by reference.

contain the values 1000 and 1002, when we execute the following statements

```
temp = *firstp;
*firstp = *secondp;
*secondp = temp;
```

we are really performing

```
temp = contents at location 1000;
location 1000 = contents at location 1002;
location 1002 = temp;
```

Note that the **main** function could have been rewritten as follows:

```
main()
{
    int v1, v2;
    int *v1p, *v2p;
    v1p = &v1;
```

```
        v2p = &v2;
        read values into v1 and v2
        swap(v1p, v2p);
}
```

The `main` function shown above is essentially the same as the `main` function we wrote earlier. Both pass the addresses of the variables, which need to be interchanged, to the function `swap`.

This above example illustrates how we can *fake* call by reference by using call by value and pointers. Realize that the basic mechanism used to pass arguments to the function is still call by value. When we passed addresses as function arguments, we passed the addresses by value. That is, the value of the pointers were copied into the formal parameters by using call by value. Thus it is incorrect to say that C uses call by reference. We merely work around the problems of call by value by using pointers.

The summary of steps required to implement call by reference is outlined in the following Box 10.1.

- Declare arguments as pointers to the appropriate data type.
- Initialize the pointer values to point to the variables.
- Pass the pointer values to the function at invocation time. The above two steps may be bypassed, as in `swap` function, by supplying the address values directly.
- Declare the arguments as pointers to the appropriate data type in the function header.
- Dereference the pointer values to access the actual variables inside the function body.
- Any modifications made through the pointer variables inside the function body will affect the variables in the calling environment.

Box 10.1 Summary of steps to implement call by reference

10.2b Functions vs. macros

Are you a little curious as to why the macro SWAP that we implemented earlier worked correctly, whereas the the original version of the function swap did not?

The reason for this is that a macro is replaced before compilation by the preprocessor. Thus the macro code is really contained in the caller's body, and the arguments to the macro are really working on the same variables in the calling code. The following example clearly shows what happens if we use a macro called SWAP, as opposed to function swap. We will show the program before and after preprocessing to illustrate macro expansion.

```
/* Before preprocessing */
#define SWAP(a,b)   {                   \
                    int temp;           \
                    temp = a;           \
                    a = b;              \
                    b = temp;           \
                    }

main()
{
   int v1, v2;
   v1 = 24;
   v2 = 46;
   printf("Before swap v1 = %d, v2 = %d\n", v1, v2);
   SWAP(v1,v2);
   printf("After swap v1 = %d, v2 = %d\n", v1, v2);
}
```

The preprocessed output of the above program is shown below:

```
/* After preprocessing */
main()
{
   int v1, v2;
   v1 = 24;
   v2 = 46;
   printf("Before swap v1 = %d, v2 = %d\n", v1, v2);
```

```
    {
        int temp;
        temp = v1;
        v1 = v2;
        v2 = temp;
    };
    printf("After swap v1 = %d, v2 = %d\n", v1, v2);
}
```

Since the preprocessor merely replaces the macro, before it is passed to the compiler, there is no function call involved, and call-by-value semantics are not applicable here.

10.2c   Returning more than one value from a function

One of the limitations of functions is that the `return` statement can only return one value to the user. But you just learned how to manipulate the memory location in the caller from the callee. We will use this technique to simulate returning multiple values to the caller from the callee. The idea is fairly simple: allocate variables and pass their addresses to the function. The function will fill in values by using the indirection operator.

The following program illustrates how we can simulate the returning of two values by a function. The program uses a function called `find_square` that takes two arguments. The first argument is an *in parameter* (one that is used to send a value into the function). The function computes the largest square that is less than or equal to its first parameter. It returns the computed largest square using the `return` statement. It also returns the remainder (input minus its largest square) as the *out parameter* (one that is used to send a value out from the function to the caller) by using the second parameter. This requires that the caller pass an address as the second argument, where the function may place the remainder, indirectly.

For testing purposes, if you input 9, the largest square is 9 (3^2) and the remainder is 0. If you input 18, the largest square is 16 (4^2) and the remainder is 2.

```
/* Example: Find largest square <= input value
 * and the remainder
 */
```

Function Arguments: Call by Value

```
#include <stdio.h>
#include <math.h>

main()
{
   int input;
   int lsquare;   /* Largest square */
   int remainder, *ptr_rem;
   int find_square(int, int *); /* Prototype */

   ptr_rem = &remainder;   /* Initialize the pointer */
   printf("Enter a value: ");
   scanf("%d", &input);
   lsquare = find_square(input, ptr_rem);
   printf("The largest square is %d and remainder is %d\n",
          lsquare, remainder);
}

int find_square(int val, int *rem)
{
   int sq;
   sq = (int) sqrt((double)val); /* From the math library */
   *rem = val - (sq * sq);
   return(sq * sq);
}
```

Note that the largest whole square is returned as the return value and the remainder is returned as the out parameter of the function. When you compile the above program, don't forget to include the math library!

Now we will take the mystery out of putting the **&** in front of the argument variables in **scanf** functions. Since we need to receive values back from **scanf**, this is the only way to do it!

Note *It is possible to pass arguments to the **main** function as well. Passing arguments to **main** is discussed in Chapter 13, Section 13.2.*

10.2d Exercises

1. Write a function called **get_random_pair**, which, when called, returns *two* random numbers. Use two variables called **high** and **low**, from the main function, to receive the values from the function. When the function returns, the largest of the two random numbers must be placed in the variable **high** and the smallest, in the variable **low**.
   Use the **get_random_pair** function to implement the math tutor program shown earlier in this chapter.

2. Write a function that when given an integer value returns its lowest common denominator and its highest common denominator.

10.2e Arrays as function arguments

We noted earlier that using call by value is a very inefficient method of passing arrays as arguments to functions. However, we can avoid the problem by using pointer variables to implement call by reference and pass the array to the function by reference, rather than copying all the individual values.

Recall that the array name represents the address of the beginning of the array. Thus we can just pass the name of the array to a function. Inside the callee function, array elements can be accessed either through pointer operations or through the subscript operator (which are equivalent operations). To refresh your memory, for an integer array **a** and a pointer variable **ptr_a** initialized to the beginning of the array,

```
a[0]    is equivalent to ptr_a,
a[1]    is equivalent to ptr_a + 1,
a[2]    is equivalent to ptr_a + 2,
etc.
```

The following example illustrates how arrays can be passed as arguments to a function by writing a program that reads student grades into an array and uses a function to compute the average.

```
/* File average.c: Computes the average score
 * of an exam */
#include <stdio.h>
```

```c
#define NO_STUDENTS 12

main()
{
   int grades[NO_STUDENTS], *gradesp;
   int index;
   int average_score(int *);/* Function for average */

   gradesp = grades; /* Initialize the pointer */
   for (index = 0; index < NO_STUDENTS; index++)
   {
      printf("Enter Grade for Student %d: ",index);
      scanf("%d",gradesp++);
   }
   printf("The average score is %d\n",
           average_score(grades));
}
```

Now there are two ways to write the function **average_score**. The first version uses pointers to access the array, and the second version uses subscripts.

```c
/* Version 1. Using pointers */
int average_score(int *array_ptr)
{
   int index, sum;
   for (index = 0, sum = 0; index < NO_STUDENTS; index++)
      sum = sum + *array_ptr++;
   return (sum / NO_STUDENTS);
}


/* Version 2. Using subscripts */
int average_score(int array[])
{
   int index, sum;
   for (index = 0, sum = 0; index < NO_STUDENTS; index++)
      sum = sum + array[index];
   return (sum / NO_STUDENTS);
}
```

10.2f Functions: A complete example

The following program uses several small functions to keep track of the minimum, maximum, average and sum of a list of floating point numbers, input at the keyboard. Each time a value is input, the program displays the above-mentioned statistics about all the numbers input so far.

We will use the following functions in the program. The prototype of each function and the intended use are outlined in the following table:

Function prototype	Intended use
`void print_info(void)`	Print information about program.
`void print_heading(void)`	Print the heading for data.
`void print_data(int, float, float, float, float, float)`	Print the data statistics.
`float minimum(float, float)`	Compute the smallest of its arguments.
`float maximum(float, float)`	Compute the largest of its arguments.

```
/* File stats.c: Contains all the functions and the main
 * program for the elementary statistics program
 */
#include <stdio.h>
#include <float.h> /* For FLT_MAX and FLT_MIN below */
/* Function to compute minimum of two values */
float minimum(float x, float y)
{
    return x < y ? x : y;
}
/* Function to compute maximum of two values */
float maximum(float x, float  y)
{
    return x > y ? x : y;
}
```

Function Arguments: Call by Value

```c
/* Function to print information about program */
void print_info(void)
{
   printf ("\n%s\n%s\n",
           "This program computes and prints cumulative",
           "statistics on n floating point numbers");
}
/* Function to print heading of the table items */
void print_heading(void)
{
   printf("\n%5s%12s%12s%12s%12s%12s\n",
          "count", "item", "minimum", "maximum", "sum",
          "average");
}
/* Function to print data value */
void print_data(int count, float item, float min,
                float max, float sum, float average)
{
   printf ("%5d%12.5f%12.5f%12.5f%12.5f%12.5f\n",
           count, item, min, max, sum, average);
}
```

Next, the main program:

```c
/* Now the main program to put it all together */
#define MAX_ITEMS 100

main()
{
   int count, i, ret_val;
   float x, min, max, sum;
   /* Function declarations */
   void print_data(int, float, float, float, float, float);
   void print_info(void), print_heading(void);
   float minimum(float, float), maximum(float, float);

   min = FLT_MAX; /* Initialize to very high value */
   max = FLT_MIN; /* Initialize to very low value */
   sum = 0; /* Initialize sum */
```

```
        print_info(); /* Print the heading */
        for (i = 1; i <= MAX_ITEMS; i++)
        {
           printf ("Enter item %d: ", i);
           ret_val = scanf ("%f", &x);
           if (ret_val == EOF)
              break;

           min = minimum (x, min);
           max = maximum (x, max);
           sum = sum + x;
           print_heading();
           print_data(i, x, min, max, sum, sum/i);
        }
    }
```

When compiled and run, the program produces the following output.

```
This program computes and prints cumulative
statistics on n floating point numbers
Enter item 1: 12

count         item       minimum       maximum            sum       average
    1      12.00000      12.00000      12.00000       12.00000      12.00000
Enter item 2: 23.4

count         item       minimum       maximum            sum       average
    2      23.40000      12.00000      23.40000       35.40000      17.70000
Enter item 3: 16

count         item       minimum       maximum            sum       average
    3      16.00000      12.00000      23.40000       51.40000      17.13333
Enter item 4: 0

count         item       minimum       maximum            sum       average
    4       0.00000       0.00000      23.40000       51.40000      12.85000
Enter item 5: <control-d>
```

Note *The program will not compile correctly without an ANSI C compiler or a compiler that understands ANSI C function prototypes. If you get numerous* errors in trying to compile this program, you probably don't have an ANSI C compiler. Appendix B, at the end of this workbook, contains the program, modified to compile under older C compilers.

Note *Some systems do not contain the header file* **float.h**. *If your system does not contain* **float.h**, *include the header file* **limits.h** *and modify the two statements that initialize* `max` *and* `min` *as shown below:*

```
min = (float)INT_MAX; /* Initialize to very high value */
max = (float)INT_MIN; /* Initialize to very low value */
```

❏ **Functions with variable number of arguments**

It is possible to write a function that takes a variable number of arguments, such as the function `printf`. Consider the following two statements:

```
printf("Hello world\n");
printf("Average score = %d\n", average(grades));
```

In the first statement, `printf` has one argument, a string. The second statement has two arguments: a string and type of the return value from the function `average`. Assuming that the function `average` returns an `int`, the prototypes for these two statements can be written as follows:

```
int printf(char *); /* Prototype for first
                     * printf statement */
int printf(char *, int); /* Prototype for second
                          * printf statement */
```

Obviously, it is impossible to list the prototypes for all the statements that we may be using the `printf` function for. In old C, this is not a problem, as the function prototype does not include any information about the arguments. ANSI C provides a syntactic form to declare functions that take a variable number of arguments. In ANSI C, an ellipsis (...) can be used to specify a function that takes a variable number of arguments. Using the ellipsis form, the prototype for the `printf` function can be specified as shown:

```
int printf(...);
```

How do we write the code for a function that takes a variable number of arguments? The standard library provides a facility known as *varargs* (variable arguments) that can be used to implement such functions. Discussion of the *varargs* mechanisms is outside the scope of this workbook.

10.2g Exercises

1 Add a new function called **range** to the above program. The function **range**, when called with two arguments (the maximum and minimum values seen so far), should return the absolute difference. Modify the **print_heading** and **print_data** routines to also print out the range of the maximum and minimum values on each line. Of course, modify the **main** program to compute the range and pass it to the routine **print_data**.

2 Modify the parking permit program which you wrote in Chapter 7, to use a function called **print_permit**. The prototype of **print_permit** is

```
void print_permit(TicketType, int);
```

where **TicketType** is an enumerated type that represents faculty, staff and students and the second argument is the fee to be printed.

10.3 Functions: Separate Compilation

All of the functions and the **main** program need not be resident in the same file. Often, it is highly impractical to place all the functions in a single file if the application is relatively large.

If the functions are placed in different source files, they can be compiled separately to produce *object modules* that are linked together to make an executable program. When a modification is made to the program, it may not be necessary to recompile all the separate source files: Relinking the object modules may suffice.

It is often advantageous to put tested and nonchanging functions into separate source files, as they need not be compiled every time a source file changes. Usually, utility programs such as **make** manage the compilation of multiple source files. The program `make` is available on most UNIX systems, and similar programs are available for DOS and other operating systems. Description of `make` is beyond the scope of this workbook. However, `make` is a very useful utility, and you are encouraged to learn it on your own.

We will use our earlier statistics example to show how we can split the program into multiple source files, compile them separately and *link* them together to make the executable program. The actual details of the compilation and linking vary among compilers.

Consider splitting the file `stats.c` into two files as follows:
- A file called `statfns.c` that contains all the function code
- A file called `statmain.c` that contains the `main` function

Compile the file `statfns.c`, and produce an *object module*. On C compilers running on UNIX systems the **-c** option to the C compiler will create an object module, as shown below:

```
cc -c statfns.c
```

On other compilers, issue the appropriate command. For example, for the Borland C++ compiler (which also compiles C programs), issue the following command:

```
tcc -c statfns.c
```

The above command, if successful, creates an object file. On compilers running on UNIX, the object file will be created with the same names as the source file but with a **.o** suffix instead of the **.c**. On the Borland C compiler, the suffix is **.OBJ**.

Similarly, compile the file **statmain.c**, and create an object file.

```
cc -c statmain.c
```

Now link both the object files together, and make an executable program. On UNIX systems use the following command:

```
cc -o stat statfns.o statmain.o
```

Note   *The file **statfns.c** need not be recompiled every time **statmain.c** changes. Likewise, if only **statmain.c** has been changed, **statfns.c** need not be recompiled. But, if there are dependencies between the two source files that relate them more closely, simply relinking the two object files may not suffice. Read the documentation about utilities, such as* `make`, *on how to specify relationships between source files.*

If you are only recompiling one file, you make modifications in the source file and recompile that source file and relink it with the object file of the unmodified source file. For example, if you changed **statfns.c**, you can make a new executable file as shown below:

```
cc -o stat statfns.c statmain.o
```

10.3a   Exercises

1   Using your editor, split the statistics example program file into two files, as described above, compile them separately and link them together to create the executable program.

2   Use the `make` program to manage your source files.

10.4 Function Prototypes: ANSI C vs. Old C

If your compiler is non-ANSI-compliant, you will encounter problems with function prototypes. This is especially bothersome if you use the same code on different platforms. One solution to this problem is to modify the code each time, before compiling it on a different compiler. A better solution is to use the conditional compilation feature of the C preprocessor.

The conditional compilation feature allows us to conditionally compile parts of a program, based on a flag that we pass to the C compiler. Conditional compilation can also be accomplished by using the predefined macros supported by the preprocessor. In this section, we will outline two different techniques that can be used to compile your code under old C and ANSI C.

10.4a Conditional compilation to manage code

The preprocessor commands that implement conditional compilation are outlined in the following table:

Preprocessor command	Meaning
`#if` *constant-expression*	Conditionally include text below, terminated by a **#endif**, based on the value of the constant expression.
`#ifdef` *macro-name*	Conditionally include text below and up to an **#endif**, based on whether the name *macro-name* has been defined.
`#ifndef` *macro-name*	Conditionally include text below and up to an **#endif**, if the name *macro-name* has not been defined.
`#elif` *constant-expression*	Conditionally include text below and up to an **#endif**, depending on the value of the *constant-expression*, if the previous **#if**, **#ifdef** or **#ifndef** failed.

Preprocessor command	Meaning
#else	Include text below and up to an #endif, if the the previous #if, #ifdef or #ifndef failed.
#endif	Terminate conditional inclusion.

The following program shows how to use the preprocessor commands shown above to conditionally include the macros **EXIT_SUCCESS** and **EXIT_FAILURE** along with our programs. Recall that these macros were introduced by ANSI C and may not be available in older C compilers. We will use the preprocessor **ifndef** command to test whether the macro **EXIT_SUCCESS** is defined or not. If it is not defined, we will define **EXIT_SUCCESS** and **EXIT_FAILURE** and give them appropriate values.

Put the following lines in your header file **my_defs.h**:

```
#ifndef EXIT_SUCCESS      /* If EXIT_SUCCESS is not defined */
#define EXIT_SUCCESS     0 /* Define it and give it value 0 */
#define EXIT_FAILURE     1 /* Define EXIT_FAILURE as well */
#endif
```

We have been including debugging output in our programs. If we need to turn of such output after the program has been tested, we can use the preprocessor **ifdef** command, as shown:

```
#ifdef DEBUG    /* If DEBUG has been defined */
/* Verify that original scores and names have
 * been stored correctly (from Chapter 9) */
printf("%-25s\t%d\n", namelist[student], scores[student]);
#endif DEBUG
```

To turn on debugging, we can define the name DEBUG in the program itself, or through a command line option to the compiler. To do the former, place the following line before the debugging statement shown above:

```
#define       DEBUG
```

Function Prototypes: ANSI C vs. Old C 315

When the program is compiled again, preprocessor will check whether the name `DEBUG` has been defined or not. In this case, since the name has been defined, the lines enclosed by the `#ifdef` and its corresponding `#endif` will be included with the program. It is also possible to define the name `DEBUG`, using a command line option. In this case, there is no need place the line `#define DEBUG` in the program text. On UNIX systems, most compilers allow the name to be defined, as shown:

```
$ cc -o prog -D DEBUG prog.c
```

The **-D** option instructs **cc** to pass the name `DEBUG` to the preprocessor. This will cause the the macro name to be *defined*. Thus the preprocessor will include the text following the `#ifdef DEBUG` with the program.

Note *Read your compiler's documentation on how to pass a macro name to the preprocessor.*

We can use the techniques discussed here to conditionally compile code so that it may be compiled under an ANSI C compiler as well as a K&R compiler. To test code for ANSI compliance or noncompliance, we can use a predefined macro called `__STDC__` which has the value 1 on ANSI C compilers only. Testing for this value in our program enables us to write and compile code without passing any flags to the preprocessor.

The following example shows how to to use the value of the predefined macro `__STDC__` to conditionally compile code.

```
/* File average.c: Computes the average score of an exam.
 * The file has been modified so that it can compile under
 * old C as well as ANSI C compilers.
 */
#include <stdio.h>
#define NO_STUDENTS 12

main()
{
   int grades[NO_STUDENTS], *gradesp;
   int index;
```

```c
#ifdef __STDC__
   /* This compiler is ANSI compliant */
   int average_score(int *);/* ANSI prototype */
#else
   /* Compiler is not ANSI */
   int average_score();/* OLD C prototype */
#endif

   gradesp = grades; /* Initialize the pointer */
   for (index = 0; index < NO_STUDENTS; index++)
   {
      printf("Enter Grade for Student %d: ",index);
      scanf("%d",gradesp++);
   }
   printf("The average score is %d\n",
          average_score(grades));
}

#ifdef __STDC__
/* Compiler is ANSI compliant: use ANSI style header */
int average_score(int *array_ptr)
#else
/* Use old style header */
int average_score(array_ptr)
int *array_ptr;
#endif

{
   int index, sum;
   for (index = 0, sum = 0; index < NO_STUDENTS; index++)
   {
      sum = sum + *array_ptr++;
   }
   return (sum / NO_STUDENTS);
}
```

10.5   Common Problems

1. The potential for a lot of compile time syntactic errors exists if you are using an older, non-ANSI C compiler. Make sure that the type of prototyping that you use is in compliance with the type of compiler that you have.

2. Lack of function prototyping in older C compilers introduces a major problem in argument passing. Consider the following program, written using older C function prototype:

    ```
    main()
    {
        double sqrt();  /* Older C prototype */
        double value;

        value = sqrt(16);
    }
    ```

    The above program will not work as expected. The problem is that the real prototype of function **sqrt** is

    ```
    double sqrt(double);
    ```

    The function **sqrt** expects that the value passed to it will be a **double**. However, the compilation of the program shown above causes the compiler to treat the value **16** as an integer (as it should be), and an integer value gets passed to the function **sqrt**. This causes **sqrt** to return an incorrect value.

    This problem does not exist under ANSI C compilers, as the prototype also includes the type of the argument. On non-ANSI compilers, the correct version of the program is as shown:

    ```
    main()
    {
        double sqrt();  /* Older C prototype */
        double value;
    ```

```
        value = sqrt((double)16);
}
```

3. Non-ANSI C compilers also introduce the potential to call a function with the wrong number of arguments. Since the function prototype for non-ANSI compilers does not list information about arguments, the compiler has no way of checking to see if the function is being called with the right number of arguments.

4. In programs written for non-ANSI C compilers, the arguments to a function go through a process known as *argument widening*, or *promotion*, before they are copied into formal parameters. In argument widening, `char` and `short` parameters to a function are converted to `int`s; `float`s are converted to `double` before they are copied into formal parameters. If the formal parameters are smaller in size than the promoted types, information may be lost. While this may not cause any problems in normal programs, programmers must be aware of the automatic widening of arguments in compiling programs with older C compilers. Even in ANSI C compilers, the use of ellipses to avoid the specification of arguments introduces automatic promotion of parameter values.

11
User-Defined Data Types: Structures

So far, we have programmed with all of C's built-in data types, such as `int`, `float` and `char`. We have also seen derived data types, such as arrays and pointers. We know that whole numbers can be represented by `int`s, strings can be realized by using an array of `char`s, etc. But how do we represent data that cannot be represented by these simple data types? You might ask, "What kind of data?"

Consider a typical database program. Our university database maintains information about students. Hence a logical data-item in the database is a type called a `student`. But what is a `student` data type? A student may be represented by a name (string), a social security number (`long` or string), current grade point average (`float`) and such. Thus the data type `student` could be a collection of individual data types. Obviously, it would be a lot easier to deal with this *aggregate* as one logical unit rather than a loose collection of individual data types. The derived data type `struct` in C provides the framework for building user-defined data types, such as `student`, from basic data types.

In this chapter, you will learn how to define your own data types by using `struct` definitions. The examples in this chapter will show you how a simple database containing student records can be set up. In parallel, you will be developing a simple card file program that maintains address records.

11.1 Structure

A structure is a collection of one or more variables, of possibly different types, grouped together to form a *user-defined* data type. In database lingo, a structure is known as a *record*.

A structure representing a student record is depicted in Figure 11.1.

The components of the structure in Figure 11.1 can be represented by the following basic data types:

```
char name[24];         /* Student name */
unsigned long id;      /* Student ID */
float gpa;             /* Grade point average */
int classification;    /* Classification code: freshman,
                        * sophomore, junior, senior */
```

We will use these individual declarations to define a new data type. Once the new data type is defined, variables of the the newly defined type can be declared.

Syntax   **Defining a structure data type**

```
struct structure-name
{
    data-type variable-name1;
    data-type variable-name2;
    etc.
};
```

Figure 11.1 A student record.

Note *Note the semicolon at the end of the closing curly brace.*

Example **Defining a `student` data type**

```
struct student
{
    char name[24];            /* Name of student */
    unsigned long  id;        /* ID of student */
    int classification;       /* Code for academic standing */
    float gpa;                /* Current grade point */
};
```

The above definition specifies a new data type called `struct student`, with the components (or *members*) `name`, `id`, `classification` and `gpa`. Once the new data type has been defined, variables of the type can be declared. The variables of the user-defined type are commonly known as *instances*, or *objects*.

Example **Declaring an instance of the user-defined type**

```
struct student student1, student2;
```

In the declaration shown above, two variables called `student1` and `student2` of type `struct student` will be allocated.

Note that `struct student` is not a variable. It is the name of a data type. In other words, it is only a *template*, much the same way as `int` is a template for integer values. Using the template `struct student`, we can declare variables of type `struct student`.

Once the new data type has been defined, it can be used in any of the familiar declarations.

Example **Declaring an array of structures**

```
/* Using the template shown above */
struct student student_records[100];
```

Example **Declaring a pointer to a structure**

```
struct student *student_p;
```

We can use the **typedef** mechanism to shorten the definition and give it a more intuitive appeal.

```
typedef struct student
{
      char name[24];          /* Name of student */
      unsigned long  id;      /* ID of student */
      int classification;     /* Code for academic standing */
      float gpa;              /* Current grade point */
} student;
```

With the definition shown above, the name **student** now becomes synonymous with **struct student**. Variable declaration can be made as

```
student student1; /* Student1 is of type student */
student student_records[100]; /* Student_records is an
                               * array of students */
```

In the remainder of this chapter, we use the **typedef** mechanism along with the structure template definition.

11.1a   Accessing structure members

Members of a structure can be accessed by using the dot operator (.), as shown next.

Example   Accessing a structure member

structure-variable-name.member

Given a structure variable **student1**, we can access the individual fields as

```
student1.name
student1.id
student1.classification
etc.
```

Example **Accessing a structure member**
```
/* Printing the student name */
printf("Name: %s\n", student1.name);
student1.classification = 2; /* 2 is code for junior */
```

In the case of array of structure instances, accessing members is done through the use of array subscripts:

Example **Accessing a member of an array of structures**
```
#define NO_STUDENTS    30

student student_records[NO_STUDENTS];
int index;

for (index = 0;index < NO_STUDENTS;index++)
{
   printf("Enter name for student %d ", index);
   fgets(student_records[index].name, 24, stdin);
   printf("Enter GPA ");
   scanf("%f", &(student_records[index].gpa));
}
```

Example **Printing all the student names**
```
int index;

for (index = 0; index < NO_STUDENTS;index++)
{
   printf("Student %d - %s\n",
          index, student_records[index].name);
}
```

For the next example, we will set up the declaration for the member **classification** more abstractly. We will also put the following definitions in the header file **student.h** and include the file in our programs.

```
/* Header file student.h: Contains the structure
 * templates and macros.
 */
```

```c
typedef enum { FRESHMAN, SOPHOMORE, JUNIOR, SENIOR } status;
typedef unsigned long ulong;

#define NO_STUDENTS             30
#define NAME_SIZE               24

typedef struct student
{
   char    name[NAME_SIZE];
   ulong   id;
   status  classification;
   float   gpa;
} student;
```

With the declaration of the member **classification** as a type **status**, we can write statements such as

```c
        student1.classification = FRESHMAN;
```

Recall that the **enum** definition assigns integer values, starting at zero, to its members. Thus **FRESHMAN** will be assigned the value **0**, **SOPHOMORE 1**, etc. The following example shows the assignment of values to student records.

```c
#include <stdio.h>
#include "my_defs.h" /* Commonly used definitions */
#include "student.h"

main()
{
   student student_records[NO_STUDENTS];
   int index;

   /* Input data into the records */
   for (index = 0; index < NO_STUDENTS; index++)
   {
      printf("****Record %d ****\n", index);
      printf("Name? ");
      fgets(student_records[index].name, NAME_SIZE, stdin);
      printf("ID? ");
      scanf("%ld", &student_records[index].id);
```

```
        printf("Status (0 = Freshman, 1 = Sophomore,\
2 = Junior, 3 = Senior) ? ");
        scanf("%d", &student_records[index].classification);
        printf("GPA? ");
        scanf("%f", &student_records[index].gpa);
    }
    exit(EXIT_SUCCESS);
}
```

Type in and run the program. If the program does not work as you expected, read on!

❏ Problem with mixing formatted and unformatted I/O

You may have observed a curious phenomena. After the first student record has been populated (record 0), during the second iteration of the **for** loop, the program does not wait for you to enter the student's name. The **fgets** statement seems to have been skipped over.

This is a problem that occurs when formatted input (**scanf**) meets unformatted input functions (**gets, fgets, getchar**, etc.). In our case, the problem is due to the last **scanf** statement at the end of the **for** statement and the subsequent **fgets** statement at the beginning of the loop. Here is what happens. When the statement

```
scanf("%f", &student_records[index].gpa);
```

is executed, the program waits for your input. If you enter input at the keyboard, followed by a carriage return, the input stream contains input characters plus the character corresponding to the carriage return. Since a carriage return is a valid input separator, **scanf** merely reads the characters *up to* the carriage return, performs the format conversion and returns. The input stream now contains a carriage return.

Next, when the **fgets** statement

```
fgets(student_records[index].name, NAME_SIZE, stdin);
```

is executed, the carriage return becomes valid input for **fgets**, and the function returns immediately, after reading the carriage return, converting it to a new line character and placing it in the buffer `student_records[index].name`.

Tip *It is a bad idea to mix functions which perform input conversion (such as `scanf`) with character-oriented input functions (such as `gets`, `getchar`).*

To fix this problem, we use unformatted I/O and perform any necessary format conversion ourselves by using conversion functions available in the standard library.

The commonly used string to number conversion functions in the standard library are shown in the following table. From now on, we will use the prototype of the function to show you its intended usage. To access the following functions, you need to include the header file **stdlib.h**.

Function name	Purpose
`int atoi(char *)`	Converts from string to `int`
`long atol(char *)`	Converts from string to `long`
`double atof(char *)`	Converts from string to `double`
`long strtol(char *, char **, int)`	Converts from string to `long`
`long strtoul(char *, char **, int)`	Converts from string to `unsigned long`
`double strtod(char *, char **)`	Converts from string to `double`

The last three functions in the table shown above are more general versions of the first three. They take two or three arguments. The first argument corresponds to the string to be converted, and the second argument is an out parameter that will contain the position of the first character of the string following the converted part of the string. If a third argument is present, it specifies the base of the numbers to be converted (`10` for decimal, `8` for octal, etc.). Detailed description of these functions is beyond the scope of this workbook. Please refer to your compiler's documentation or the system manual.

Structure

Back to the main topic: We will rewrite **main** program to use unformatted input and perform conversions by calling the appropriate conversion function. We will use a function called **input_record** to input one student record at a time to the array **student_records**.

Structures can be passed as arguments to functions, just like any ordinary variable. Structures can also be returned as the return value from functions. Return value can be assigned to a structure variable of the same type. C allows the assignment operator to be applied to structures. The following is a valid assignment:

```
student_records[5] = student_records[1];
```

When one structure variable is assigned to another, its members are copied, one by one, into the receiving structure. Thus the above assignment is equivalent to

```
strcpy(student_records[5].name, student_records[1].name);
student_records[5].id =  student_records[1].id;
student_records[5].classification =
                         student_records[1].classification;
student_records[5].gpa = student_records[1].gpa;
```

The rewritten program is shown below.

```
#include <stdio.h>
#include <stdlib.h>
#include <float.h>
#include "my_defs.h"       /* Our header file */
#include "student.h"       /* Our header file */

#define BSIZE    12        /* Size of buffer to hold string to
                            * be converted */
main()
{
   student student_records[NO_STUDENTS];
   char scratch[BSIZE]; /* Scratch variable */
   int index, ret_val;
   student input_record(void); /* For record entry */
   void print_record(student s);
```

```c
      for (index = 0; index < NO_STUDENTS; index++)
      {
         printf("****Record %d ****\n", index);
         /* Call function and assign the return value to
          * the appropriate index
          */
         student_records[index] = input_record();
         if (strlen(student_records[index].name) <= 1)
            break; /* User has terminated input */

#ifdef DEBUG
         /* Call function and pass it the student record
          * so that the callee may print it
          */
         print_record(student_records[index]);
#endif
      }
      exit(EXIT_SUCCESS);
}

/* Function input_record: Prompts the user for input and
 * enters input to the buffer supplied by main. Notice how
 * the input entry is terminated by checking for a carriage
 * return for the name entry
 */

student input_record(void)
{
   student s;
   char scratch[BSIZE]; /* Scratch variable */

   printf("Name? ");
   fgets(s.name, NAME_SIZE, stdin);
   if (strlen(s.name) <= 1)
   {
      /* User may have typed a new line, which is
       * converted to a null character (length 1)
       */
      return s; /* Out of the for loop */
```

```
            }
            printf("ID? ");
            fgets(scratch, BSIZE, stdin); /* Get the ID in
                                           *  string form */
            /* Convert from string to long using strtol */
            s.id = strtol(scratch, NULL, 10);
            /* Specify NULL for the second argument, since we
             * don't care to find out where the conversion ended.
             * Pass 10 as the base
             */
            printf("Status (0 = Freshman, 1 = Sophomore, \
    2 = Junior, 3 = Senior) ? ");
            fgets(scratch, BSIZE, stdin);
            /* Convert from ASCII to int */
            s.classification = (status) atoi(scratch);
            printf("GPA? ");
            fgets(scratch, BSIZE, stdin);
            /* Convert to float */
            s.gpa = (float) strtod(scratch, NULL);
            return s;
        }
```

11.1b Exercises

1 At the end of input, print all the student structures by using a function called **print_record**.

2 Print the number of students with a grade point average above 3.5.

11.1c Structures and files

It would be a lot more convenient to input all the student information into a text file and read from the file into the records. For example, we could create a text file called **STUDENT.TXT**, which contains a bunch of student records, as shown below:

```
Oxford Ox
12345678
0
```

```
2.3
Audry Owl
45612398
3
3.5
etc.
```

Note that the information in the file corresponds to the order in which we populate the records: name, ID, status and grade point average. We could modify our program, as shown below, to read the input from a file called **STUDENT.TXT**, which contains data, as shown above. We will also modify the function **input_record** to take input from a file. Thus we can use the same function to read input from **stdin** as well as a disk file.

```
#include <stdio.h>
#include <stdlib.h>
#include "my_defs.h"
#include "student.h"

#define BSIZE    12
#define INPUT    "STUDENT.TXT"   /* Input file */

main()
{
   void print_record(student s);
   student student_records[NO_STUDENTS];
   int index, ret_val;
   FILE *handle;
   student input_record(FILE *);

   if ( (handle = fopen(INPUT, "r")) == NULL)
   {
      perror(INPUT);
      exit(EXIT_FAILURE);
   }
   for (index = 0; index < NO_STUDENTS; index++)
   {
      student_records[index] = input_record(handle);
      if (strlen(student_records[index].name) <= 1)
         break; /* User has terminated input */
```

```c
#ifdef DEBUG
      /* For debugging, print the record */
      print_record(student_records[index]);
#endif
   }
   exit(EXIT_SUCCESS);
}

/* Function input_record: Reads input from a file, the
 * handle for which is supplied by main, and enters input
 * into the buffer supplied by main. Notice that since
 * the input may be coming from a disk file, we no longer
 * prompt. An exercise at the end of this section deals
 * with prompting the user if the handle is stdin
 */
student input_record(FILE *ihandle)
{
   char scratch[BSIZE]; /* Scratch variable */
   student s;

   /* Read the name */
   if (fgets(s.name, NAME_SIZE, ihandle) == NULL)
      return s;

   /* Read the ID */
   if (fgets(scratch, BSIZE, ihandle) == NULL)
   {
      s.name[0] = '\0'; /* Null out the name */
      return s;
   }

   /* Convert from string to long using strtol */
   s.id = strtol(scratch, NULL, 10);
   /* Read the status */
   if (fgets(scratch, BSIZE, ihandle) == NULL)
   {
      s.name[0] = '\0'; /* Null out the name */
      return s;
   }
```

```
        s.classification = (status) atoi(scratch);
        /* Read the gpa */
        if (fgets(scratch, BSIZE, ihandle) == NULL)
        {
            s.name[0] = '\0'; /* Null out the name */
            return s;
        }
        s.gpa = (float) strtod(scratch, NULL);
        return s;
    }
```

11.1d Exercise

Modify the function `input_record` to prompt the user so that we can input from the keyboard. A common way to do this is to pass another argument to `input_record` from the `main` to indicate whether prompting should be on or off.

11.1e Structures and binary files

The student data can be stored in files in binary format as well. If the information is stored in binary form, we can use the **fread** and the **fwrite** functions to read or write the record(s) directly into memory, without any input conversions. Reading and writing using binary format is more efficient. But the efficiency comes at the expense of portability. A binary file created on one machine cannot be used directly by a program running on a machine of a different architecture and operating system.

The next example shows how to create a binary file containing the student records by using **fwrite**. Reading the records by using **fread** will be left as an exercise for you.

```
/* File student.c: Reads input from the keyboard and
 * writes to a file called "STUDENT.DAT" in binary format.
 */
#include <stdio.h>
#include <stdlib.h>
#include "my_defs.h"
#include "student.h"
```

```
          #define    BSIZE       12
          #define    OUTFILE     "STUDENT.DAT"

          main()
          {
             void print_record(student s);
             student student_records[NO_STUDENTS];
             int index, ret_val;
             FILE *ofhandle;
             student input_record(FILE *);

             if ( (ofhandle = fopen(OUTFILE, "w")) == NULL)
             {
                perror(OUTFILE);
                exit(EXIT_FAILURE);
             }
             for (index = 0; index < NO_STUDENTS; index++)
             {
                printf("****Record %d ****\n", index);
                student_records[index] = input_record(ofhandle);
                if (strlen(student_records[index].name) <= 1)
                   break; /* User has terminated input */

#ifdef DEBUG
             /* For debugging, print the record */
             print_record(student_records[index]);
#endif

             } /* End for loop */
             /* At this point, all records have been input, and
              * index contains the number of records input.
              * Write all the records, in one shot, into the file
              */
             ret_val = fwrite((void *)student_records,
                              sizeof (student), index, ofhandle);
             if (ret_val != index)
             {
                perror("fwrite");
                exit(EXIT_FAILURE);
             }
```

```
        fclose(ofhandle);
        exit(EXIT_SUCCESS);
} /* Function input_record not shown: Use
   * from the previous exercise */
```

When the program shown above is compiled and run, it creates a binary file called **STUDENT.DAT** that contains all the records. Note that **fwrite** writes the entire array in one operation. Notice the use of the **sizeof** operator to get the size of one record.

11.1f Exercises

1. Write a program that reads the binary file created by the program shown above. Using **fread**, read the file into an array of structures. Use the return value from **fread** to count the number of individual records read. Make sure that you declare an array of structures large enough to hold all the records.

2. Design your own format and display the student records. At the end of the program, print the number of students with a grade point average greater than 3.5.

11.1g Structures and pointers

Pointers can be used with an array of structures the same way as with arrays of any other data type. When a pointer to a structure is used, individual members of the structure can be accessed through the *indirect member selection operator* (->).

Syntax **Member selection using a pointer to a structure**

`structure-ptr->member`

The following example shows how to traverse an array of structures by using a pointer.

Example **Accessing members through pointers**

```
/* Declarations */
student student_records[NO_STUDENTS]; /* The array */
```

```
    student *student_ptr;           /* A pointer */
    int index;

    student_ptr = student_records;  /* Initialize the pointer to
                                     * the beginning of array */
    for (index = 0; index < NO_STUDENTS; index++, student_ptr++)
    {
       printf ("Student name %s, GPA %3.2f\n",
               student_ptr->name, student_ptr->gpa);
    }
```

Recall that address arithmetic is different from integer arithmetic. Due to pointer arithmetic when we increment **student_p** by one, it points to the next record in the array. Thus

```
        student_ptr++   ≡   student_ptr + sizeof(student)
```

Amazing, isn't it?

The next example shows our earlier program which creates a binary file containing the records, rewritten with pointers.

```
#include <stdio.h>
#include <stdlib.h>
#include "my_defs.h"
#include "student.h"
#define BSIZE     12
#define OUTFILE   "STUDENT.DAT"

main()
{
   void print_record(student s);
   student student_records[NO_STUDENTS];
   student *student_ptr;
   int count = 0;
   int ret_val;
   FILE *ofhandle;
   int input_record(student *, FILE *);

   if ( (ofhandle = fopen(OUTFILE, "w")) == NULL)
   {
```

```c
            perror(OUTFILE);
            exit(EXIT_FAILURE);
        }
        student_ptr = student_records; /* Initialize pointer */
        while(1)
        {
            printf("****Record %d ****\n", count);
            ret_val = input_record(student_ptr, stdin);
            if (ret_val == 0)
                break;

#ifdef DEBUG
            print_record(*student_ptr);
            /* Note the * before student_ptr. Since the function
             * print_record expects the whole structure to be
             * passed, we take the contents at the address and pass
             * it.
             */
#endif
            student_ptr++; /* Point to the next array element */
            count++;       /* Increment count */
            if (count >= NO_STUDENTS)
            {
                fprintf(stderr, "No more room in array\n");
                break;
            }
        } /* End while */
        /* At this point, all records have been input (or
         * the array is full), and count contains the number
         * of records. Write all the records into the file
         */

         ret_val = fwrite((void *)student_records,
                         sizeof (student), count, ofhandle);
        if (ret_val != count)
        {
            perror("fwrite");
            exit(EXIT_FAILURE);
        }
        fclose(ofhandle);
```

```
        exit(EXIT_SUCCESS);
    }

    int input_record(student *stu_ptr, FILE *infile)
    {
        char scratch[BSIZE]; /* Scratch variable */
        printf("Name? ");
        fgets(stu_ptr->name, NAME_SIZE, infile);
        if (strlen(stu_ptr->name) <= 1)
            return 0;

        printf("ID? ");
        fgets(scratch, BSIZE, infile);
        stu_ptr->id = strtol(scratch, NULL, 10);
        printf("Status (0 = Freshman, 1 = Sophomore, \
    2 = Junior, 3 = Senior) ? ");
        fgets(scratch, BSIZE, infile);
        stu_ptr->classification = (status) atoi(scratch);
        printf("GPA? ");
        fgets(scratch, BSIZE, infile);
        stu_ptr->gpa = (float) strtod(scratch, NULL);
        return 1;
    }
    void print_record(student s)
    {
        char *standing[4] = { "FRESHMAN", "SOPHOMORE", "JUNIOR",
                              "SENIOR" };
        printf("Name: %s", s.name);
        printf("ID: %8d\t", s.id);
        printf("Academic Standing: %-24s",
                              standing[s.classification]);
        printf("GPA: %3.2f\n", s.gpa);
    }
```

11.1h Exercises

1 Modify the previous exercise to use a pointer to the array of structures.

2 Define a structure for an address record. The definition should contain the following fields:

```
First name, 12 characters
Last name, 12 characters
Street Address, 32 characters
City, 16 characters
State, 16 characters
Zip Code, 10 characters
Country, 16 characters
Telephone Number, 16 characters
```

Put the structure definition in a header file called **address.h**. Next, create a text file containing data in the following form:

```
Lastname, firstname
Street address
City, State, Zip Code
Country
Telephone Number
```

If any of the fields are omitted in the file, a blank line must be substituted in its place.

Next, write a program that reads input from the text file and fills in the array of records. After all the records have been input, print the addresses. Later, we will modify the program to build a full-fledged card file.

Notice that we will have to parse lines of input. For example, the name in our text file has the form

Lastname, firstname

We need to separate the line into its component fields, so that we can copy each field into the structure member. If you are tempted to run off and write a long and complicated parsing program, don't! There is a function in the standard library called `strtok` that will do all the parsing for us. The function `strtok` splits a string into a sequence of zero or more component strings (*tokens*), separated by a span of one or more characters from a delimiter string. The prototype of **strtok** is given below:

```
char *strtok(char *s1, char *s2);
```

In the above prototype, **s1** is the original string and **s2** is the string containing the delimiter characters.

The first call to **strtok** returns a pointer to the first token, properly appended with a null character at the end. If subsequent calls are for more tokens from the same string **s1**, the first argument to **strtok** must be **NULL**. It is possible to change the delimiter set each time **strtok** is called.

The following example shows how a line containing input of the form

```
Millington, New Jersey, 07903
```

can be parsed into a city, state and Zip code. After the input line has been read into your program using **fgets**, the buffer containing the line will appear as shown.

```
---------------------------------
|Millington, New Jersey, 07903\n|
---------------------------------
```

The token separators and valid calls to **strtok** to get pointers to the beginning of the tokens are

Order	Delimiter	Call
First time	,	strtok(buf, ",")
Second time	,	strtok(NULL, ",")
Third time	\n	strtok(NULL, "\n")

Compile and run the following program, and then incorporate it into your card file program.

```c
#include <stdio.h>
#include <string.h>
#include "my_defs.h"

main()
{
   char buf[80];    /* To read from keyboard */
   char *token_ptr; /* Token pointer */
   printf("Enter City, State, Zipcode: ");
   fgets(buf, 80, stdin); /* Read from stdin */
   /* The first token is the city, and the
    * delimiter is a comma (,)
    */
   token_ptr = strtok(buf, ","); /* First time */
   printf("city is %s\n", token_ptr);
   /* Next, read the state, using the same delimiter.
    * Since we are using the same string in buf,
    * the first argument should be a NULL
    */
   token_ptr = strtok(NULL, ",");
   printf("State is %s\n", token_ptr);
   /* Finally, read the Zip code. The new delimiter
    * is the new line character at the end of the string */
   token_ptr = strtok(NULL, "\n");
   printf("Zip code is %s\n", token_ptr);
}
```

Compiling and running the program, with the input line shown above, produces the following output:

```
Enter City, State, Zipcode: Millington, New Jersey, 07903
City is Millington
State is New Jersey
Zip code is 07903
```

To copy a token to a structure member, you may use **strcpy** or **strncpy**. Assuming that the array of structures is called **addresses** and that the member for holding a city name is called **city**, here is how you can copy a city field, parsed as shown above, into the structure.

Structure

```
        token_ptr = strtok(buf, ","); /* First time */
        printf("City is %s\n", token_ptr); /* Debug */
        /* Copy into structure member: up to 16 characters
         * or till a null character is encountered
         */
        strncpy(addresses[count].city, token_ptr, 16);
        addresses[count].city[15] = '\0'; /* Terminate with
                                           *  null character */
```

11.1i Structures as function arguments

Structures can be passed as function arguments the same way as other data types are passed: By value.

To print an individual record, we could employ a function called **print_record** with the following prototype:

```
        void print_record(student);
```

The function **print_record** may be written as shown in the following example:

Example **Structures as function arguments**

```
/* Function print_record: Prints one student record */
void print_record(student s)
{
    char *standing[4] = { "FRESHMAN", "SOPHOMORE", "JUNIOR",
                          "SENIOR" };
    printf("Name: %s", s.name);
    printf("ID: %8d\t", s.id);
    printf("Academic Standing: %-24s",

standing[(int)s.classification]);
    printf("GPA: %3.2f\n", s.gpa);
}
```

From the main program, the function **print_record** may be called as follows:

```
student student1;
input to student1
print_record(student1);
```

In the example shown above, call-by-value semantics apply, and the structure **student1** is *memberwise copied* into the formal parameter **s** in the callee function.

Note *If you have a non-ANSI C compiler and the statement shown below causes compilation problems*

```
char *standing[4] = { "FRESHMAN", "SOPHOMORE", "JUNIOR",
                      "SENIOR" };
```

move the statement out of the body of the function and place it on top of the file before the function name. Older C compilers do not allow automatic arrays to be initialized at run-time. You will learn about automatic variables in the next chapter.

If an array of structures needs to be passed to a function, call by value could be very inefficient. In this case, we will resort to our old trick of faking call by reference by passing the address of the array to the function.

The example below illustrates passing structures by reference. From the **main** function, we call a function named **honor_roll**, which scans through the array of records for students with grade point averages greater than or equal to 3.5. If a match is found, the function prints the names, GPAs and, at the end, the total count.

```
/* Function to count no. of students with GPA >= 3.5 */
void honor_roll(student_record *stp)
{
   int count, i;
   for (i = 0; i < NO_STUDENTS; i++, stp++)
   {
      if (stp->gpa >= 3.5)
      {
         printf("%s\t%f\n", stp->name, stp->gpa);
         count = count + 1;
      }
```

```
        }
        printf("%d students on honor roll\n", count);
}
```

From the main program, we can simply pass the name of the structure array as the argument to the function. Recall that the name of an array contains its address.

```
student student_records[100];
input values into the student record
honor_roll(student_records);
```

Note *The above program has a deliberate bug. Can you catch it by reading the code?*

11.1j Exercise

Write a function called `print_address` to print an address record. Use it from the `main` function to display the addresses after they have been input.

11.1k Searching through the records

Next, we will add a simple search feature to the database. After all the records have been read into memory, the program will ask you to enter a student's name. When the name is input, the program will scan the records for a matching name, and if a match is found, it will print the student's record.

Assuming that a file called **STUDENT.DAT** contains the student records, we will open the file and read the records into an array large enough to hold the records. Next, we will prompt the user to input a name. We will search the array for a matching name, and if found, we will call the function `print_record` to print the record.

The program is given below:

```
/* File search.c: Reads records from a file named
 * STUDENT.DAT into an array of structures. Next,
 * the program prompts the user for a name and if
 * found in the array records, it prints the record.
 */
```

```c
#include <stdio.h>
#include <stdlib.h>
#include "my_defs.h"
#include "student.h"
#define    INFILE    "STUDENT.DAT"

main()
{
   student student_records[NO_STUDENTS], *student_p;
   char buf[80];           /* To read keyboard input */
   int index, ret_val;
   FILE *ifhandle;
   void print_record(student);

   if ( (ifhandle = fopen(INFILE, "r")) == NULL)
   {
      perror(INFILE);
      exit(EXIT_FAILURE);
   }
   student_p = student_records; /* Initialize the pointer */
   ret_val = fread((void *)student_p, sizeof (student),
                    NO_STUDENTS, ifhandle);
   fprintf(stderr, "%d records read and initialized \n",
           ret_val);
   printf("Enter search name ");
   gets(buf); /* Note that gets null-terminates a line */
   for (index = 0; index < ret_val; index++, student_p++)
   {
      if (strncmp(buf, student_p->name, strlen(buf)) == 0)
      {
         fprintf(stderr, "Match found at index %d\n",
                 index);
         print_record(student_records[index]);
         exit(EXIT_SUCCESS);
      }
   }
   printf("Record for name %s was not found\n", buf);
   exit(EXIT_FAILURE);
}
/* Function print_record not shown */
```

Structure

11.1l Exercises

1 Modify the card file program as follows:

Implement a menu interface to the card file program. The menu should allow the user, given a first name or a last name, to search for an address. Search the database for matching records, and output all the records that match the names. A sample run of the program should be as follows:

```
$ cardfile
23 entries in the card file

    Options:
 1. Locate an address by first name
 2. Locate an address by last name

Enter selection: 2
Enter the last name: Kangaroo

*******************************************************
* Karen Kangaroo                                       *
* 78 Down Under Blvd.                                  *
* Outbackville, Canberra 100678                        *
* Australia                                            *
* 1-234-567-8901                                       *
*******************************************************
```

2 Modify the above program to ignore the case (upper or lower case) when searching for a match.

11.1m Structure containing structures

A structure definition may contain definition of other structures. However, a structure definition should not contain a variable of the type of the structure being defined. The following examples show valid and invalid structure definitions.

Example **Structure containing definition of another structure**

```
typedef struct address
{
   char street[32];
   char city[16];
   char state[16];
   char zip[10];
} address_t;  /* An address type */


typedef struct student
{
   char name[NAME_SIZE];
   ulong id;
   status classification;
   float gpa;
   address_t home; /* Valid. Different type of structure */
} student;
```

The above definition is valid, since a structure may contain a definition of another structure. To access a member of the nested structure, we can use the dot (.) operator, as before. For example, to input the street address, we can use the following statement:

```
student student1; /* Declare student1 of type student */
fgets(student1.home.street, 32, stdin);
```

The above statement selects the member **home** of **student** and further selects **street** of the **home** member of **student1**.

The following definition is invalid, since a structure may not contain an instance of itself.

```
typedef struct address
{
   char street[32];
   char city[16];
   char state[16];
```

```
      char zip[10];
      address_t dorm; /* Invalid. cannot contain
                       *  an instance of self */
} address_t;
```

However, structures are allowed to contain a pointer to themselves. Thus the following is a valid structure definition:

```
struct student
{
   char name[NAME_SIZE];
   ulong id;
   status classification;
   float gpa;
   address_t home;
   student *next; /* Valid: Pointer to a type student */
};
```

Structures containing pointers to themselves are useful for implementing such data structures as *linked lists*, a list containing a collection of records strung together using pointers. So far, we have been using an array to represent a collection of records. However, arrays have the limitation that all memory needed to hold the records has to be declared at compile time. But in practice, this is not often possible, as we cannot predict, *a priori*, the number of records in our program. Allocating a very large array in anticipation of the maximum number of records is impractical.

We will study dynamic memory allocation and linked lists in Chapter 13.

11.1n   **Exercise**

This exercise has been designed to show you how to use the numerous functions available in the standard library. Some of these functions expect structures as arguments and/or return structures or pointers to structures as the return value. While it is a tall order to show you examples of how these functions may be used, it is certainly necessary to show you how to read these function prototypes and use these functions correctly.

The C library provides a variety of functions to deal with *time*. For example, the function called `time` returns a value of type `time_t` (which is type-defined to `long` on most systems). The value returned by `time` is the current calendar time encoded as an integer value. The encoded time value is not comprehensible without processing through other functions. Compile and run the following small program to see the output from the `time` function.

```
#include <stdio.h>
#include <time.h>
main()
{
  time_t current_time; /* To hold return value */
  current_time = time(NULL);
  printf("Current time is %d\n", current_time);
}
```

To access the `time` function, the header file **time.h** must be included. The prototype of the time function is

```
time_t time(time_t *ptr);
```

The above declaration is to be read as follows:

> `time` is a function that takes an argument of type pointer to a `time_t` and returns a value of type `time_t`.

Thus, as an argument to the function, we must pass a pointer to a variable of type `time_t` (or the `NULL` pointer, as the case may be). We can assign the return value from `time` to a variable of type `time_t`. The description of the function mentions that the argument of the function is an *out parameter* that also stores the return value, for whatever reason (strange reasons, if you ask us!). We won't bother about the return through the out parameter and will pass a `NULL` pointer instead (which is allowed, according to the documentation).

The program shown above, when compiled and run on a Sun SPARCstation 1, produced the following output:

```
Current time is 716403098
```

The number displayed is usually the number of seconds elapsed since some arbitrary date in the past. January 1, 1970, is a popular choice among most UNIX systems. In any case, this number is not comprehensible, and we need to convert it into a more usable form. The function `localtime` comes to our rescue. The function **localtime** converts a time value returned by **time** and stores the decoded values in a structure of type **tm**, defined in the header file **time.h**. The structure definition is as shown:

```
struct tm
{
    int   tm_sec;
    int   tm_min;
    int   tm_hour;
    int   tm_mday;
    int   tm_mon;
    int   tm_year;
    int   tm_wday;
    int   tm_yday;
    int   tm_isdst;
    char  *tm_zone;
    long  tm_gmtoff;
};
```

The member **tm_sec** contains the seconds, **tm_min** contains the minutes, etc. (Read the documentation for a complete description of all fields.) Your job is to call the function **localtime** with the value returned by **time**, decode the structure returned by **localtime** and print the time as *min:sec, date, year*.

The prototype of **localtime** is as given below:

```
struct tm *localtime(time_t *t);
```

From the above prototype declaration, notice that the function **localtime** expects an argument of type **time_t**, which is the value returned by **time**. The return value is a pointer to **struct tm**. This pointer can be assigned to a variable of the same type, and the individual members of the structure can be accessed.

11.2 Unions

C provides a derived data type, called a *union*, that is used to hold objects of different types and sizes. This allows a memory location that holds a variable of a certain type to be treated as a different type in the program.

To understand where the **union** type may be used, consider the following example. We wish to modify the student record to add one more field: the address of the student. We will use a structure to define the address, as shown:

```
struct address
{
   char street[32];
   char city[16];
   char state[16];
   char zip[10];
};
```

But there is a problem. Students living in the dormitory have their address in a different format. For them, the address structure will look like

```
struct address
{
   char dormname[24];    /* Dorm name */
   char roomnum[7];      /* Room number */
};
```

How do we maintain these two addresses? That's where the **union** data type is useful. We can declare a **union** that is composed of the two definitions shown above. This allows us to access the address, either in the home address or dorm address format.

The syntax for defining a **union** data type is similar to that of a structure definition.

Syntax   **Union data type**

```
union union-name
{
    data-type variable-name1;
```

```
            data-type variable-name2;
            etc.
    };
```

Unlike structures, a union can contain only one of its member values at a time. An example will illustrate this more clearly. We will modify the two structure definitions shown above and turn them into a **union** as follows:

```
    /* Define a home address structure */
    struct off_campus
    {
       char street[32];
       char city[16];
       char state[16];
       char zip[10];
    };

    /* Define a dorm address structure */
    struct on_campus
    {
       char dormname[24];    /* Dorm name */
       char roomnum[7];      /* Room number */
    };
```

Next, we will define the union as

```
    union address
    {
      struct off_campus home;
      struct on_campus  dorm;
    };
```

We will use the **typedef** mechanism on unions, to make it more convenient.

```
    typedef union address
    {
      struct off_campus home;
      struct on_campus  dorm;
    } address_t; /* Define an address type */
```

Now, we will modify the student structure as follows. In addition to the fields defined so far, we also need a field to indicate which *type* of address is stored in the union: `off_campus` or `on_campus`. Create a new header file **student1.h** and put the following declarations in it.

```
/* Header file student1.h: contains the structure
 * templates and macros.
 */
typedef enum { FRESHMAN, SOPHOMORE, JUNIOR, SENIOR } status;
typedef enum {HOME, DORM} residence;
/* Define a home address structure */
struct off_campus
{
   char street[32];
   char city[16];
   char state[16];
   char zip[10];
};
/* Define a dorm address structure */
struct on_campus
{
   char dormname[24];    /* Dorm name */
   char roomnum[7];      /* Room number */
};

typedef union address
{
   struct off_campus home;
   struct on_campus  dorm;
} address_t; /* Define an address type */

#define NO_STUDENTS         30
#define NAME_SIZE           24

typedef struct student
{
   char      name[NAME_SIZE];
   ulong     id;
   status    classification;
```

```
        float     gpa;
        residence res_code;
        address_t location;
} student;
```

Once the structure has been defined, we can access and store information in either the dorm address format or the home address format. To access either, we use the dot operator (.).

```
student student1;
/* Input an address in dorm address format */
printf("Enter the dorm address ");
gets(student1.location.dorm.dormname);
printf("Enter the room number ");
gets(student1.location.dorm.roomnum);
```

Alternatively, we may use the home address format. Realize that for one record, we can use either the home address or the dorm address format, but not both. The **union** data type contains enough memory to hold the largest of its components, but not for the aggregate of the components. In the common memory, the individual components are overlaid.

The code for inputting the address information in the student record is shown below:

```
#include <stdio.h>
#include <stdlib.h>

#include "my_defs.h"
#include "student1.h" /* New header file */

main()
{
   char buf[80]; /* To read keyboard input */
   student student_records[NO_STUDENTS];
   int index;

   for (index = 0; index < NO_STUDENTS;index++)
   {
      /* Code for inputting all other members of the
       *  structure is the same as before and is not
```

```
             * shown here
             */
            printf("Enter address code (0 for HOME, \
    1 for DORM)? ");
            gets(buf);
            student_records[index].res_code =
                                        (residence) atoi(buf);
            /* Now depending on the code, enter address in
             * dorm format or home format
             */
            switch (student_records[index].res_code)
            {
               case HOME:
                printf("Street Address? ");
                gets(student_records[index].location.home.street);
                printf("City? ");
                gets(student_records[index].location.home.city);
                printf("State? ");
                gets(student_records[index].location.home.state);
                printf("Zip Code? ");
                gets(student_records[index].location.home.zip);
                break;
               case DORM:
                printf("Dorm Name? ");
                gets(student_records[index].location.dorm.dormname);
                printf("Room Number? ");
                gets(student_records[index].location.dorm.roomnum);
                break;
               default:
                printf("Invalid code: Skipping record\n");
                break;
            }   /* End switch */
       }  /* End for */
    }  /* End main */
```

Note how we access the member fields of the address structure. For example, the statements such as:

```
gets(student_records[index].location.home.state);
    or
gets(student_records[index].location.dorm.dormname);
```

11.2a Exercises

1. Incorporate the code shown above into the function **input_record**.

2. Write a function called **print_student**, which prints the student records, including the addresses, in the right format.

11.3 Common Problems

Common problems at this stage of program development are:

1. Syntactic errors due to the omission of the semicolon at the end of the structure definition.

2. When declaring a pointer to a structure it is often easy to overlook the fact that the pointer needs to be initialized to point to a valid structure in memory. It is incorrect to use a pointer to a structure as shown below:

    ```
    struct student *student_p;

    student_p->gpa = 3.5;
    ```

    Notice that the variable **student_p** does not contain any memory for the structure: *It is merely a pointer to a structure.* Before using the pointer, it must be initialized, as shown:

    ```
    struct student s, *student_p;

    student_p = &s;
    student_p->gpa = 3.5;
    ```

    In the example shown above, **s** contains the memory to hold the structure and **student_p** is initialized with the address of **s**.

3. Another common problem is the use of the dot operator where an indirect member selection operator may be necessary, and vice versa. The rule is quite simple: If the variable on the left-hand side of these operators is an aggregate (i.e., contains the whole structure), the dot operator is to be used. If the variable is a pointer to a structure, the indirect member selection operator is to be used, as shown below:

```
struct student s;              /* An aggregate */
struct student *student_p;     /* A pointer */

student_p = &s;                /* Initialize pointer */
s.gpa = 3.5;                   /* Dot operator for aggregate */
student_p->gpa = 3.5;          /* Selection operator
                                * for pointer */
```

4. Problems due to mixing **gets** and **fgets**. The function **gets** replaces the new line at the end of the input with a null character, whereas **fgets** appends a null character after the new line. Thus if you are searching for a name in the address structure (which was entered using **fgets**) by using a key value entered using **gets**, the match may never be found. The makeup of the two character strings will be as shown for the sample name "Oxford Ox":

```
Name read using fgets:   Oxford Ox\n\0
Name read using gets:    Oxford Ox\0
```

What is the solution? There are many:

- Stick consistently with one version of the function.

- Discard the new line before storing.

- Compare only up to **strlen** − 1 character.

12
Types of Memory

In our dealings with memory, in the form of variables, we were only concerned about one attribute: the type of the memory. The type (`int`, `float`, etc.) specifies what type of values may be stored in the variable. In C, the memory to hold the variables has one additional attribute, called its *storage class*. Depending on where the memory is allocated for a variable, the variable may exhibit different behavior.

So far, we have been declaring variables inside the body of the programs. Such variables are called *automatic variables*. Automatic variables have the important property that memory for the variables is created when their declaration is encountered inside a block (started with a {) and destroyed when the block is exited (ended with a matching }). C provides three additional storage classes, called `extern`, `static` and `register`. In this chapter, you will learn about the properties of these storage classes and how to use variables of these classes effectively.

12.1 Automatic Variables

Even though the keyword `auto` is new to us, the storage class `auto` is nothing new: We have been using `auto` variables all along. The storage class `auto` is applicable to variables that are declared within a block. Any variable declared within a block, without any key words affixed, are `auto` by default. Hence the key word `auto` is almost always omitted.

Example **Declaring `auto` variables**

```
{
    char c; /* Default is auto */
    int i, j, k;
    statements
}

/* Above declaration is same as */
{
    auto char c;
    auto int i, j, k;
    statements
}
```

The most important property of the `auto` storage class is that an `auto` variable is only created when the block which contains it is entered. Recall that a block begins with an open curly brace (`{`) and ends with a matching close brace (`}`). A block could be the start of a function body, the start of a `for`, `while` or `do` loop or `if-else` statement, or, simply, enclosing a set of statements. When a block is entered, memory is allocated for the variables declared inside the block (C permits variables to be declared inside any block but before any executable statements inside the block). Upon the block being exited, the memory allocated for the any variables inside the block is destroyed.

Thus, in the above example, memory for the variables `c`, `i`, `j`, and `k` is destroyed when the block is departed. Consequently, any values contained in these variables are lost. Next time the block is reentered, the variables will not contain their previous values.

The compiler allocates the memory for holding an `auto` variable in a temporary region (called a *stack*). The contents of this memory are not automatically initialized to zeros. Thus when a function is entered, unless you explicitly initialize the variables yourselves, the `auto` variables in your programs will contain garbage values.

The following examples show incorrect and correct versions of a program that uses `auto` variables.

Automatic Variables

```
/* Program that computes the sum of numbers 1 to N */
main()
{
   int number, sum;

   printf("Enter the number :");
   scanf("%d", &number);

   do
   {
      sum = sum + number;
      number--;
   } while (number > 0);
}
```

By reading the program, can you tell if there is anything wrong with it? If not, try running **lint** on the program for a hint. The problem of course is that in the line

```
sum = sum + number;
```

the initial value of **sum** is undefined.

Compile and run the program for smaller inputs so that you can verify the result. You may get correct results if you are lucky! To be precise, you might get correct results if the memory area where **sum** was allocated *happened to contain a zero*. But since memory is allocated from a temporary area, which could change each time the program is run, there is no guarantee that once you get a zero in that memory location, you will always get a zero. In short, this program may work on Wednesdays and Tuesdays but never on Monday afternoon when your boss is looking or when you submit the assignment and the teacher's assistant runs it.

Note *Forgetting to initialize automatic variables is the number-one cause of bugs in C programs. Even experienced programmers fall prey to this, sometime or other, in their programming careers.*

The correct version of the above program is:

```
/* Program that computes the sum of numbers 1 to N */
main()
{
   int number, sum = 0;   /* Initialize sum */

   printf("Enter the number :");
   scanf("%d", &number);
   do
   {
      sum = sum + number;
      number--;
   } while(number > 0);
}
```

12.2 External Variables

So far, the only kind of variables that we have seen are automatic variables, declared within the body of a function. Memory for storing these variables is tied closely with the block in which the variables are declared (recall Figure 10.2 for call by value) and are inaccessible to any statement outside the block. The *visibility* of these variables is said to be limited to within the *scope* of the block in which they are declared.

Definition **Visibility**

Visibility of a variable defines whether you can access the value of the variable from elsewhere in the program, from other functions, within or outside the source file in which the variable is declared.

Definition **Scope**

The scope of a variable/function is defined as its visibility with respect to the rest of the program.

External variables define another class of storage. External variables are variables declared outside any block (including function definitions). Memory for variables declared outside any block is allocated once and remains allocated for the life of the program. Any value placed in such a variable remains available until it is overwritten. Since they are not "tied" to any one

External Variables

function, these variables are visible to all the functions in the program. Due to their global visibility, they are also called *global variables*.

Declaring external variables is quite simple: Declare the variable outside any block.

Example **Declaring external variables**

```
int Value1, Value2; /* External variables */
main()
{
   local (auto) declarations
   statements
   Value1 = random() % 20;
   Value2 = random() % 20;
   etc.
}
```

To access an external variable, functions in the same file in which the variable is declared need not make any further declaration (assuming that the external variable's definition is *before* any statement that uses it). Otherwise, to access the external variable, the variable must be declared, and the declaration must be prefixed with the key word **extern**. This tells the compiler that the variable has been defined (allocated memory) elsewhere and not to allocate private (**auto**) memory for the variable. When all the files are compiled and linked together, the *link editor* will ensure that all references to the variable are directed to the same global memory location.

In this text, we will always redeclare any external memory explicitly, by using the key word **extern**, even if it may not be technically necessary. This is a good practice to follow, as we can tell by reading a declaration which variables are global. Also, note that we chose to capitalize the first letter in the names of the global variables. This is a convention that we will follow in this text to distinguish global variables from all other types of variables.

12.2a Functions and external variables

Since external variables can be accessed by statements inside any function, they provide a means of sharing information between functions without passing them as arguments. Thus, external variables provide an alternative to function arguments and return values. To use external variables in place of function arguments, all we need do is declare the variables externally and access them from inside any function.

Variables **value1** and **value2** in the function **foo** are the same as the variables **value1** and **value2** in **main**.

The following program illustrates how we can implement the function **swap** by using external variables in place of arguments.

```
int First, Second;   /* Global variables */


main()
{
    extern int First, Second;
    void swap(void);

    /* Assign some values to First and Second */
    First = 24;
    Second = 46;
    printf("Before swap: First = %d, Second = %d\n",
            First, Second);
    swap(); /* Notice: no arguments */
    printf("After swap: First = %d, Second = %d\n",
            First, Second);
}

void swap(void)   /* Notice: no arguments */
{
    int temp; /* A local variable */
    extern int First, Second;

    temp = First;
    First = Second;
    Second = temp;
}
```

Figure 12.1 illustrates how the storage allocated to the external variable is accessed by both **main** and the function **swap** to effect the exchange of the two values.

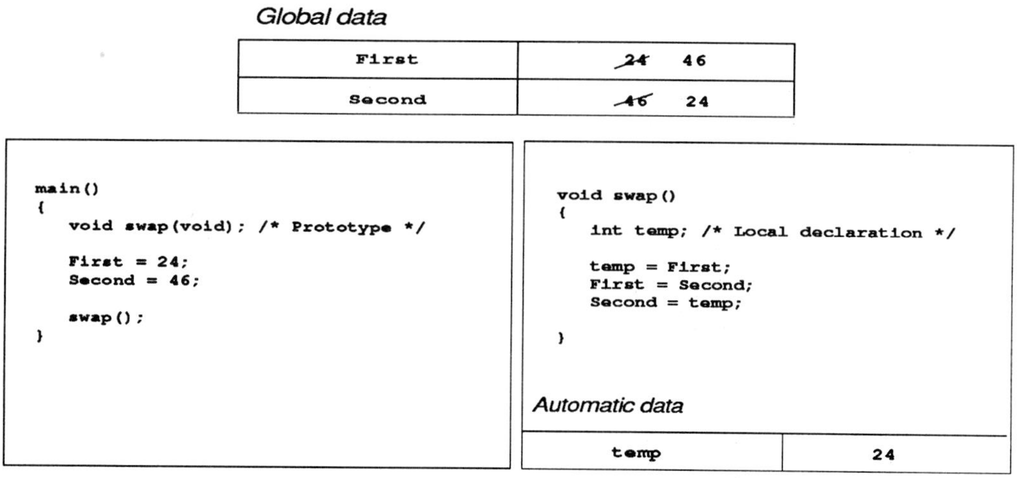

External Variables

Global data

| First | ~~24~~ 46 |
| Second | ~~46~~ 24 |

```
main()
{
    void swap(void); /* Prototype */

    First = 24;
    Second = 46;

    swap();
}
```

```
void swap()
{
    int temp; /* Local declaration */

    temp = First;
    First = Second;
    Second = temp;
}
```

Automatic data

| temp | 24 |

Figure 12.1 Global variables in place of arguments.

The following example illustrates how we can use external variables to avoid the copying overhead of passing by value. The **main** function fills in a global array and then calls a function, called **average_score**, to compute the average test scores. We wrote two versions of the function **average_score**, in Chapter 10. In this program, we will write a third version and use external variables.

```
#include <stdio.h>
#define NO_STUDENTS 12

int grades[NO_STUDENTS];   /* Global array */

main()
{
    int *gradesp;
    int index;
    int average_score(void);/* Function to compute average */

    gradesp = grades; /* Initialize the pointer */
    for (index = 0; index < NO_STUDENTS; index++)
    {
        printf("Enter Grade for Student %d ",index);
```

```
        scanf("%d",gradesp++);
    }
    printf("The average score is %d\n", average_score());
}

/* Version 3, using external variables */
int average_score(void)
{
    int index, sum;
    int *gradesp; /* Pointer to array grades */

    gradesp = grades; /* Initialize the pointer */
    for (index = 0, sum = 0; index < NO_STUDENTS; index ++)
    {
        sum = sum + *gradesp++;
    }
    return (sum / NO_STUDENTS);
}
```

Functions are always external. That is, in a program consisting of multiple files, any function is visible to any other function and can be called from anywhere. To compile a program file that contains a call to a function in another file, we can declare the function to be **extern** and later link the files together to make the executable program.

Even though global variables are a convenient alternative to function arguments, using external variables for functions is not always safe. Since every function in the program has access to the variable, it may be inadvertently modified by other functions. Thus it is not a good idea to always use global variables as a substitute for function arguments. A common and acceptable use of global variables is to set a value in a variable that may be used by many functions. For example, if we set a character string with the current date, functions using the date in a print string may look at the value of the date variable without issuing a call each time the date is needed.

12.2b Exercises

1 Modify the statistics program, which we wrote earlier, to eliminate the numerous arguments that we pass to the function **print_data**, and, instead, use global variables.

12.3 Storage Class `register`

2 Write version 4 of the `average_score` function to use array subscripts and external variables.

3 Write a function called `get_random_pair`, which, when called, places the largest of two random numbers in a global variable called `High` and the smallest in a variable called `Low`. Use the `get_random_pair` function to implement the math tutor program.

C provides a storage class called `register` that can be used to speed up execution in time-critical applications. Certain variables that are used heavily in programs (such as loop variables) can be placed in high-speed registers in the CPU, if possible, by instructing the compiler to do so.

The following program illustrates how we may attempt to speed up the execution of a program by requesting the compiler to place in a register a variable that is heavily used.

Example Using a `register` variable

```
/* Since loop variable i will be accessed many
 * times, place i in a register if possible */
register int i;
for (i = 0; i <large_value; i++)
{
    statement-list
}
```

The `register` declaration indicates to the compiler that the programmer wishes the value of the variable to be stored in high-speed memory register, provided it is possible to do so. The number of registers available depends on the machine architecture. Thus, there is no guarantee that the variable will actually be placed in a register. If the compiler cannot place the value in a register, the declaration defaults to `auto`.

Note *It is not possible to take the address of a register variable.*

12.4 Storage Class `static`

The next and perhaps most interesting storage class is `static`. The storage class `static` has two interesting properties:
- Declared within a block, it allows the variable to retain its value, even when the block is exited (contrast this with `auto` variables). In this sense, a `static` variable looks like an `auto` variable but acts like a global variable.
- The `static` variables and functions declared in a program file are only visible to the functions within that file (`static` variables declared inside a block are only visible within that block, anyway). An external `static` variable (a static variable declared outside any function block) declared in a program file is not accessible from any other file. This hiding provides a convenient mechanism whereby functions in one source file may share some external variables without risking their modification by other functions in the rest of the program.

The declaration of a `static` variable or function is shown below:

Syntax **Static variables and functions**

```
static data-type variable-name
;    or
static data-type function-declaration;
```

Example **Declaring static variables**

```
static int value;  /* A static int variable */
static void my_func(void);  /* A static function */
static char buffer[100];    /* A static character array */
```

The following example illustrates the use of a `static` array that retains its value between function calls. The program uses a function called `parse` that returns a word separated by a delimiter into an array specified by the caller. The prototype of `parse` is

```
void parse(char *string, char delimiter, char *dest_buffer);
```

where `string` is the original buffer containing the string to be parsed, `delimiter` is a one-character delimiter between words and `dest_buffer` is an array to hold the word. Each time the function **parse** is called, **parse** needs to "remember" where it was the last time **parse** was called. This is accomplished by using a **static** array that contains the string to be parsed and a static pointer that indicates the end of the last word returned to the user.

To parse a string into component words, the function **parse** is called with the **string** as the first argument. To continue parsing the same string, the function **parse** is to be called with **NULL** as the first argument so that **parse** may continue from where it left off last time. The function **parse** is shown below:

```
#include <stdio.h>
#include <string.h>

void parse(char *string, char delimiter, char *dest)
{
    static char buf[1024];   /* To hold the string
                              * to be parsed */
    static char *bufptr;     /* To keep track of the
                              * current pointer */
    int i, length;           /* Local variables */

    /* Copy the string into a static buffer */
    if (string != NULL)
    { /* New string to be parsed */
      strcpy(buf, string); /* Copy string to own buffer */
      bufptr = buf; /* Set bufptr to beginning of string */
    }
    /* Otherwise, use the previous value of bufptr */
    length = strlen(bufptr); /* Length of remaining string */
    /* Look for delimiter in the string */
    printf("Unprocessed string is \"%s\", length %d\n",
            bufptr, length);
    for (i = 0; i < length; i++)
    {
       if (*bufptr == delimiter)
       {
         bufptr++; /* Advance past the delimiter */
         break; /* If delimiter found */
       }
```

```
        /* Otherwise, copy character to destination string */
        *dest++ = *bufptr++; /* Increment after copying */
} /* End for loop */
/* String length depleted or delimiter found */
*dest = '\0'; /* End with null character */
}
```

Now, a sample main program to show the usage of the **parse** function.

```
main()
{
   char *test = "A test string";
   char buf[24]; /* To hold a word */

   /* Initialize parse with the string */
   parse(test, ' ', buf); /* Get word separated
                           * by blank, in buf */
   printf("got string: %s\n", buf); /* Debug */
   /* To parse the same string, use NULL
    * as first argument */
   do
   {
      parse(NULL, ' ', buf);
      printf("Got word: %s\n", buf);
   } while (buf[0] != '\0');
}
```

Compiling and running the program gives the following output:

```
Unprocessed string is "A test string", length 13
Got word: A
Unprocessed string is "test string", length 11
Got word: test
Unprocessed string is "string", length 6
Got word: string
Unprocessed string is "", length 0
Got word:
```

The array **buf** retains its contents across function calls. The pointer variable **bufptr** retains the position of the array past the last word returned.

Note   *The function* `strtok` *available in the standard library is a more advanced version of the* `parse` *function shown above.*

The next example shows how to generate our own random numbers by using the *linear congruential method.*[*] In this algorithm, successive numbers in the random sequence are generated by the recurrence relation:

$$x_{n+1} = (ax_n + c) \% m, \quad n >= 0$$

The initial value x_0 is known as the *seed*, the constant `a` is the *multiplier*, the constant `c` is the *increment*, `%` is the modulus operator and, `m`, the *modulus*. The selection of values for these constants has a dramatic effect on the *quality* of the random numbers generated. We will take the mathematicians' word for it and use values that have been found to produce good random numbers.

Note that the algorithm computes a random number by using the previous value of the random number and applying the multiplier, the increment and the modulus. Thus if we were to use a function called `my_random` to generate the random number, the previous random number generated must be accessible to the function. To jump-start the random number generator, we will use an initial `seed value` as the value of x_0. Once we compute a random number, we will use that as the seed for the next number.

If the seed is declared as a local variable in the function `my_random`, its value will be lost when the function call returns. The choices are between making the seed variable a static and a global. Since the `static` variable cannot be accessed from outside the file in which it is contained, the correct choice is `static`, as it offers more security than global variables.

```
/* File myrand.c: Pseudo-random number generator using the
 * linear congruential method
 */

/* Define constants for multiplier, increment and modulus */
#include <stdio.h>
```

---

[*] Lehmer, D. H., *Proceedings of the Second Symposium on Large-Scale Digital Computing Machinery,* Cambridge, Mass.: Harvard University Press, 1951.

```
#include <limits.h>

#define    MULTIPLIER     65541
#define    INCREMENT      65539
#define    MODULUS        INT_MAX
#define    INITIAL_SEED   255

/* Code for my_random */
int my_random(void)
{
   static unsigned int random_value = INITIAL_SEED;

   random_value = (MULTIPLIER * random_value + INCREMENT)
                       % MODULUS;
   return (random_value);
}
```

Now, from the main program, we can call the function **my_random** to return a random number.

```
main()
{
   register int i;
   int random1, random2;
   int my_random(void);
   random1 = my_random() % 20;
   random2 = my_random() % 20;
   statement-list
}
```

In the function **my_random**, notice the line

```
static unsigned int random_value = INITIAL_SEED;
```

It would appear that each time the function **my_random** gets called, this line would be executed, resetting the value of variable **random_value** to **INITIAL_SEED**. If that were the case, then we would end up with the same random number every time, and that would not be very random at all!

Luckily, the property of static variables states that the next time the function is reentered, the previous value will be retained. So the second time the function `my_random` is called, the *value from the previous invocation is retained in the variable*. Thus a new random number will be generated each time the function `my_random` is invoked.

Static variables are similar to global variables in that the memory holding the variables is created on a global area and is not destroyed when the block that contains the variable is exited. The initialization is performed once, when the memory is created, and is not performed each time the block is entered. Thus the static variable *looks like an* `auto` variable but *acts like* a global variable. Since the `static` variable can be declared inside a block (unlike global variables, which are declared outside any block), it does not have global visibility like external variables.

A static variable can also be declared outside any block. If it is declared outside any block, it becomes similar to external variables and is accessible by other functions.

But the second property of static variables guarantees that the variables will be visible only to functions in the same file in which they are declared.

Functions also can be declared as static. If a function is declared `static`, it can only be invoked from the source file in which the code for the function is contained.

12.4a Exercises

1. Compile and run the random number program. Change the declaration of the variable `random_value` from `static` to `auto`. Compile and run the program again to see its effect.

2. Reimplement the function `my_random` so that you don't have to use a static variable at all yet get random numbers on each invocation of the function.

3. Modify the function `parse` to take care of removing multiple delimiters of the same type separating two words. For example, you should be able to parse the following string correctly:

    ```
    "A     test     string"
    ```

into component words "A", "test" and "string".

12.5 Scope Rules

Since we are on the topic of figuring out who has access to what variable/function, this is the right place to talk about C's *scope rules*. As mentioned before, the scope of a variable/function is defined as its visibility with respect to the rest of the program.

Visibility of a variable defines whether you can access the value of the variable from elsewhere in the program, from other functions, within or outside the source file in which the variable is declared. If you access a variable declared outside your block and the variable is *not visible* to you, an error message will be issued by the compiler or when the program is linked together to make an executable file.

Using the storage classes discussed in this chapter, we can limit the visibility of variables, as shown below.

12.5a Global visibility

Global variables are accessible from the rest of the program. Functions have global visibility. To achieve global visibility, variables need to be declared outside any block. To access the variables or the functions from elsewhere, you can redeclare them, as **extern** prior to access. This is shown below in Figure 12.2.

12.5b Block visibility

The visibility of **auto** variables is limited to the block in which they are declared.

```
{
    block-declarations    /* Visible to all statements in
    statements             * this block only */
}
```

```
global-declarations          extern {necessary global
main()                         declarations}
{                            /* Globally declared variables
    local-declarations        * from File 1 are accessible
    statements                * from these functions
}                             */
                             func2()
func1()                      {
{                                local-declarations
    local-declarations           statements
    statements               }
}
```

Figure 12.2 Illustrating global visibility.

Auto variables introduce interesting scoping problems. To explain this, let us review C's block-structured nature.

Since C is a block-structured language, the programmer can introduce a new block anywhere in the program.

A block is a set of statements enclosed within a pair of curly braces. We have seen the blocks that enclose the function body inside which we declare all our local variables. We have also used blocks that associate a set of statements with a loop structure such as the **while** statement or a decision-making construct such as the **if** statement. In this case, we used the block as a means to bind more than one statement with the **while** loop or the **if** statement.

```
foo()
{
   /* Outer block in a function */
   local declarations
   while (...)
   {
      /* Inner block */
      statements
      if (...)
```

```
            {
                /* Innermost block */
                statements
            } /* End innermost block */
        } /* End inner block */
    } /* End outer block */
```

Binding a set of statements to a construct is not the only capability that the block-structured nature of the language provides. Each time a block is entered, a new *activation record* is created, which, among other things, contains the memory for local variables within that block. What that signifies is that any time a block is started, variables can be declared in the block. For example, the following is valid in C:

```
void foo()
{
    int count;
    statements
    {   /* Start a new block */
        int count; /* New local variable */
        statements
    }
}
```

The memory for the inner variable count is distinct from the memory for the outer variable count. This naturally paves the way for the following question: When we access count in the function foo, which count are we accessing?

The answer is simply this: *It depends*. It depends on where in the program we are accessing count. Sounds complicated? It isn't. The basic rule is simple:

Identifiers are accessible only within the block in which they are declared.

Thus in the above program, when we access count in the inner block, we are accessing the inner variable count. Outside that block (above the inner block or below it), we will be accessing the outer variable count. Let us illustrate this with the aid of a simple program. Compile and run this program, and verify the results. Write the output values next to the statement that prints it.

Example   Illustrating block visibility

```
main()
{
   int a = 5;                /* Outer block a */
   printf("a contains %d\n", a);
   {
      int a = 2;             /* Inner block a */
      printf("a contains %d\n", a);
   }
   printf("a * a = %d\n", a*a);
}
```

When a block is exited (upon encountering the closing "}"), the activation record for the block is destroyed and all the memory allocated for the variables in that block will be freed. Thus, in the above example, once we exit the inner block, the variable **a** that we access is, once again, the outer variable **a**.

Note   *In reality, no one should be writing programs like the example shown above. The example is meant for illustrative purposes only. If you need to allocate a variable in the inner block, choose a name that does not conflict with any other variable name within the same function.*

12.5c   File visibility

We can limit the visibility of variables and functions to the files they are declared in by using the storage class **static**. To limit the visibility of variables to a file, declare them as **static** and place them outside any block. To limit the visibility of functions to a file, simply append the key word **static** before the function header.

12.5d   Storage classes: A complete example

The next example illustrates using all the storage classes we studied in this chapter. In this example, we develop the stubs for a generalized unit conversion program. When the program runs, it issues a prompt and the user can type a command line of the form

```
unit to unit
```

and the program will display the conversion from the first unit to the second. A sample session is shown below:

```
$ unit
units> inch to cm
To convert from inches to centimeters, multiply centimeters
by 2.54
units>
```

To implement the unit conversion program, we use a technique that you haven't seen before. We will create a structure that contains a *pointer to a function* as the first member and a string containing the type of conversion as the second member. When the user types a conversion command, we use the command string to search an array of structures, comparing the second member of each element to the command. If a match is found, we invoke the function whose pointer is in the first member. This requires that we be able to store a function pointer as a variable member of the structure, initialize the variable with a function name and invoke the function indirectly. To parse the line typed by the user, we use the function **parse** that we developed earlier in this chapter.

To declare a variable as a pointer to a function, the **typedef** mechanism can be employed:

Example   **Declaring a variable to be a pointer to a function**

```
extern void my_function(void)
typedef void (*function_name)();

function_name ptr_to_fn;
ptr_to_fn = my_function;
```

Read the above **typedef** as

```
function_name is a      /* Start with the name */
    pointer to a        /* Cannot go right due to (),
                         * so go left */
    function returning a /* After (), go right */
        void
```

Thus the name **function_name** has been defined as a data type that stands for a pointer to a function returning a void. Now, variables of type **function_name** can be declared.

```
function_name   ptr_to_fn;
```

This declaration declares a variable called **ptr_to_fn** to be of type **function_name**. Now, the variable can be initialized to contain the pointer to a function of the same type, as shown:

```
ptr_to_fn = my_function;
```

The statement shown above assumes that you have already declared a function called **my_function**, which returns a **void** (returns nothing). Just like arrays, the name of a function indicates its starting address (i.e., where it is loaded in memory). The function **my_function** is as shown:

```
void my_function()
{
    code implementing my_function
}
```

Notice that in the initialization

```
ptr_to_fn = my_function;
```

the parentheses enclosing the arguments are missing. If the parentheses are placed, this implies an actual function call, which causes a type mismatch. The type of the variable on the left-hand side is **function_name** and the type of the variable on the right-hand side is **void** (which is the type of the return value of the function).

Now, to invoke the function indirectly, using the pointer variable, we can use the following form:

```
(*ptr_to_fn)();
```

Back to our units program. Shown below is the definition of the command structure:

```
typedef  void (*FNPTR)();  /* FNPTR is a pointer to a
                            * function returning void */

typedef  char FNAME[24];   /* FNAME is a an array of 24
                            * characters */

typedef struct table
{
   FNPTR func_addr; /* Func_addr is of type FNPTR */
   FNAME func_name; /* Func name is of type FNAME */
} func_table;
```

The complete program is shown below. First, we write two functions that display the conversion from inches to centimeters and centimeters to inches.

```
void inch_to_cm()
{
   printf("To convert from inches to centimeters, \
multiply inches by 2.54\n");
}

void cm_to_inch()
{
   printf("To convert from centimeters to inches, \
divide centimeters by 2.54\n");
}
```

Next is a function called **init_func_table**, which initializes the command structure. Since the command array needs to be accessed from the **main** as well as **init_func_table**, we declare the command structure array as global and static.

```
static func_table functions[20]; /* A global structure
                                  * array */
static int count;    /* Global, indicating number
                      * of entries */

void init_func_table()
{
   extern static func_table functions[];
   extern static int count;
```

Scope Rules

```
        strcpy(functions[0].func_name,"inchtocm");
        functions[0].func_addr = inch_to_cm;
        strcpy(functions[1].func_name,"cmtoinch");
        functions[1].func_addr = cm_to_inch;
        /* If more functions are added, update count */
        count = 2;
}
```

The **main** function is shown next.

```
main()
{
    char buf[80];  /* To read input from user */
    char word[20]; /* To store a parsed word */
    char match_buf[80]; /* To create a match string */
    int length, i;
    void init_func_table(); /* Prototype declaration */
    extern void parse(char *, char, char *); /* Prototype */

    init_func_table(); /* Initialize command array */
    while(1)
    {
       printf("units> "); /* Prompt */
       gets(buf); /* Read input */
       if (strlen(buf) <= 1)
          break; /* Exit, if user typed carriage return */

       length = 0;
       /* Next, we parse the line input by the user,
        * which is of the form:
        *      unit to unit
        */
       parse(buf, ' ', word); /* Get the first unit */
       memset(match_buf,'\0',80); /* Zero out the
                                   * match_buf */
       strcpy(match_buf, word); /* Copy first word
                                 * into match_buf */
       length = strlen(word);   /* Count length of
                                 * first word */
```

```
            parse(NULL, ' ', word); /* Get the next word */
            strcat(match_buf+length, word); /* Put at the end
                                             * of previous */
            length = length + strlen(word); /* Count the
                                             * new length */
            parse(NULL, ' ', word); /* Get the next word */
            strcat(match_buf+length, word); /* Put at the end */
            puts(match_buf); /* Debug statement */
            /* We now have a string that we can use
             * to search the command array for a match.
             * At this point, an input such as
             *        inch to cm
             * has been modified to inchtocm in match_buf
             */
            /* Search for a match in command array */
            for (i = 0; i < count; i++)
            {
               if (strncmp(match_buf, functions[i].func_name,
                                    strlen(match_buf)) == 0)
                  {
                     (*functions[i].func_addr)(); /* Call the
                                                   * function */
                     break; /* Get out of for loop */
                  }
            }
            if (i == count)
               printf("Conversion not found\n");
      } /* End while loop */
      exit(EXIT_SUCCESS);
}
```

Note that it is possible to initialize a variable to hold a function address at compile time, as opposed to run-time. Often, it is practical to create a table containing function pointers at compile time and use the table to call the appropriate function, at run-time. The following small program illustrates how a table containing function pointers can be initialized at compile time.

```
int function_a(int arg1)
{
   /* Code for function_a */
```

```
      printf("function_a called with arg %d\n", arg1);
      return 0;
}

int function_b(int arg2)
{
   /* Code for function_b */
   printf("function_b called with arg %d\n", arg2);
   return 0;
}

typedef int (*FNPTR)(int);
/* FNPTR is a pointer to a function which
 * takes an int argument and returns an int
 */
/* Initialize at compile time */
FNPTR table[2] = { function_a, function_b };

main()
{
   int i;
   for (i = 0; i < 2; i++)
   {
      /* Call the function indirectly */
      (*table[i])(i);
   }
}
```

When the program is compiled and run, it will produce the following output:

```
function_a called with arg 0
function_b called with arg 1
```

If the element of the table is a structure, it is still possible to initialize the member fields at compile time. For example, we can initialize the table **functions**, at compile time, as follows:

```
static func_table functions[] = { {"inchtocm", inch_to_cm},
                                  {"cmtoinch", cm_to_inch} };
```

Note that within each inner set of curly braces, we supply the values to the structure members in the order in which we declared the members.

What is the advantage of compile-time initialization? Quite simply, it saves some time in the execution speed of the program, since most of the work is done while the program is compiling. It also makes the program somewhat more readable, since we can see the declarations at the top of the program listing.

12.5e Exercises

1. Modify the files **stats.c** and **statmain.c** to use global variables called **Min** and **Max**, which contain the minimum and maximum of all values seen so far. Declare these variables in **statmain.c**, and use these variables in the file **stats.c**. Compile these files and link them together to make a new executable file and test your program.

2. Change the declaration of the variables **Min** and **Max** to **static**. Compile and run the program. What happens?

3. Modify the units program as described below:

   a. Add one more field to the command structure to include a verbose description of the type of conversion. Initialize the new member at initialization time. If the user types a conversion for which a match cannot be found, call a function called **print_help_table** that prints the description of all types of conversions implemented by the program.

   b. Add more conversions to the table: kilometers to miles, miles to kilometers, Fahrenheit to Celsius, etc.

   c. Modify the individual functions that display the conversion method to accept an integer argument corresponding to a value to be converted. For example, the user should be able to perform the following:

   ```
   $ units
   units> inch to cm 4
   4 inches equals 10.064 cm (inch times 2.54)
   ```

12.5f   Quick sort: A complete example

In this example, we will use quick sort to sort arrays of elements. The quick-sort algorithm sorts an array of elements *in place*. That is, there is no extra space required to sort the array (such as another array to hold elements to be sorted). Rather than writing our own algorithm, we will use the **qsort** function provided by the C library. The **qsort** function is very versatile: You just tell it how to compare two elements, and it will do the rest of the work. This is achieved by writing a function that compares two elements (of any type) and passing the name of the function (its address) to **qsort**.

Since it is our responsibility to write the function to compare two elements, the elements can be of any type. Thus we can use the **qsort** function to sort arrays of integers, floating point numbers, strings or even structures. In this example, we will show you how to sort an array of **float**s and an array of strings (a list of names). In the following exercise, you will sort an array of structures.

The prototype for **qsort** is shown below:

```
void qsort(const void *array_base,
           size_t count, size_t width,
           int (*comparison_function) (const void *e1,
                                       cont void *e2) );
```

The prototype looks pretty complicated, but when you use the function, it isn't all that bad! Here is what the arguments mean:

array_base: The beginning of the array containing the elements to be sorted.

count: The number of elements in the array.

width: The size, in bytes, of each element of the array.

comparison_function and arguments *e1* and *e2*: The name of the function, supplied by the user (that's you!), that is used for comparing two items of the array. This function must return an integer value less than zero, zero, or greater than zero, depending on if the first item *e1* is less than, equal to, or greater than the second item *e2*.

Let's write the program, and you will see that things are not as complicated as it sounds here. First, we write a program to sort an arrays of **float**s. We start with the comparison function that we must write:

```
#include <stdio.h>
#include <stdlib.h>

/* Function to compare two floating point values */
int float_compare(float *first, float *second)
{
   if (*first < *second)
       return(-1);
   if (*first > *second)
       return(1);
   return(0); /* Must be equal */
}

/* Next, the main program to test the sorting */
main()
{
   int i;
   /* Create an array, for testing */
   float farray[10] = { 34.6, 18.3, 0.36, 100.0, 12.2,
                        19.3, 3.14, 0.3786, 9.9, 236.78 };
   /* Next, call qsort to sort the array, in-place */
   qsort(farray, 10, sizeof(float), float_compare);
   /* After qsort returns, the array is sorted. Print out
    * for testing
    */
   for(i = 0; i   10; i++)
   {
      printf("%f\n", farray[i]);
   }
}
```

Notice how the arguments are passed in the call to **qsort**. Who calls our function **float_compare**? The answer is: **qsort** does. When **qsort** calls

float_compare, it will pass two elements of the array at a time. Since **qsort** has no idea of the type of the elements, it assumes that it is a pointer to a void (**void *e1, void *e2**, in the prototype). But since we declared the incoming parameters to be of type **float ***, the values will be automatically converted to the right type.

Compiling and running the above program produces the following sorted output.

```
0.360000
0.378600
3.140000
9.900000
12.200000
18.299999
19.299999
34.599998
100.000000
236.779999
```

In case you are wondering why the arguments of our function are pointers, the next example will clarify it. In this example, we use **qsort** to sort an array of strings. Thus each of our array elements is a string. We start by writing a function to compare two strings. But wait a minute! Isn't that what the function **strcmp** is supposed to do? Reading the documentation of **strcmp** should reveal that it returns an integer value less than zero, zero, or greater than zero, according to whether its first argument is less than, equal to, or greater than the second argument. Thus we just substitute **strcmp** in place of the function that we are supposed to write.

```
/* Program to test sorting an array
 * of names by using qsort */

char names[5][24] = { "Karen Kangaroo", "Lionel Lion",
                      "Audry Owl", "Charley Horse",
                      "Calvin Cow" };
main()
{
   int i;
   extern int strcmp(const char *, const char *);
   printf("\tNames, before sorting\n");
```

```
        for(i = 0; i < 5; i++)
           printf("\t%s\n", names[i]);

        /* Call qsort and pass it strcmp as function to compare
         * strings. Note that the width is 24
         */
        qsort(names, 5, 24, strcmp);
        printf("\n\tNames, after sorting\n");
        for(i = 0; i < 5; i++)
           printf("\t%s\n", names[i]);
}
```

Compiling and running the program produces the following result:

```
    Names, before sorting

    Karen Kangaroo
    Lionel Lion
    Audry Owl
    Charley Horse
    Calvin Cow

    Names, after sorting

    Audry Owl
    Calvin Cow
    Charley Horse
    Karen Kangaroo
    Lionel Lion
```

12.5g   Exercises

1 Modify the above program to sort by the last name. To achieve this, write your own function to perform the string comparison.

2 Write a program to input 10 student records with GPA information. After the records have been input, sort the records by the GPA, from lowest to highest, using the `qsort` function. After sorting, print all the records.

12.6 Common Problems

The relationship between arrays and pointers is often misunderstood, even by experienced C programmers. Some programmers tend to believe that arrays and pointers are synonymous. While this is mostly true, there is one significant difference between arrays and pointers, which shows up when using arrays as external variables. In this section, we outline the significant difference by using a small example.

12.6a Near, but not complete, equivalence of arrays and pointers

In Chapter 9, Section 9.2, Pointers and Arrays, we mentioned that the name of an array contains the address of the beginning of the array (the position of the first element). Contrast this with any ordinary variable: *The name of a variable contains the value stored in the variable and not the variable's address*. Thus array names are treated differently by the compiler.

So, to make things work properly, the compiler needs to know whether a variable is an array name or not. If the variable is an array name, the compiler gives us the location of the variable when the variable is referenced. Otherwise, it gives us the value. The next example illustrates how things can go wrong if we don't take this information into account when our programs use arrays.

In the example shown below, the `main` function and the function `print_array` should be split into two separate files. Type in the program, as shown, into two files. Compile them separately and link them together to make an executable file.

```
/* main.c */

#include <stdio.h>

int myarray[2]; /* Global array of 2 elements */

main()
{
   extern void print_array(void);
```

```
    /* Put some sample values in the array */
    myarray[0] = 24;
    myarray[1] = 46;


    /* Call function print_array to print the
     * contents of the array. We use external
     * variables in place of arguments
     */
    print_array();
}
```

Next, we write the function **print_array**. Assuming that arrays and pointers are the same thing, we treat the array named **myarray** as a pointer variable in function **print_array** (as we did in the program in Chapter 10, Section 10.2d).

```
/* func.c: Prints the elements of an array */
#include <stdio.h>

extern int *myarray;   /* Myarray is a pointer to an int */

void print_array(void)
{
   int i;

   printf("Array elements are\n");
   for (i = 0; i < 2; i ++)
      printf("%d\n", *myarray++);
   printf("\n");
}
```

Now compile the two files and link them together and make an executable program file. When run on a Sun SPARCstation 1, the program produces the following output:

```
Array elements are
Memory fault(coredump)
```

What went wrong? Let's find out by adding a debug statement in the main function and the function **print_array**.

Common Problems

```c
/* main.c */
int myarray[2]; /* Global array of 2 elements */

main()
{
   extern void print_array(void);

   /* Put some sample values in the array */
   myarray[0] = 24;
   myarray[1] = 46;
   /* Call function print_array to print the
    * contents of the array. We will use external
    * variables in place of arguments
    */
   printf("(main) The name of the array contains %d\n",
          &myarray);
   print_array();
}

/* func.c: Prints the elements of an array */
extern int *myarray;   /* Myarray is a pointer to an int */

void print_array(void)
{
   int i;

   printf("(print_array) The name of the array \
          contains %d\n", &myarray);
   printf("Array elements are\n");
   for (i = 0; i < 2; i ++)
      printf("%d\n", *myarray++);
   printf("\n");
}
```

Compiling and running the program produces the following output.

```
(main) The name of the array contains 102168
(print_array) The name of the array contains 24
Array elements are
Memory fault(coredump)
```

The problem here is that when compiling the function **print_array**, the compiler has no idea that the variable **print_array** is an array. Thus, it treats **print_array** as an ordinary variable. We know by now that when an ordinary variable is referenced, we get the contents at the location that the variable occupies. In this case, the contents at the location is **24** that we placed into the first location. The number **24** happens to be an invalid address, and when dereferenced, it causes a memory fault.

Note *The above program may not generate a memory fault on all machines.*

How do we fix this problem? Just instruct the compiler to treat the variable name **myarray** as an array. We can do this as follows:

```
/* func.c: Prints the elements of an array */
#include <stdio.h>

extern int myarray[];   /* Myarray is a an array, not
                         * an ordinary variable */

void print_array(void)
{
   int i;

   printf("(print_array) The name of the array \
contains %d\n", &myarray);
   printf("Array elements are\n");
   for (i = 0; i < 2; i ++)
      printf("%d\n", myarray[i]);
   printf("\n");
}
```

Compiling and running the program produces the following output.

```
(main) The name of the array contains 101872
(print_array)   The name of the array contains 101872
Array elements are
24
46
```

Now, let's turn our attention again to a program that we wrote in Chapter 10, Section 10.2d, and see how it works. The program is shown below:

```
#define NO_STUDENTS 12

main()
{
   int grades[NO_STUDENTS], *gradesp;
   int index;
   int average_score(int *);/* Function for average */
   gradesp = grades; /* Initialize the pointer */
   for (index = 0; index < NO_STUDENTS; index++)
   {
      printf("Enter Grade for Student %d ",index);
      scanf("%d",gradesp++);
   }
   /* gradesp now points past the end of the array. Reset
    * it to point to the beginning again
    */
   gradesp = grades;
   printf("The average score is %d\n",
            average_score(gradesp));
}
/* Version 1. using pointers */
int average_score(int *array_ptr)
{
   int index, sum;
   for (index = 0, sum = 0; index < NO_STUDENTS; index ++)
   {
      sum = sum + *array_ptr++;
   }
   return (sum / NO_STUDENTS);
}
```

In this program, we treat the array as a pointer in the function **average_score**, and yet this program works. How?

This program works because when the function **average_score** is called from **main**, the value of **gradesp**, which is the address of the array, is passed to the parameter **array_ptr** in the function **average_score**. There is no extra compiler magic going on in this case. The function `average_score` receives the correct address of the beginning of the array.

13
Best of the Rest

In the final chapter of the workbook, you will learn about allocating memory at run-time, passing command line arguments to the `main` function, recursive functions, random access of data in files and bit-wise operators.

13.1 Dynamic Memory Allocation

In programming with C, the single biggest limitation that you may have observed is in the way memory is allocated to programs. So far, we have been forced to declare all the memory needed for the programs when the program is written. But in practice this is not often possible. Consider the case of our student database program. How can we tell, *a priori*, the number of students in our database? Allocating a very large array to hold the records is wasteful.

What we need is a way to allocate memory to a program at *run-time*, rather than at *compile time*. The standard library provides a set of routines that facilitate allocation of memory at run-time. Using these routines, you can request blocks of memory when the program is running and release the blocks when they are no longer needed.

ANSI C has a set of four basic memory allocation routines, shown in the following table:

Function name	Purpose
`void *malloc(size_t s)`	Allocates memory of size *s* and return a pointer to it or **NULL** if request cannot be satisfied
`void *calloc(size_t n, size_t s)`	Allocates memory to hold *n* objects of size *s* and initializes them to zero
`void *realloc(void *b, size_t s)`	Enlarges or shrinks a previously allocated memory beginning at *b* to size *s*
`void free(void *b)`	Releases previously allocated memory beginning at *b*

These routines can be accessed by including the header file **stdlib.h**. The data type `size_t` is `typedef`ed appropriately.

The following example shows how to allocate an array at run-time to read a number of student test scores.

Example **Dynamically allocating an array**

```
#include <stdlib.h>
#include <stdio.h>

main()
{
   int *array_p, *array_begin;
   int no_students, index;

   printf("Enter the number of students ");
   scanf("%d", &no_students);
   array_begin = (int *) malloc(sizeof(int) * no_students);
   if (array_begin == NULL)
   {
      perror("malloc");
      exit(EXIT_FAILURE);
   }
   array_p = array_begin;
```

Dynamic Memory Allocation

```
      for (index = 0; index < no_students; index++,
                                           array_p++)
      {
         printf("Enter grade for student %d: ", index + 1);
         scanf("%d", array_p);
      }
   }
```

Notice the use of the cast operator to cast the type of the memory returned from **void *** to the type of the data that will be stored in it.

The next example illustrates allocating a **student** record at run-time.

Example   **Request memory for a student record**

```
student *record_p;
record_p = (student *) malloc(sizeof(student));
if (record_p == NULL)
{
   perror("malloc");
   exit(EXIT_FAILURE);
}
```

After casting the right-hand side to be of the same type as the left-hand side, we can use the memory, pointed to by the pointer variable **student_p**, the same way as we are used to:

```
      student_p->gpa = 3.2;
      printf("Name = %s\n", student_p->name);
```

We can use **calloc** to request more than one unit of the allocation size. In addition, **calloc** also initializes the contents of the memory to all zeros.

The next example shows using **calloc** to allocate and initialize 100 student records.

Example   **Allocating and initializing records by using calloc**

```
student *student_p;
student_p = (student *) calloc(100, sizeof(student));
if (student_p == NULL)
{
```

```
        perror("calloc");
        exit(EXIT_FAILURE);
    }
```

On successful return, `student_p` will point to an initialized array of 100 student records.

Since memory is allocated by the system from a finite *heap*, memory no longer needed should be returned to the heap by using the `free` function. The function `free` requires that the pointer to the memory block passed to it be the address of a block of memory, which was allocated by earlier calls to `malloc`, `calloc` or `realloc`. Otherwise, the function will fail.

Example **Freeing previously allocated memory**

```
/* Free the memory allocated
 * by the previous calloc */
free(student_p); /* No return value (ANSI) */
```

13.1a Dynamic memory allocation and linked lists

Using statically allocated arrays to hold the student records was very convenient, due to the contiguous nature of the array elements. It was possible to traverse the entire array of structures by using array subscripts or simple pointer arithmetic.

Unfortunately, such luxury is lost when memory is allocated dynamically (at run-time). Each time a request for a block of memory is made, the memory may be allocated from different locations within the heap. The library makes no guarantee that two immediate allocations will be from a contiguous area. Hence, array subscripting or pointer arithmetic will not work across dynamically allocated memory. It is the programmer's responsibility to keep track of where all these different memory locations are.

Sounds complicated? It isn't! Earlier we mentioned that structures may contain pointers to themselves, called *self-referential structures*. We can use these pointers to form a *linked list* of structures allocated all across the heap memory.

In the example we will build, the unit of allocation will be a `student`. Thus we will have `student` records scattered throughout the memory, and we will need to keep track of it. We will devise a scheme that given any **student** record, we will know where the *next* **student** record is allocated (if there is any). To do this, we need to add a pointer to a **student** record to the structure definition, as shown:

```
typedef struct student_record {
    char    name[16];
    ulong   id;
    status  classification;
    float   gpa;
    struct  student_record *next;
} student;
```

Using the pointer **next**, we can connect all the memory blocks containing the **student** records, as shown in Figure 13.1. The figure shows two calls to **malloc** and how the structures are connected to form a linked list. Since we have only one connection, going forward, the list of records is called a *singly linked list*.

How do we get to to the first item in the list? To get to the first item, we keep a global variable (called **Head**) that contains the address of the first item in the list. Thus starting with the global variable, we can get to the first record, and by following the **next** pointer, we can access all the subsequent records. Similarly, we allocate a global pointer (called **Tail**) to point to the last item in the list so that we can easily add a new record to the end.

The code for building a singly linked list is shown below:

```
/* File lnklist.c: Builds a singly linked list of student
 * records. After all records have been input, list
 * the records
 */

#include <stdio.h>
#include <stdlib.h>
#define BSIZE   12
#define FALSE   0
#define TRUE    1

typedef unsigned long ulong; /* Shorthand for
                              * unsigned long */
```

```c
typedef enum { Freshman, Sophomore, Junior, Senior }
status;typedef struct student_record {
   char    name[16];
   ulong   id;
   status  classification;
   float   gpa;
   struct student_record *next;
} student;

student *Head = NULL; /* Global pointer to first record */
student *Tail = NULL; /* Global pointer to last record */

main()
{
   student *student_p;
   int input_one_record(student *);
   void print_database();

   while(1)
   {
      /* Allocate memory for a record, check for error */
      student_p = (student *) malloc(sizeof(student));
      if (student_p == NULL)
      {
         perror("malloc");
         exit(EXIT_FAILURE);
      }
      /* Call the function input_one_record to input the
       * record. If input succeeded, the function will
       * return TRUE. Otherwise, it will return FALSE
       */

      if (input_one_record(student_p) == FALSE)
      {
         /* Free the last block of memory allocated */
         free(student_p);
#ifdef DEBUG
         fprintf(stderr, "Record entry complete\n");
         print_database();
#endif
```

```
            exit(EXIT_SUCCESS);
         }
         /* Next, build the list */
         if (Head == NULL)
         {
            /* If it's the first record, set the head
             * and tail to point to the record
             */
            Head = student_p;
            Tail = student_p;
         }
         else
         {
            /* Head is unchanged. Record is added
             * to the end of Tail, and Tail is updated
             */
            Tail->next = student_p;
            student_p->next = NULL;
            Tail = student_p;
         }
      } /* End while */
      exit(EXIT_SUCCESS);
   }

   int input_one_record(student *rec_p)
   {
      char scratch[BSIZE];

      printf("Name? ");
      gets(rec_p->name);
      if (strlen(rec_p->name) <= 1) /* No more input */
         return(FALSE);

      printf("ID? ");
      fgets(scratch, BSIZE, stdin);
      rec_p->id = strtol(scratch, NULL, 10);
      printf("Status (0 = Freshman, 1 = Sophomore, \
2 = Junior, 3 = Senior) ? ");
      fgets(scratch, BSIZE, stdin);
      rec_p->classification = (status) atoi(scratch);
```

```
        printf("GPA? ");
        fgets(scratch, BSIZE, stdin);
        rec_p->gpa = (float) strtod(scratch, NULL);
        return(TRUE);
}
```

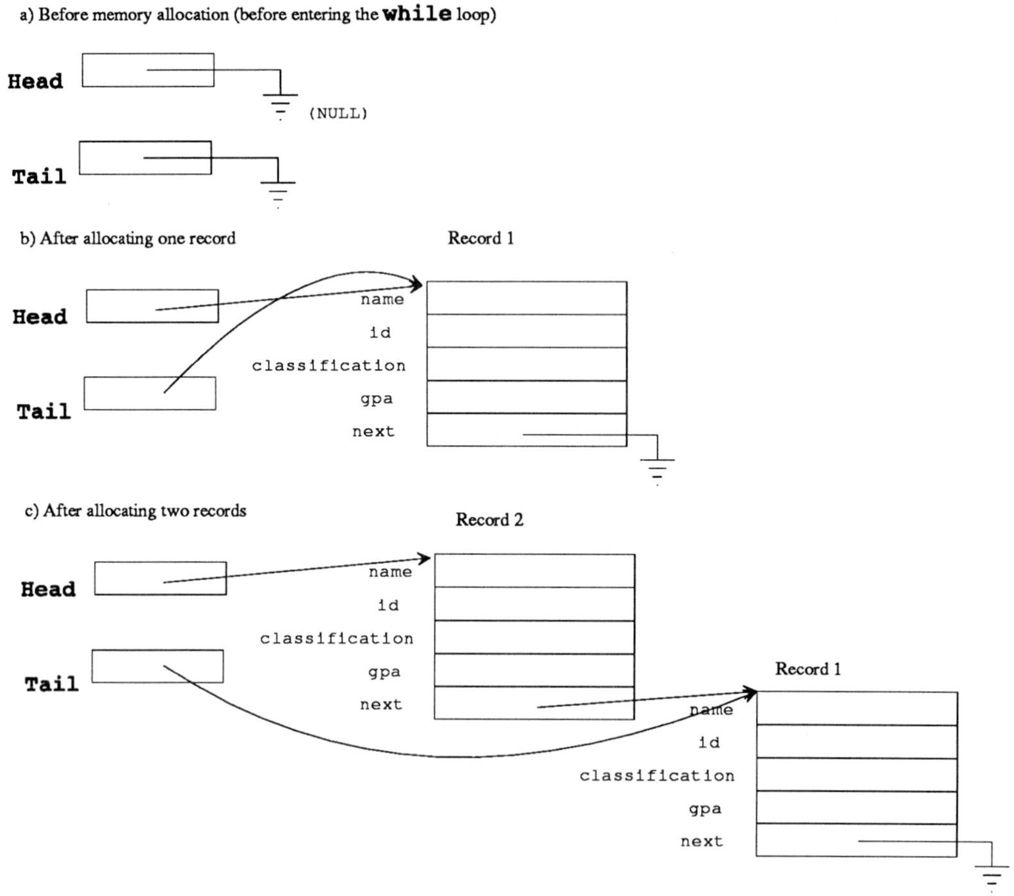

a) Before memory allocation (before entering the **while** loop)

Head

(NULL)

Tail

b) After allocating one record

Record 1

Head

name
id
classification
gpa
next

Tail

c) After allocating two records

Record 2

Head

name
id
classification
gpa
next

Tail

Record 1

name
id
classification
gpa
next

Figure 13.1 Building a linked list

To see how the list is traversed, we will write a routine called `print_database`, which will traverse the list and print the information about all the students in the database.

```
void print_database()
{
   student *record_p;
   void print_one_record(student *);
   record_p = Head;
   while(record_p != NULL)
   {
      print_one_record(record_p);
      record_p = record_p->next;
   }
}

/* Function to print one record */
void print_one_record(student *student_p)
{
   printf("Name=%s, ID=%d, Class=%d, GPA=%f\n",
             student_p->name,
             student_p->id,
             student_p->classification,
             student_p->gpa);
}
```

We use a temporary variable called `record_p` to traverse the list. Initially, `record_p` points to the beginning of the list, and once that record is printed, `record_p` is set to point to the next member, which is available through the `next` pointer in the structure. This will continue until there are no more structures (indicated by the NULL value in the structure's `next` pointer).

13.1b Exercise

1. Allocating memory to hold the student records one block at a time may be very inefficient due to the large number of calls made to `malloc`. Modify the program to allocate memory in blocks of 10 at a time. Keep track of the number of blocks used to input the records and allocate more blocks, 10 at a time, when necessary.

2. A doubly linked list is a list that contains a pointer to the next record and a pointer to the previous record. A doubly linked list can be implemented by using another pointer in the structure definition. Modify the program shown above to implement a doubly linked list. After the input is complete, print the records backwards, using the backward link starting from the `Tail`.

13.2 Command Line Arguments

In this section, we discuss the techniques for passing arguments to the `main` function. Earlier we mentioned that the `main` function is similar to any other function except that program execution always begins at `main`. This implies the following:

- It should be possible to pass arguments to `main`.
- Since `main` is called by the system, the system is responsible for packaging and passing the command line options, typed in by the user, as arguments to `main`.

Have we seen examples of programs that accept arguments in `main`? Of course. Our C compiler is such a program, written in C, which inevitably has a `main`. The C compiler is compiled just like any other program. How do we run the compiler? On UNIX systems, we invoke the compiler to compile a program called **test.c**, as shown:

```
cc -o test test.c
```

The file **cc** is the executable program that contains the `main` function, and the rest of the line in the command line are all arguments to `main`. Thus `main` in **cc** should have been written to accept arguments.

The arguments in the command line are separated by white space. In the case of the example above, the arguments are:

```
-o
test
test.c
```

In addition, the environment passes the name of the program itself as the first argument. Thus the arguments that will be passed to the **main** function are:

```
cc
-o
test
test.c
```

Arguments are passed as null-terminated character strings. Thus the arguments really look like:

```
"cc\0"
"-o\0"
"test\0"
"test.c\0"
```

But how does **main** know how many arguments are passed to it? In addition to the actual arguments, the number of arguments are also passed to it. We have been using **main** without any formal parameters. The function **main** has two different prototypes:

```
int main(void);                        /* Prototype 1 */
int main(int argc, char *argv[]); /* Prototype 2 */
```

We have been using the first form up to this point. In the second form, the intended usage of **main** is as follows:

```
int main(no_of_arguments, array of arguments);
```

The formal parameter **argc** contains the argument count and the variable **argv** contains an array of strings. Since the C compiler represents string constants as a pointer to the string's first element, **argv** is really an array of pointers. When the array of pointers is passed as a function argument, it is passed as a pointer to the first element. Thus **argv** is really a pointer to a pointer. If you are confused, just think of it as an array of pointers.

```
int main(int argc, char **argv)
            or
int main(int argc, char *argv[])
```

The second form is preferred. Notice that the function can also return an integer value to the environment. The convention used is that if the program succeeded in accomplishing its task, a value of 0 is returned to the environment. Otherwise, a positive value is returned to the environment. The return value is available for perusal (for example, on UNIX systems, using the Korn shell or Bourne shell, the shell command **echo $?** shows the return value from the *previous command*).

For the example shown above, `argc` will be 4 and `argv` will be as shown below:

```
argv[0] = "cc"      /* Null not shown but is implied */
argv[1] = "-o"
argv[2] = "test"
argv[3] = "test.c"
```

The following program displays the command line arguments passed to it.

Example **Displaying command line arguments**

```
int main(int argc, char *argv[])
{
   int i;
   for (i = 0; i < argc; i++)
   {
      printf ("Argument %d: %s\n", i, argv[i]);
   }
   return(0);
}
```

Compile the program, create an executable file called **listargs** and run the program for the following input:

```
$ listargs one 2 buckle my shoe
```

The output will be:

```
Argument 0: listargs
Argument 1: one
Argument 2: 2
Argument 3: buckle
```

```
        Argument 4: my
        Argument 5: shoe
```

In the next example, we modify the database program that we wrote in Chapter 11 (file **student.c**) to pass to it the name of the file to open, rather than using a default file.

```c
/* File database.c: Reads input from the keyboard and writes
 * to a file specified by the user as a command line option.
 */

#include <stdio.h>
#include <stdlib.h>
#include "student.h"      /* Our header file */
#define BSIZE    12       /* Size of buffer to hold string to
                           * be converted */
#define NO_STUDENTS 5
#define NAME_SIZE   24

int main(int argc, char *argv[])
{
   int count; /* Number of students input */
   student student_records[NO_STUDENTS];/* Memory to hold
                                         * records */
   int create_database(student *, char *);

   if (argc == 1)
   {
      fprintf(stderr, "Usage: %s filename\n", argv[0]);
      exit(EXIT_FAILURE);
   }
#ifdef DEBUG
   printf("Name of file to open is %s\n", argv[1]);
#endif
   count = create_database(student_records, argv[1]);
#ifdef DEBUG
   printf("%d number of students were input", count);
#endif
   exit(EXIT_SUCCESS);
}
```

```c
int create_database(student student_records[],
                    char *filename)
{
   FILE *ofhandle;
   char scratch[BSIZE]; /* Scratch variable */
   int index;
   int ret_val;

   if ((ofhandle = fopen(filename, "w")) == NULL)
   {
      perror(filename);
      fprintf(stderr, "Create database failed\n");
      exit(EXIT_FAILURE);
   }

   for (index = 0; index < NO_STUDENTS; index++)
   {
      printf("****Record %d ****\n", index);
      printf("Name? ");
      fgets(student_records[index].name, NAME_SIZE, stdin);
      if (strlen(student_records[index].name) <= 1)
         break; /* Out of the for loop */

      printf("ID? ");
      fgets(scratch, BSIZE, stdin); /* Get the ID */
      student_records[index].id = strtol(scratch, NULL, 10);
      printf("Status (0 = Freshman, 1 = Sophomore, \
2 = Junior, 3 = Senior) ? ");
      fgets(scratch, BSIZE, stdin);
      student_records[index].classification =
                                 (status) atoi(scratch);
      printf("GPA? ");
      fgets(scratch, BSIZE, stdin);
      student_records[index].gpa =
                          (float) strtod(scratch, NULL);
   }
   /* At this point, all records have been input,
    * and index contains the number of records input
    */
```

```
        /* Write all the records, in one shot, into the file */
        ret_val = fwrite((void *)student_records,
                         sizeof(student), index, ofhandle);
        if (ret_val != index)
        {
           perror("fwrite");
           fprintf(stderr, "create database failed\n");
           fclose(ofhandle);
           exit(EXIT_FAILURE);
        }
        fclose(ofhandle);
        return(index);
    }
```

Now, the program can be invoked as

$ **database STUDENT.DAT**

where the name of the executable file is **database** and the name of the data file is **STUDENT.DAT**.

13.2a   Exercises

1. Modify the database program so that if the user does not enter the name of the database file in the command line, it uses a default file named **DATABAS.DAT**.

2. Modify the `main` function for the database program so that if the user enters the command line option **-p**, the database will be printed after all the records are input. For example

    $ **database -f STUDENT.DAT -p**

    should create a data file called **STUDENT.DAT** and print the database after all the records are entered.

3. Modify the math tutor program by adding a command line interface. It should be possible to invoke the tutor program by giving it the type of test to administer and the number of tests. For example, the command line

```
tutor add 5
```

must be supported; it indicates that the addition test must be performed five times.

Since command line options are passed as strings, you will have to convert from string to integer to obtain the numeric value of the second argument to tutor.

13.3 Recursive Functions

Functions that call themselves are known as *recursive functions*. Certain classes of algorithms can be very elegantly coded by using recursive functions. Any function whose operation can be expressed in terms of itself is a candidate for recursion. For example, consider the following recursive definition of the factorial function:

$$n! = n * (n - 1) * (n - 2) * (n - 3) * \ldots 2 * 1$$

or

$$n! = n * (n - 1)!, n > 0 \quad (0! \text{ is } 1, \text{ by definition})$$

In the above expression, the factorial on the left-hand side is defined in terms of the factorial on the right-hand side. Thus if we write a function for computing the factorial, it would appear as follows:

```
factorial(int n)
{
    int fact;

    fact = n * factorial (n - 1);
    return fact;
}
```

There is, however, one little problem. How do we terminate the recursion? As written, this function will keep calling itself forever or until it runs out of memory. To avoid this problem, there should be a test condition inside the function with which we can terminate the recursion. Terminating the recursion by using a predefined test condition is known as *bottoming out* from the recursion.

In our case, notice that every time the function `factorial` is entered, the value of `n` will be reduced by 1. When `n` becomes 0, there is no need to continue and we can terminate the recursion. We will modify the code to do this:

```
factorial(int n)
{
    int fact;
    if (n == 0)
    {
        /* 0! is 1, by definition */
        return 1;
    }
    fact = n * factorial (n - 1);
    return(fact);
}
```

Let us trace the execution of the `factorial` function by using an example. We will use the following main program:

```
#include <stdio.h>
main()
{
    printf("3! is %d\n", factorial(3));
}
```

The program looks quite simple and innocuous. But under the surface, a lot goes on. Figure 13.2 illustrates what happens when the function `factorial` is called from `main` with 3 as the argument (the name of the function has been shortened to `fact`, to fit the page).

The important thing to remember about recursive functions is that each time the function is called, memory for the automatic variables is created. Since the function only starts returning when it bottoms out, several instances of the automatic variables may exist at any time. In the factorial example, once we bottom out and start returning from the function, the return value from the innermost invocation is passed to its caller, which then uses it to compute its return value and returns. This goes on till we unwind all the calls and get back to the top level (in `main`).

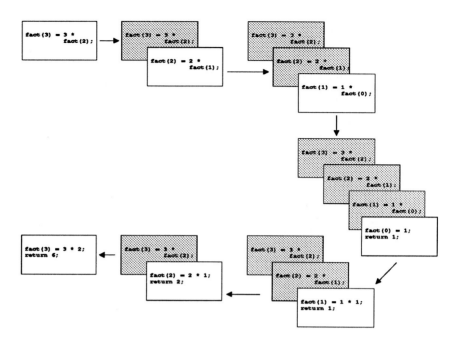

Figure 13.2 Execution trace of factorial function.

To understand the significance of the automatic variable creation and destruction, consider the following example. In our math tutor program, we wish to call a function called **get_random_number**, which will return a nonzero random number. We will write the function **get_random_number** with a small, but deliberate, bug to show the significance of block entries and exits.

From our discussion on recursive functions, here's how we may be tempted to code the **get_random_number** function:

```
int get_random_number(int upperbound)
{
    int number;

    number = random() % upperbound;
    /* If the generated number is zero, simply
     * call get_random_number again until we
     * get a good number
     */
```

Recursive Functions

```
        if (number == 0)
        {
            get_random_number(upperbound);
        }
        return number;
    }
```

The function `get_random_number` looks okay, intuitively. However, it will not work at all. Can you reason why?

To understand why this function does not work, let us trace the execution of the program. First, we will show a `main` program to test our `get_random_number`. If we call the function `random` with the same seed each time, we will get the same random number. To avoid this problem, we will get the value of the system time by using the library function `time` and use the time value as the seed. The complete program is shown below:

```
/* File my_rand.c */
#include <stdio.h>
#include <time.h>   /* To use time function */
int main(void)
{
    time_t seedval;    /* Seed for the generator */
    int high = 10;     /* Largest random number that we want */
    int get_random_number(int); /* Our function */
    time(&seedval);    /* Get the time in variable seedval */
    srandom(seedval);  /* Use it to seed the generator */
    printf("%d\n", get_random_number(high));
}

int get_random_number(int upperbound)
{
    int number;
    number = random() % upperbound;
    /* If the generated number is zero, simply
     * call get_random_number again until we
     * get a good number
     */
    if (number == 0)
    {
        fprintf(stderr, "Got a zero; recursion forced\n");
```

```
        get_random_number(upperbound);
    }
    return number;
}
```

Compiling and running this program repeatedly produces the following output:

```
$ my_rand
2

$ my_rand
8

$ my_rand
Got a zero; recursion forced
0
```

Assume that during the first call to the `get_random_number` function, the variable `number` gets the value 0 (we will refer to this variable as $number_1$). This causes a recursion, which results in calling `get_random_number` again. When `get_random_number` is called again, memory for the automatic variable `number` is created again (we will refer to this instance as $number_2$). If we get a nonzero value in $number_2$, we return from the function to the caller. At the time we return from the function, $number_2$ is destroyed. When we return to the caller, $number_1$ is active again, and it still contains the value **0** (surprise, surprise!). This is the value we return to the user.

The key to understanding and using recursive functions is the knowledge that each invocation of the function causes a new *activation record* to be created, which contains memory for all the automatic variables. There is no sharing of the automatic variables, and any sharing needs to be achieved by using global variables or static variables.

We can fix the above problem by modifying `get_random_number` as follows:

```
int get_random_number(int upperbound)
{
    int number;

    number = random() % upperbound;
```

```
        /* If the generated number is zero, simply
         * call get_random_number again until we
         * get a good number
         */
        if (number == 0)
        {
            fprintf(stderr, "Got a zero; recursion forced\n");
            number = get_random_number(upperbound);
        }
        return number;
}
```

In this case, when get_random_number with the variable $number_2$ returns, we assign the return value into $number_1$, which is returned to the user. Compiling and running the above program produces the following output:

```
$ my_rand
8

$ my_rand
Got a zero; recursion forced
7
```

13.3a Binary search: A complete example

In this section, we will use recursion to implement the binary search algorithm. The binary search algorithm is an efficient algorithm that can be used to search for a value in a presorted array. We discussed the iterative algorithm for binary search in Chapter 8.

The basic idea behind the recursive algorithm is as follows: From the main function, we call the function binsearch, passing to it the beginning index of the array, the ending index and the value to be searched for. The function binsearch compares the element at the middle of the array with the value to be searched for. If the element at the middle of the array is larger than the value to be searched for, we can eliminate the upper half of the array from the search. This is done by computing a new ending index and calling binsearch again. If the element lies in the second half, the first half of the array is eliminated from the search. Thus during each call of the function `binsearch`, the number of elements to be searched is halved.

The complete program is given below, with debug statements to show the execution of the program.

```c
/* File bsearch.c: Implements binary
 * search algorithm by using recursion
 */
#include <stdio.h>
#include <math.h>

#define EXIT_SUCCESS    0 /* For non-ANSI compilers */
#define EXIT_FAILURE    1

/* For testing, use a 10 element presorted array */
int sorted_array[] = { 0, 2, 6, 7, 8, 11, 14, 19, 23,
                       99, 4000 };

int main(void)
{
   int value;     /* Value to be searched for */
   int position;  /* Position of value in array */
   int binsearch(int lower, int upper, int value);

   printf("Enter value to be searched for: ");
   scanf("%d", &value);
   position = binsearch(0, 10, value);
   if (position  0)
   {
      printf("Value %d not found in array\n", value);
      exit(EXIT_FAILURE);
   }
   else
   {
      printf("Value %d found in array at index %d\n",
             value, position);
      exit(EXIT_SUCCESS);
   }
}
```

```c
int binsearch(int first, int last, int key)
{
   int mid_point, index;

   mid_point = (first + last) / 2;
   if (key == sorted_array[mid_point])
   {
      /* Value has been found */
      return(mid_point);
   }
   if (first >= last && key != sorted_array[mid_point])
   {
      /* We have narrowed down search to one element
       * and still haven't found it
       */
      return(-1);
   }

   /* Debug output */
   fprintf(stderr, "Midpoint of the array contains %d\n",
           sorted_array[mid_point]);

   /* Now find which half of the unchecked array
    * the key may be in
    */
   if (key > sorted_array[mid_point])
      first = mid_point + 1;
   else
      last = mid_point - 1;
   /* Debug output */
   fprintf(stderr, "first = %d, last = %d, mid = %d\n",
           first, last, (first+last)/2);
   index = binsearch(first, last, key);
   return(index);
}
```

Compiling and running the above program with some sample test values yields the following output.

```
$ bsearch
Enter value to be searched for: 7
Midpoint of the array contains 11
first = 0, last = 4, mid = 2
Midpoint of the array contains 6
first = 3, last = 4, mid = 3
Value 7 found in array at index 3

$ bsearch
Enter value to be searched for: 3000
Midpoint of the array contains 11
first = 6, last = 10, mid = 8
Midpoint of the array contains 23
first = 9, last = 10, mid = 9
Midpoint of the array contains 99
first = 10, last = 10, mid = 10
Value 3000 not found in array
```

Note *C standard library provides a function called bsearch, which is a much more versatile version of the function shown here.*

13.3b Exercises

1 Modify the program that builds a singly linked list of student records (**lnklist.c**) to print all the student records recursively. After all the records have been input, call the recursive function `print_database`, passing to it the first record of the list (the **Head** pointer). The function `print_database` should recursively call itself with the next link in the records until it reaches the end (null pointer is detected). Once it reaches the end, start popping back and print each record.

2 Modify the program to print from the **Tail** pointer backwards.

13.4 Random Access

So far, when we access data in a file, we have been using sequential access. That is, data is accessed (read or written) sequentially, from beginning to end. Using random access, it is possible to access the data at any location within a file.

Random access is achieved by moving the current location indicator to an arbitrary location within a file and then accessing the data. Recall that when we open a file, the current location indicator points to the top of the file. When data is read or written, the current location is incremented by the size of the of data.

Using a library call named `fseek`, it is possible to move the current location indicator to any position within the file, without reading or writing any data. When accessing individual records within a file, random access is very efficient, as it avoids the unnecessary disk access required in sequential access.

The library functions implementing random access are outlined in the table below:

Function name	Purpose
`int fseek(FILE *file, long offset, int from)`	Moves the current location within the file. Returns nonzero for failure.
`long ftell(FILE *file)`	Returns the position of the current location within the file.
`void rewind(FILE *file)`	Resets the current location to the beginning of the file.

The function `fseek` moves the current location to a position within the file, as dictated by its arguments *offset* and *from*. The argument *offset* is a signed long integer specifying the number of bytes to be advanced, relative to a code specified by *from*. The valid codes are:

SEEK_SET (the value 0) indicates that the advancing should be with respect to the top of the file.

SEEK_CUR (the value 1) indicates that the advancing should be with respect to the value of the current location.

SEEK_END (the value 2) indicates that the advancing should be with respect to the end of the file.

The following examples illustrate the use of `fseek` function.

Example **Seeking to the end of the file**
```
FILE *handle;
open the file, etc.
if (fseek(handle, 0L, SEEK_END) != 0)
{
   perror("fseek failed");
   exit(EXIT_FAILURE);
}
```

Notice that `rewind` is simply `fseek(handle, 0L, SEEK_SET);`

Note *In addition to the functions listed above, ANSI C also provides two functions `fgetpos` and `fsetpos`, which are useful in implementing random access. Describing these functions is beyond the scope of this book. Please refer to the library documentation for more detail.*

13.4a Random access: A complete example

In this example, we develop our student database further to incorporate random access.

We have a new requirement for the database program. Given a student ID, we need to display the student's record in detail. Without random access, we would have to read each record into memory, scan the records in memory till we find a record that matches the given ID, and then print the record. This is an obviously unacceptable solution, considering the amount of disk I/O wasted just to read one record.

Random Access

A better solution is to open the file containing the records, seek to the record that contains the student ID, and read just that record. But there is a problem: We don't know where the record lies in the file, and consequently, we don't know how much to seek.

A common technique used to solve such problems is to store a small amount of information with each file, which will allow us to find the position of all records within the file. In our case, storing the ID of each student, in the order in which the student records are written to the file, will enable us to find an individual record easily. After the file is opened, we read all the IDs into memory. Next, we search the IDs to find a match for our given ID. If a match is found, we found an index, which will be the relative index for our record in the file. This information will suffice in calculating the *offset* value for seeking within the file. This method of accessing a record (using information stored in the file) is commonly known as *indexed key access*.

The layout of the file with the keys stored at the top of the file is shown in Figure 13.3. In the figure, notice that finding the position of the given ID in

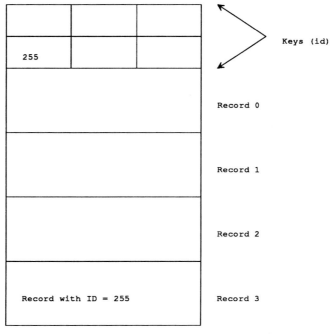

Figure 13.3 File format for random access.

the keys (position 4) enables us to find the record within the file. Specifically, the beginning of a given record within a file, given an index (`index`) of its key, will be

```
offset = sizeof key_table + index * sizeof record
```

where *key_table* is the table that holds all the keys at the top of the file.

We will modify our student database program to incorporate this file layout. The program is given below:

```c
#include <stdio.h>
#include <stdlib.h>
#include "student.h"

#define BSIZE    12
#define OUTFILE  "DATABAS.DAT"
#define INFILE   "DATABAS.DAT"

/* The main function inputs all the records into a
 * file in binary format. Next, it closes the file
 * and calls a function named query_database that
 * implements querying by ID of the student.
 */

int main(void)
{
   student student_records[NO_STUDENTS];
   int index;
   FILE *ofhandle;
   int ret_val;
   student *student_p;
   int input_record(student *, ulong *, FILE *);

   student_p = student_records;

   if ( (ofhandle = fopen(OUTFILE, "w")) == NULL)
   {
      perror(OUTFILE);
      exit(EXIT_FAILURE);
   }
```

```c
      for (index = 0; index < NO_STUDENTS; index++)
      {
         printf("****Record %d ****\n", index);
         /* Call input record to input the student info
          * and store it into the array. Also, store the
          * keys into the key array. Notice that we pass
          * the addresses of the records and the key entry
          * so that the function may place a value into it
          * for our use
          */
         if (input_record(&student_records[index],
                                  &key[index], stdin) == 0)
            break;
      }
      /* Write the index first */
      ret_val = fwrite((void *)key, sizeof(ulong),
                    NO_STUDENTS, ofhandle);
      if (ret_val != NO_STUDENTS)
      {
         fprintf(stderr, "Error in writing keys to file %s\n",
               OUTFILE);
         exit(EXIT_FAILURE);
      }
      /* At this point, all records have been input and index
       * contains number of records input.
       * Write all the records, in one shot, into the file
       */
      ret_val = fwrite((void *)student_records,
                    sizeof (student), index, ofhandle);
      if (ret_val != index)
      {
         fprintf(stderr, "Error in writing records to file \
                    %s\n", OUTFILE);
         exit(EXIT_FAILURE);
      }
      fclose(ofhandle);  /* To ensure that data gets
                          * written to file */

      /* Next, call function query_database */
```

```c
      if (query_database() == 0)
      {
         printf("Record not found\n");
         exit(EXIT_FAILURE);
      }
      exit(EXIT_SUCCESS);
}

/* Function to input student records */
int input_record(student *bufp, ulong *key_value, FILE *fh)
{
      char scratch[BSIZE];

      printf("Name? ");
      fgets(bufp->name, NAME_SIZE, fh);
      if (strlen(bufp->name) <= 1)
        return 0;
      printf("ID? ");
      fgets(scratch, BSIZE, fh);
      bufp->id = strtol(scratch, NULL, 10);
      *key_value = bufp->id;
      printf("Status (0 = Freshman, 1 = Sophomore, \
2 = Junior, 3 = Senior ?");
      fgets(scratch, BSIZE, fh);
      /* Convert from ASCII to int */
      bufp->classification = (status) atoi(scratch);
      printf("Status = %d\n", bufp->classification);
      printf("GPA? ");
      gets(scratch);
      /* Convert to float */
      bufp->gpa = (float) strtod (scratch, NULL);
      printf("GPA = %f\n", bufp->gpa);
      return 1;
}

/* Function to implement querying the database by ID */
int query_database()
{
   int key_value;
   char scratch[BSIZE];
```

```c
      ulong key_array[NO_STUDENTS];
      int index, offset, ret_val;
      student buf;
      FILE *fh;
      ulong key[NO_STUDENTS]; /* To read keys into memory */
      void print_record(student);

      if ( (fh = fopen(INFILE, "r")) == NULL)
      {
         perror(INFILE);
         exit(EXIT_FAILURE);
      }
      printf("Enter the student number\n");
      fgets(scratch, BSIZE, stdin);
      key_value = strtol(scratch, NULL, 10);

      /* Read the key table into array */
      ret_val = fread((void *)key_array, sizeof(ulong),
                  NO_STUDENTS, fh);
      if (ret_val != NO_STUDENTS)
      {
         perror("fread");
         exit(EXIT_FAILURE);
      }
      for (index = 0; index < ret_val; index++)
      {
         if (key_value == key_array[index])
            break;
      }
      if (index == NO_STUDENTS) /* Key not found */
         return 0;

#ifdef DEBUG
      fprintf(stderr, "found key at index %d\n", index);
#endif DEBUG

      /* Compute the offset:
       * Size of key table (size of ulong * NO_STUDENTS) plus
       * index * size of each record
       */
```

```
        offset = sizeof(ulong) * NO_STUDENTS +
                 sizeof(student) * index;

        /* Seek to the right place within the file */
        if (fseek(fh, offset, SEEK_SET) != 0)
        {
           /* Seek failed */
           perror("fseek failed");
           exit(EXIT_FAILURE);
        }

        /* Read the record */
        if (fread(&buf, sizeof(student), 1, fh) != 1)
        {
           perror(fread);
           exit(EXIT_FAILURE);
        }

        /* Print the record. print record function not shown */
        print_one_record(buf);
        return 1;
    }
```

13.4b Exercises

1 Modify the database program to maintain the keys in a separate file.

2 Sort the keys in memory, and use a binary search to locate a key.

13.5 Bitwise Operators

In addition to the arithmetic, logical and relational operators that we discussed in Chapter 4, C provides a variety of operators for manipulating bits within a word. The bitwise operators in C provide an alternative to programming in assembly language. This is one of the reasons for C's popularity among systems programmers.

The bitwise operators are shown in the following table.

Operator	Purpose	Example
&	Bitwise AND	x & 7
|	Bitwise OR	x | y
^	Bitwise exclusive-OR	x ^ 3
<<	Left shift	x << 1
>>	Right shift	x >> 2
~	One's complement	~x

As mentioned above, these operators are bitwise; i.e., they operate on bits within a word. When dealing with bits, it is easier to represent data as hexadecimal (base 16) or octal (base 8). Let us examine the octal and the hexadecimal systems in more detail.

13.5a Octal and hexadecimal representation of data

The reason why the octal and hexadecimal systems are popular among systems programmers is that since 16 and 8 are integral powers of 2, it is easier to represent and interpret a byte (which is 8 bits wide) in octal or hexadecimal. Each hexadecimal digit can represent 4 bits, and each octal digit can represent 3 bits. Note that there is no integral bit representation for decimal digits.

In the octal representation, the only digits are those from 0 to 7. The example below illustrates counting in octal:

Decimal: 0 1 2 3 4 5 6 7 8 9 10 11 12 13 13 15 16 17 18 19 20 ...
Octal: 0 1 2 3 4 5 6 7 10 11 12 13 14 15 16 17 20 21 22 23 24 ...

Note *Read the octal counting as "zero," "one," "two," "three," "four," "five," "six," "seven," "one zero" (not "ten"), "one one," "one two," etc.*

In the hexadecimal system, the base is 16. We count in hexadecimal as

Decimal: 0 1 2 3 4 5 6 7 8 9 10 11 12 13 13 15 16 17 18 19 20 ...
Hexadecimal: 0 1 2 3 4 5 6 7 8 9 A B C D E F 10 11 12 13 14 ...

An integer constant can be represented as an octal value or a hexadecimal value (in addition to decimal value) by placing an appropriate prefix in front of the digits.

If a constant begins with 0 (zero), it is assumed to be octal. For example, `050` is octal 50, which has decimal value $(5 * 8^1) + (0 * 8^0)$, or 40. If a constant begins with `0x` or `0X`, it is assumed to be hexadecimal. For example, `0x345` (or `0X345`) is hexadecimal 345, which has the decimal value $(3 * 16^2) + (4 * 16^1) + (5 * 16^0)$, or 837.

The next number is not a Grateful Dead logo — `0XDEAD` is a valid hexadecimal number which has the decimal value $(13 * 16^3) + (14 * 16^2) + (10 * 16^1) + (13 * 16^0)$, or 57,005.

We can also use `scanf` and `printf` to input and output octal and hexadecimal values. The following format specifiers can be used in `scanf` and `printf` statements to specify the base of the input or output item.

Format sequence	Use
%o, %O	Normal integer format (octal system)
%x, %X	Normal integer format (hexadecimal system)

The following simple program illustrates reading an input value in hexadecimal and displaying the value in decimal.

```
#include <stdio.h>

main()
{
   int value;

   printf("Enter a hexadecimal value: ");
   scanf("%x", &value);
   printf("Value is %d\n", value);
}
```

Shown below is a sample input and the displayed result:

```
Enter a hexadecimal value: dead
Value is 57005
```

13.5b Bitwise AND, OR and exclusive-OR

The bitwise AND, OR and exclusive-OR operators are binary operators that operate on individual bits within a word.
- The bitwise AND (&) operator yields 1 only if both the operands (which are bits) are 1. Otherwise, it yields 0.
- The bitwise OR (|) operator yields 1 if either of its operands is a 1. Otherwise, it yields 0.
- The bitwise exclusive-OR (^) operator yields 1 if both of its operands are different (0 vs. 1 or 1 vs. 0). If both the operands are the same, it yields 0.

The operations of these three operators are summarized in the following table:

x	y	x & y	x | y	x ^ y
0	0	0	0	0
1	0	0	1	1
0	1	0	1	1
1	1	1	1	0

Example **Bitwise AND operation**

```
binary 0110 &
binary 0101
yields 0100
```

Example **Bitwise OR operation**

```
binary 0110 |
binary 0101
yields 0111
```

Example **Bitwise exclusive-OR operation**

```
binary 0101 ^
binary 0011
yields 0110
```

The following program tests whether the first 4 bits (bit positions 0 through 3, where bit 7 is the most significant bit and bit 0 is the least significant bit) are all set to 1. Specifically, we are looking for the pattern

```
XXXX1111
```

where X indicates that the bit may contain 0 or 1.

The operation is quite simple: We use the `&` operator to test whether the 4 bits are on. Recall that the `&` operator yields 1 only if its left and right operands are 1. Since we are interested in the low 4 bits, we will devise a *mask* to test the low-order 4 bits. The mask is as shown below in binary

```
00001111
```

The binary value shown above translates to a hexadecimal or decimal constant quite easily. To translate it to a hexadecimal constant, just group the bits into groups of four and compute its decimal value. Next, translate from decimal to hexadecimal.

```
binary       0000 1111
hexadecimal    0    f  ⇨2³*1+2²*1+2¹*1+2⁰*1 equals
                         15 (decimal) or f (hexadecimal)
```

Bitwise Operators

Thus the mask we are looking for is the constant `0x0f`. To arrive at a mask in octal (if we need to), group the bits in groups of three (from least significant to most significant) and convert to decimal and octal:

```
                  00 001 111
     octal         0   1   7
```

Thus, the mask can be `0x0F` or `017`. The program is given below:

```c
/* bittest.c: Program to test if the low 4 bits
 * of a byte are all ones
 */
#include <stdio.h>
#define MASK    0x0F

main()
{
   int value;
   printf("Enter a hexadecimal value: ");
   scanf("%x", &value);

   if ((value & MASK) == MASK)
      printf("Low 4 bits are all ones\n");
   else
      printf("Low 4 bits are not all ones\n");
}
```

A sample run of the program is shown below:

```
Enter a hexadecimal value: 0f
Low 4 bits are all ones

Enter a hexadecimal value: ff
Low 4 bits are all ones

Enter a hexadecimal value: f0
Low 4 bits are not all ones
```

13.5c Shift operators

The left shift and right shift operators shift the bits in their left operand to the left or the right by the desired number (the right operand). In the left shift operation

```
x << y
```

the bit representation of **x** is shifted **y** positions to the left. On the low-order end, 0s are shifted in. In the right shift operation

```
x >> y
```

the bit representation of **x** is shifted **y** positions to the right. If **x** is an unsigned value, 0s are shifted in at the high end. For signed values, what gets shifted in is machine dependent: Some machines shift 0s; others shift sign bits.

Example **Left shift operation**

```
0x0F << 4 gives 0xF0
```

Let us examine how the above operation works. As mentioned earlier, a hexadecimal digit can be represented as a series of 4 binary digits. Hence we convert `0x0F` to binary 0000 1111 (0000 for the first hexadecimal digit 0, 1111 for the hexadecimal digit F). Next, we shift all the bits by four positions to the left. The operation is shown as:

```
0000 1111 << by 1 yields
0001 1110 << by 1 yields  /* Note: 0 enters from left */
0011 1100 << by 1 yields
0111 1000 << by 1 yields
1111 0000, which is hexadecimal 0xF0
```

The next program illustrates how to use the shift operators to count the number of 1 bits in an unsigned integer value. To count the number of 1 bits, we repeatedly test the rightmost bit, using an appropriate mask, and shift the bit pattern to the right by one until the bit pattern becomes all 0s.

```
/* File bitcnt.c: Counts the number
 * of 1 bits in an integer value
 */
```

```c
#include <stdio.h>

#define MASK    1

main(int argc, char *argv[])
{
   unsigned int bit_value;
   int count;

   if (argc == 1)
   {
      /* No argument given by the user */
      fprintf(stderr, "Usage: %s number\n", argv[0]);
      exit(EXIT_FAILURE);
   }

   bit_value = atoi(argv[1]); /* Convert to integer */
   for (count = 0; bit_value != 0; bit_value >>= 1)
   {
      /* Test the rightmost bit */
      if ((bit_value & MASK) == 1)
         count++; /* Increment count */
   }
   printf("Number of 1 bits = %d\n", count);
}
```

Running the program with a few sample inputs is shown below:

```
$ bitcount
Usage: bitcount number

$ bitcount 1
Number of 1 bits = 1

$ bitcount 2
Number of 1 bits = 1

$ bitcount 3
Number of 1 bits = 2
```

```
$ bitcount 7
Number of 1 bits = 3
```

Notice the funny looking operator **>>=** in the expression

```
bit_value >>= 1
```

This is a compound operator that combines an assignment with a shift operation. We haven't discussed compound assignment operators yet! The above expression is equivalent to

```
bit_value = bit_value >> 1
```

"Compound" assignment operators are discussed in the next section.

13.5d Assignment operators

It is possible to combine an assignment operation with any of the arithmetic and bitwise operators. The general form of the assignment operators is

```
variable operator= value
```

where *operator* is an arithmetic operator or a bitwise operator. The list of assignment operators is shown in the following table.

Operator	Purpose	Example
=	Assignment	i = 10
+=	Assignment, after addition	i += 10
-=	Assignment, after subtraction	i -= 10
*=	Assignment, after multiplication	i *= 10
/=	Assignment, after division	i /= 10
%=	Assignment, after modulus	i %= 10
&=	Assignment, after bitwise AND	i &= 10
|=	Assignment, after bitwise OR	i |= 10

Operator	Purpose	Example
^=	Assignment, after bitwise exclusive-OR	i ^= 10
<<=	Assignment, after left shift	i <<= 10
>>=	Assignment, after right shift	i >>= 10

Example   Assignment operators

```
count += 1; /* Count = count + 1 */
k *= j;    /* k = k * j */
i <<= 4;   /* i = i << 4 */
```

Assignment operators provide a convenient shorthand notation for combining simple assignment with operators that have two operands. The notation of the assignment operator is easier to read, especially when the name of the variable on the left-hand side is long.

13.5e   Exercises

1 Write a program to print out the bit representation of an integer value. Use command line arguments to receive an input value and display the binary representation of the input value. The program should run as follows:

```
$ binary 4
0000 0000 0000 0100
```

The above output assumes that the integer is 16 bits wide; i.e., **sizeof(int)** is 2.

2 In a program, we wish to test if the variable **x** currently contains a pattern of bits, denoted by a constant called MASK. The following program fragment is intended to test this. Would this suffice?

```
#define MASK 0x7F     /* Bits 0111 1111 */
char x;
```

```
if (x & MASK == 0)
{
    /* Rest of the program */
}
```

Hint: Examine the precedence of the operators. Use the precedence table in Appendix B.

3 Modify the program **bittest.c** so that the user can specify the number of bits to test for and the start position of the first bit. Shown below is a sample run from the program:

```
Enter a value to test: 115
Enter the number of bits to test for: 3
Enter the position of the first bit: 4
Bit positions 4 through 7 contain all ones
```

13.6 Common Problems

1 Continuous or long-running programs that use dynamic memory allocation may develop problems with *memory leaks*. Memory leaks occur when a program that allocates memory blocks dynamically does not free all the blocks (inadvertently). Thus in the long run memory utilization gradually increases and at some point, the program runs out of heap memory. This causes further `malloc`, `calloc` and `realloc` calls to fail.

Memory leaks are hard to detect and plug without the use of debuggers. One way to find if you have a leak is to increment a counter whenever a block is allocated and decrement it when a block is freed. Periodically print the counter value. If the counter value increases gradually, you have a potential problem. Static analysis (plain code reading) may find the problem or you may have to resort to debuggers specifically written to find memory leaks.

2 When using random access, it is possible that a file may get corrupted due to incorrectly moving the read and write location by using `fseek`. The layout of the records on the file should be designed and documented. Code should be examined side by side with the file layout design to see whether the records are being written at the correct location.

3 The most common problem with recursion is due to the lack (or incorrect specification) of a *bottoming-out* criteria. This problem manifests itself as a program that goes into an infinite loop or runs out of memory.

Appendix A

A
ASCII Character Codes

Mnemonics of commonly used codes are shown in the following table.

Mnemonic	Meaning
NUL	Null character
BEL	Bell character
BS	Back space
HT	Horizontal tab
NL	New line
CR	Carriage Return
ESC	Escape
SP	Space bar

The ASCII character codes are shown on the next page.

Appendix A

Table A.1 - ASCII character codes

0 NUL	1 SOH	2 STX	3 ETX	4 EOT	5 ENQ	6 ACK	7 BEL
8 BS	9 HT	10 NL	11 VT	12 NP	13 CR	14 SO	15 SI
16 DLE	17 DC1	18 DC2	19 DC3	20 DC4	21 NAK	22 SYN	23 ETB
24 CAN	25 EM	26 SUB	27 ESC	28 FS	29 GS	30 RS	31 US
32 SP	33 !	34 "	35 #	36 $	37 %	38 &	39 '
40 (	41)	42 *	43 +	44 ,	45 -	46 .	47 /
48 0	49 1	50 2	51 3	52 4	53 5	54 6	55 7
56 8	57 9	58 :	59 ;	60 <	61 =	62 >	63 ?
64 @	65 A	66 B	67 C	68 D	69 E	70 F	71 G
72 H	73 I	74 J	75 K	76 L	77 M	78 N	79 O
80 P	81 Q	82 R	83 S	84 T	85 U	86 V	87 W
88 X	89 Y	90 Z	91 [	92 \	93]	94 ^	95 _
96 `	97 a	98 b	99 c	100 d	101 e	102 f	103 g
104 h	105 i	106 j	107 k	108 l	109 m	110 n	111 o
112 p	113 q	114 r	115 s	116 t	117 u	118 v	119 w
120 x	121 y	122 z	123 {	124		125 }	126 ~	127 DEL

Appendix B

B

Function Example for K&R Compilers

Function example from Chapter 10, converted to run on older compilers that do not understand function prototypes introduced in ANSI C.

```
/* File stats.c (from chapter 10): Modified to run
 * under K&R C compilers.
 * Contains all the functions and the main
 * program for the elementary statistics program
 */
#include <stdio.h>
#include <float.h> /* For FLT_MAX and FLT_MIN below */
/* Note: if the above file does not exisit on your
 * machine (gives a compile error), delete the #include
 * line. The Following lines will take care of
 * defining FLT_MAX and FLT_MIN
 */
#ifndef FLT_MAX
#define FLT_MAX  1E+37
#define FLT_MIN  1E-37
#endif

#define MAX_ITEMS 100

/* Function to compute minimum of two values */
float minimum(x, y)
float x, y;
{
   return x < y ? x : y;
}
```

Appendix B

```c
/* Function to compute maximum of two values */
float maximum(x, y)
float x, y;
{
   return x > y ? x : y;
}

/* Function to print information about program */
void print_info()
{
   printf ("\n%s\n%s\n",
           "This program computes and prints cumulative",
           "statistics on n floating point numbers");
}

/* Function to print heading of the table items */
void print_heading()
{
   printf("\n%5s%12s%12s%12s%12s%12s\n",
           "count", "item", "minimum", "maximum", "sum",
           "average");
}

/* Function to print data value */
void print_data(count, item, min, max, sum, average)
int count;
float item, min, max, sum, average;
{
   printf ("%5d%12.5f%12.5f%12.5f%12.5f%12.5f\n",
           count, item, min, max, sum, average);
}

main()
{
   int count, i, ret_val;
   float x, min, max, sum;

   /* Note: function declaration does not list the
    * type of the arguments */
```

```c
        void print_data();
        void print_info(), print_heading();
        float minimum(), maximum();

        min = FLT_MAX; /* Initialize to very high value */
        max = FLT_MIN; /* Initialize to very low value */
        sum = 0; /* Initialize sum */

        print_info(); /* Print the heading */
        for (i = 1; i <= MAX_ITEMS; i++)
        {
           printf ("Enter item %d: ", i);
           ret_val = scanf ("%f", &x);
           if (ret_val == EOF)
              break;

           min = minimum (x, min);
           max = maximum (x, max);
           sum = sum + x;
           print_heading();
           print_data(i, x, min, max, sum, sum/i);
        }
}
```

Appendix C

Complete Precedence Table

Operator	Precedence	Associativity
(), [], ->, .	15 (high)	Left to right
++, --, !, ~, sizeof, (cast), + (unary), - (unary), * (indirection), & (address)	14	Right to left
*, /, %	13	Left to Right
+, -	12	Left to right
<<, >>	11	Left to right
<, >, <=, >=	10	Left to right
==, !=	9	Left to right
& (bitwise)	8	Left to right
^ (bitwise)	7	Left to right
| (bitwise)	6	Left to right
&&	5	Left to right
||	4	Left to right
?:	3	Right to left
=, +=, -=, *=, (etc.)	2	Right to left
, (comma)	1 (low)	Left to right

D

Input/Output Format Conversions

Output format conversions

```
int printf(const char *format, ...)
int fprintf(FILE *stream, const char *format, ...)
```

The above functions write the output to stream, according to the specified format. The format is composed of ordinary characters which are copied unchanged, and conversion specifications introduced by % followed by zero or more flags, optional minimum field width, optional precision, a length modifier h, l or L (h for **short int** or **unsigned short int**, l for **long int** and L for **long double**), and a character that specifies the type of conversion.

The flag characters modify the result of the conversion as follows:

'-' — Left-justification.

'+' — Result starts with plus or minus sign.

' ' — Space prefixed to the result.

'#' — Convert to "alternate form" (for o conversion, it increases the precision to force the first digit of the result to be zero; for x (or X), 0x (or 0X) is prefixed and for e, E, f, g, and G, the result contains a decimal-point character.

'0' — Leading zeros are used to pad to the field width.

Appendix D

The conversion specifiers and their meanings are:

d, i — `int` argument converted to signed decimal.

o, u, x, X — `unsigned int` argument converted to `unsigned` octal(o), `unsigned` decimal(u) or `unsigned` hexadecimal(x or X); letters `abcdef` used for x conversion and `ABCDEF` for X conversion.

e, E — The `double` argument is converted in the style `[-]d.ddde+-dd`

f — `double` argument converted in the style `[-]ddd.ddd`

g, G — Same as e (E if G) or f depending on the value converted.

c — `int` argument converted to an `unsigned char`

s — Argument is a pointer to an array of characters; characters (all if no precision is specified) from array are written excluding a terminating null character.

p — Value of the pointer (to `void`) argument converted to a sequence of printable characters.

n — Number of characters written to output stream by this call to `fprintf` is written into the argument (pointer to `int`).

% — A % is written.

INPUT format conversions

```
int scanf(const char *format, ...)
int fscanf(FILE *stream, const char *format, ...)
```

Reads input from the stream controlled by the specified format using subsequent arguments as pointers to the objects to receive the converted input. The format is composed of zero or more directives: one or more white-space characters (usually skipped); an ordinary multibyte character (neither % nor a white space character); or a conversion specification introduced by the character % followed by:

An optional assignment-suppressing character *

An optional maximum field width specification.

An optional h, l or L indicating size of receiving object.

A character that specifies the type of conversion to be applied.

The composition of a directive and its effect are:

White space character(s); read input upto first non-white-space character.

Ordinary multibyte character; read characters from stream until the character differs from one comprising the directive.

A directive that is a conversion specification defines a set of matching input sequences. If the input item is not a matching sequence, the execution of the directive fails. The conversion specifiers are:

d — Optionally signed decimal integer.

i — Optionally signed integer.

o — Optionally signed octal integer.

u — Optionally signed decimal integer.

x — Optionally signed hexadecimal integer.

e, f, g — Optionally signed floating-point number.

s — A sequence of non-white-space characters.

[— A sequence of characters from a *scanset* (not from the set if ^ follows [). Scanset is the set of characters enclosed within [,].

c — Sequence of characters specified by field width (default is 1).

p — Implementation-defined set of sequences.

n — Number of characters read so far by this call to `fscanf` is written into the argument; no input is consumed.

% — A single % is consumed.

The conversion specifiers E, G, and X are also valid.

The `fscanf` function returns value of EOF if input failure occurs before any conversion; otherwise returns number of input items assigned.

Index

. operator, 322
& (address) operator, 236
&, !, ^, <<, >>, ~ (bitwise), 425
* (indirection) operator, 237
++,--, 173
+ (unary), - (unary), 68
+, -, *, /, %, 32, 67
-> operator, 334
<, <=, >, >=, ==, != 72
= assignment, 11
=, +=, -=, *=, /=, etc., 432
== equality, 34, 72
? : operator, 155
||, &&, !, 84

activation record, 374, 412
address, 234
    invalid, 245
ANSI C, 2
arguments
    command line, 402
    See also functions
arrays, 169, 201
    accessing elements, 203
    binary search, 222
    declaration, 202
    index sorting, 218
    initialization, 214
    lack of bounds checking, 216, 232
    layout, 262
    locating elements, 204
    multidimensional, 224
    pointers, 248, 387
    sorting using bubble sort, 210
    storing order, 225
    strings, 255
    subscripts, 251
    `typedef`, 268
arrays and pointers, 387
ASCII, 48
assembler, 138
assert macro, 151
assert.h, 151
associativity of operators, 69
`atof` function, 326
`atoi` function, 188, 326
`atol` function, 326
automatic variables, 357, 409

big endian, 236
binary files
    See files
binary search, 222, 413
bitwise AND, 427
bitwise exclusive-OR, 427
bitwise OR, 427
block structuring
    See programs
block visibility, 374
break, 164
    See statements
bubble sort, 210

call by value
    See functions
`calloc` function, 393
`case` values, 167
cast operator, 395
    See also operators

Index

char
    See data types
character
    conversion, 55, 58
    character sequence, 20
comma operator, 179
command line arguments, 402
comments, 10
compilation, 5
compile-time allocation
    See memory
conditional compilation, 313
const, 44
constants, 51
    character, 51, 54
    floating point, 53
    integer, 52
    string, 51, 60
continue statement, 189
ctype.h, 58

dangling else, 65
data types, 10, 35
    char, 39, 48
    enum, 165
    struct, 319
    void, 254
    const, 44, 51
    float, 40
    int, 39
    qualifiers, 41
    union, 350
division
    floating point, 19
    integer, 19, 131
dynamic memory allocation, 393
    See also memory

enum
    See data types
escape sequences, 54
exit function, 82
EXIT_FAILURE, 314
EXIT_SUCCESS, 314
expression
    conditional, 155
extern variables, 360

fclose function, 107
fgetc function, 108
fgets function, 108
field width
    See also format specification
FILE, 105
file I/O, 103
files, 103
    binary files, 108, 117
    closing, 107
    opening, 105
    random access, 103, 417
    reading, 108
    sequential access, 103
    stdin, stdout, stderr, 127
    text files, 108
    writing, 108
float.h, 40
fopen function, 105
for loops, 175
formal parameters
    functions, 284
format specification, 16, 22, 46, 50
    precision, 17
    rounding, 18
    size modifier, 46
fprintf function, 111
fputc function, 108
fread function, 210
free function, 393
fscanf function, 111
fseek function, 417
ftell function, 417
fwrite function, 210
function prototypes
    See functions
functions, 277
    arguments, 278, 304
    call by reference, 297

448

call by value, 287, 295
declaration, 281
definition, 281, 284
evaluation, 286
external variables, 362
formal parameters, 284
function call, 281, 284
prototypes, 281, 290, 313
recursive, 408
return value, 280, 286
scope, 360
separate compilation, 310
versus macros, 301

`getc` function, 108
`getchar` function, 280
`gets` function, 188
global variables, 361, 371
`goto` statement, 195

hexadecimal representation, 425

identifiers
    See variables
`if-else`
    See statements
index sorting, 218
indexed key access, 419
input, 5, 15, 21
    file I/O, 103
    input separator, 325
    `scanf` function, 47
    stream, 325
instance, 321
`isalnum` function, 59
`isalpha` function, 59
`iscntlr` function, 59
`isdigit` function, 59
`islower` function, 59
`isprint` function, 59
`isspace` function, 59
`isupper` functions, 59

K&R C, 1
Kernighan, B., 1

limits.h, 39
linear search, 204
link editor, 139, 361
linked lists, 347, 396
little endian, 236
`localtime` function, 349
`long`, 42

macros
    predefined, 315
    See also preprocessor
`main` function, 10, 402
make utility, 311
`malloc` function, 393
math.h, 32, 303
memory
    access using pointers, 233
    address, 239
    contents, 237
    dynamic allocation, 207, 393
    leaks, 435
    static allocation, 207, 217
    types of, 357
    word, 234
memory address, 239

new line, 12
null character, 170, 255
`NULL` macro, 106
null pointer, 246
null statement, 78, 96, 177

object, 321
octal representation, 425
operators
    address of, 236
    address-of, 253
    arithmetic, 69
    array subscripts, 203
    assignment, 11, 34, 432
    bitwise, 425
    cast, 129, 395
    comma, 179
    decrement, 173

Index

dot (.), 322
equality, 34
increment, 173
indirection, 237
logical, 84
member selection, 334, 356
modulus, 32
precedence, 69
shift, 430
short circuiting, 89
output, 5, 15
    file I/O, 103
    `printf` function, 15, 46

`perror` function, 107, 149
pointer arithmetic
    See pointers
pointer arrays, 261
pointers, 233 - 234
    arithmetic, 250, 335
    arrays, 248
    declaration, 240
    initialization, 242
    null, 246
precedence of operators, 68
precision
    See also format specification
preprocessor, 137
    `assert` macro, 151
    conditional compilation, 313
    file inclusion, 139
    macro substitution, 141
    macros, 40, 145
    predefined macros, 144
    stringization operator, 149, 152
`printf` function, 12, 46
    See also output
programs
    block structuring, 358
    comments, 10
    compilation, 5
    compilation cycle, 137
    executable, 6
    file name, 28
    `main`, 10
    portability, 31
    separate compilation, 310
    style, 2
    termination, 82
`putc` function, 108

qualifiers, 41
    `const`, 44
    `long`, 42
    `short`, 42
    `signed`, 43
    `unsigned`, 43
quick sort, 383

`rand` function, 32
random access, 417
`realloc` function, 393
record, 320
recursive functions, 408
register variables, 365
reserved words, 26
`return` statement
    See statements
`rewind` function, 417
Ritchie, D., 1

`scanf` function, 47
    See also input
scope, 360
    rules, 372
`SEEK_SET`, 417
`SEEK_CUR`, 417
`SEEK_END`, 417
shift operators, 430
`short`, 42
`signed`, 43
`srand` function, 32
Standard C, 2
standard library, 12, 15
statements
    `break`, 96, 164
    `continue`, 189
    `do`, 181

    `for`, 175
    `goto`, 195
    `if-else`, 33, 73, 75
    `return`, 287
    `switch`, 161
    `while`, 73, 93
static variables, 366
stddef.h, 106
stdio.h, 10, 15
stdlib.h, 326
storage class, 357
    `auto`, 357
    `extern`, 361
    `register`, 365
    `static`, 366
`strcat` function, 259
`strchr` function, 259
`strcmp` function, 259
`strcpy` function, 259
streams, 103, 127
string.h, 259
strings, 255
    See also constants
`strlen` function, 259
`strncmp` function, 259
`strncpy` function, 259
`strtod` function, 326
`strtok` function, 339
`strtol` function, 326
`strtoul` function, 326
structures, 320
    assignment, 327
    nested structures, 345
    passing by reference, 342
    pointer, 334
    storing in file, 332
    storing in files, 329
    See also data type
switch statement, 161, 167
syntax errors, 5 - 6, 26

text files
    See files
time.h, 347

`time` function, 348
`toupper`, 111
`tolower`, 111
truth tables, 86
`typedef`, 264, 267, 322

`union`, 350
`unsigned`, 43
user defined data types, 319

variables, 11, 25
    address, 239
    attributes, 37
    `auto`, 357
    `extern`, 360
    `register`, 365
    reserved words, 26
    rules for declaring, 25
    scope, 360
    size, 37
    specifying sign, 43
    `static`, 366
    visibility, 360, 372
visibility, 360, 372
    block, 372
    file, 375
    global, 372

`while`, 93
white space, 22
word
    See memory